ETHNIC POLITICS AND CIVIL LIBERTIES

National Political Science Review

Volume 3

NATIONAL POLITICAL SCIENCE REVIEW

EDITOR
Lucius J. Barker
Stanford University

ASSOCIATE EDITOR
Michael Preston
University of Southern California

BOOK REVIEW EDITOR
Paula D. McClain
University of Virginia

ETHNIC POLITICS AND CIVIL LIBERTIES

National Political Science Review

Volume 3

Lucius J. Barker, Editor

R Routledge
Taylor & Francis Group

LONDON AND NEW YORK

First published 1992 by Transaction Publishers

Published 2017 by Routledge
2 Park Square, Milton Park, Abingdon, Oxon OX14 4RN
711 Third Avenue, New York, NY 10017, USA

Routledge is an imprint of the Taylor & Francis Group, an informa business

ISSN: 0896-629X
ISBN 13: 978-1-56000-564-3 (pbk)

Contents

NATIONAL CONFERENCE OF BLACK POLITICAL SCIENTISTS OFFICERS, 1991–1992

President
Joseph H. Silver, Sr.

President-Elect
Franklin D. Jones

Membership Secretary
Robert C. Smith

Secretary
Kathie Golden

Treasurer
Sanders Anderson

G. A. P. Inc.
Carolyn Eaglin

Parliamentarian
Nolan Jones

Historians
Jewel W. Prestage
Alex Sillingham

Editor, NPSR*
Matthew Holden, Jr.

Executive Council
Shelia Harmon-Martin

Cassie Osborne

Cheryl Miller

Alvin Thornton

Marvin Haire

Maime E. Locke

Immediate Past President
Dianne M. Pinderhughes

*Contributions for future volumes of the NPSR should be sent to the new editor, Matthew Holden, Jr. (See last page in this volume.)

Editor's Note for Volume 3

I approach this third volume of the *National Political Science Review* (NPSR) with excitement, relief, and anticipation. The excitement is spurred by seeing an idea—the need for the NPSR—develop from its initial airing into what is increasingly being recognized as a first-rate scholarly publication. The relief and anticipation reflect both sides of the same coin, i.e., relief that this volume represents the end of my three year term as editor; and anticipation, knowing that the NPSR is in the very capable hands of the new editor, Matthew Holden of the University of Virginia. His "Editor's Note" (which follows) certainly indicates an exciting and rich future for the NPSR in the scholarly and professional community.

It has been exciting to see an idea—the NPSR—develop into a scholarly publication whose continued progress seems certain to bring it into the top ranks of academic scholarship and discourse. Certainly, the two earlier issues, as well as this volume, offer convincing evidence of steadied and clear progress toward this goal. The distinctive character and quality of the NPSR are reflected well in these volumes.

The first volume—*New Perspectives in American Politics*—clearly offered fresh insights and perspectives through feature articles on liberalism and black political thought, political movements in American politics, the decisional trends and doctrinal directions of the Rehnquist Court, the impact of campaign canvassing on the black vote, and second-generation educational discrimination. The two symposia—"Iran-Contra Affair" and "Black Americans and the Constitution"—illustrated well how scholarly insights and perspectives enhance understanding of both current and continuing problems in American politics.

And I am even more attached to the view, as stated in my Editor's Note introducing the first volume, that the Book Review Section, under the editorship of Paula D. McClain, represents one of the "most thorough and innovative" developments of its kind "that can be found in any scholarly journal."

Similar observations can be made about the second volume of the NPSR— *Black Electoral Politics*. Undoubtedly this volume offered some of the most penetrating insights on black politics available in today's popular or professional writing. For example, the need and value of starting an organization to develop a "different political science," in contrast to that represented in traditional scholarship, is demonstrated vividly in speeches delivered

1

by two former presidents of the National Conference of Black Political Scientists commemorating the twentieth anniversary of the founding of that organization: Mack Jones of Prairie View A. & M. University, and Dianne Pinderhughes of the University of Illinois (Urbana). And the "need and value" of this "different political science" are exemplified well by the scholarly contributions published in that very volume, including feature articles on the impact of racial belief systems and religious guidance on African American political participation; white/black perceptions of the electability of black political candidates; electoral politics, affirmative action, and the Supreme Court; political responses to underemployment among African Americans; and the politics of desegregation in higher education. A major component of this volume, the symposium "Big-City Black Mayors: Have They Made A Difference?" is very likely to become the most definitive, perceptive, and authoritative reference base from which to continue research on these matters. And once again, the Book Review Section provides an innovative supplement to the central theme of the volume—Black Electoral Politics—through very informative bibliographic and review essays.

This brings us to the current volume—*Ethnic Politics and Civil Liberties*—whose nature and range of contributions are reflected in the table of contents. These contributions also reflect the notable progress of the *NPSR* in achieving one of its major goals as stated in the very first volume: "to expand . . . traditional political science . . . by promoting the communication and dissemination of varied research interests, methodologies, and ideas."

A final word. My term as editor would have been much less fulfilling had it not been for a number of persons who made indispensable contributions to this overall endeavor. Central to this development, of course, are the authors who allow us the opportunity to assess their work for possible publication, and the anonymous referees who make peer review come alive by offering authors many constructive suggestions about their work.

I also appreciate the many symbolic and substantive supports rendered by members of the Editorial Board, and the always cheerful help and advice given by Paula D. McClain, the book review editor, and Michael B. Preston, associate editor of the NPSR. And, of course, this effort would have been almost impossible but for the tremendous and varied supports offered by my graduate research assistants (Kevin Lyles of Washington University–St. Louis, who nurtured the publications of volumes 1 and 2 of the NPSR; and Jonathan Kaplan of Stanford University, who provided similar help in producing this current volume.

Last, and most important, I want to thank members of the National Conference of Black Political Scientists for daring to develop the NPSR, and for giving me the opportunity to be of service in this pioneering effort.

LUCIUS J. BARKER

Editor's Note for Volumes 4 and Beyond

Introduction

It is my particular honor to have been appointed editor of the *National Political Science Review* for volumes 4–6 (1992–94). Lucius J. Barker, my colleague of many years, has been brilliantly successful as the founding editor. It is sufficient challenge to maintain the high and independent intellectual standard that he has established. No major changes of policy or practice are contemplated. As before, the first requirement is careful scholarship, but no particular methodological or theoretical orthodoxy is to be enforced. *If it is political science, the NPSR is interested.* As there is a special history, however, some additional comments may be helpful. The *National Political Science Review* has been, and continues to be, particularly open to research about the political relations of African-descended groups, especially in the United States.

Note on the Intellectual Background

On the basis of published research, over the past hundred years it is fair to say that the discipline of political science, overall, has proceeded as if the political relations of African-descended groups were exotica that might be interesting possibly to blacks or to occasional white scholars.[1] On the whole, the political relations of African Americans were treated as if they presented no analytically interesting questions. They surely were not deemed significant to the central issue of political science. That is why Ralph J. Bunche could say, in 1941, that generally in political science "there isn't a very cordial reception for papers dealing with the Negro" (comments in Herskovits, 1941).

The explanation probably lies in some combination of social and intellectual history. The central intellectual concern of late-nineteenth- and early-twentieth-century political science was "popular government," restyled "democracy" later on. This political science studied, more than anything else, the law, philosophy, and history of "government," with an acute emphasis on American institutions, the governments of France, Germany, and Great Britain, and international law, with a moderate addition of Asian and colonial government. It emerged within the Anglo-centric intellectual tradition that dominated American scholarship well into the twentieth century. Woodrow Wilson, A. Lawrence Lowell, Frank

J. Goodnow and William Bennet Munro may be regarded as adequately representative figures in the tradition. The leaders of this emergent discipline more or less took for granted that the political community was essentially a white community.[2] The big question was about both the empirical and the normal role of wealth in the polity. Whether understood as group (later "pressure-group" and still later the cooled down "interest-group") politics or as class politics, with or without the Marxist variant, this treatment left no intellectually compelling issues regarding race or ethnicity. The assumption of the Anglo-centric polity remained an undisturbed feature of the canon.

The inklings of a "scientific" study of politics, notably in the work of Charles E. Merriam just after World War I, long anticipated what would occur after World War II. After World War II, political scientists came strongly to accept a more self-conscious and explicit idea of "science" and a more abstract concern with "power." This did not alter, however, the central tendency of political scientists to think of black-related questions as peripheral. They could, according to the viewpoints held, be understood fully within existing intellectual parameters. Nor did the introduction of a social science saturated with intellectual problems defined from the moral problems of central Europe make much difference for a long time. The moral and intellectual problems of the United States were substantially set aside.

Recent Work

There has been a perceptible shift, especially since about 1960 and certainly since the effects of the civil rights movement have come into academic life. (Walton, McLemore, and Gray, 1990). There is now a book literature. There is now emerging a periodical literature. The latter, especially, increasingly reflects the applications of those quantitative methods from the Angus Campbell–Warren Miller–Survey Research Center mode to the politics of nonwhite ethnic minorities. The effect is strong enough that last year there was, remarkably, another journal carrying two such articles in one such issue. (Bobo and Gilliam, 1990; McClain and Karnig, 1990). We similarly note the emergence of panels at the American Political Science Association on "Race, Gender, and Ethnicity," which suggests the emergence of a new subfield in the discipline.

This shift is important for the basic intellectual health of the discipline. The *National Political Science Review* is open to disciplined thought and substantial empirical inquiry about such relationships. Perhaps it will be helpful to suggest broadly some of the possibilities. In the first place, of course, there is the normal array of studies that are defined within existing parameters of political science: the presidency, Congress, public administration, interest groups, state and local governments, (Persons, 1987), and so forth. Beyond these, it may be worthwhile to indicate some other possibilities.

Some Possibilities for the Time

Ethnic Plurality

The *National Political Science Review* will encompass not merely African-American politics, but the political relations of other historically or presently subordinated groups and the contexts in which those relations have been manifested. The problem is not how sympathetic or unsympathetic a scholar may be to the claims of African-descended persons. It is how to explore the multiethnic dynamic, how to appraise the prospects of the racially stratified constitutional democracy, and how to forecast the political consequences of a market economy characterized by severe racial inelasticities. The underlying conceptual issues in the multiethnic polity go to the question of what is a viable (accurately predictive) theory of political integration (and its converse, disintegration). The issue also presents itself in polities that are not constitutional, in our sense, and in which the market economy does not exist, as manifested in Soviet politics of recent times.

The Internal Politics of Ethnic Groups

While "the state" is again in vogue, the editor will also welcome research grounded in other perspectives. Among other things, there is room for new work on "private politics," or the internal conduct of nongovernmental entities. What, for instance, is the decision-making mode present in "the black community," so that the preferences attributed to the African-American population are identified or changed? What is the support basis and the decision-making mode for any of the major black organizations, such as the National Association for the Advancement of Colored People, (NAACP), the National Urban League, the African Methodist Episcopal Church, or the National Baptist Convention of the U.S.A., Inc.? What is to be said of interest groups, of how they arise and change, and of what their level of efficiency is in achieving what they seek? What is the empirical knowledge of the structure of the black community in comparison to, for example, the structure of the Jewish community? Scholars might, for instance, not only choose to examine the governance of the public to which they commonly direct their attention; they might also direct their attention to the governance of the workplace in which they spend most of their lives, namely the college or university itself.

Public Policy

The editor would welcome attempts to apply political science concepts to the examination of public policy. Contributions are invited in which public policy and policy relationships to African Americans and other subordinated groups would be examined. Among the subjects on which sound research is particularly needed is the entire system of public order (or "criminal justice"). This might include study on how communal order is induced (if it is), which is both a major practical issue and a theoretical issue of far-reaching proportions. Studies of public order might include not only police and policing, but prosecution, the judicial system, the prison and penal systems, and the relationships between those systems and the social environment. Similarly, one might inquire into the systems of social insurance and public assistance, or reexamine the systems of public housing and education. The editor believes there is need for deep and thorough inquiry into the phenomenon of affirmative action, its origins, its supporting and opposing coalitions, and its intended results as well as its unintended side effects.

The foregoing items are merely illustrations. The NPSR will welcome policy studies, where the analytical and conceptual tools and problems of political science are brought to bear, without restriction as to the subject matter of the policy. The prime requirements will be that work reflect new data, thorough reexamination of old data, or some substantial new conceptualization. The editor will discourage mere expressions of opinion.

Extra-Disciplinary Connections

The present editor has a special interest in work about politics that attempts to assimilate concepts and data from other disciplines, notably anthropology, economics, geography, history, psychology, sociology, and law. The crucial requirement is that concepts or data produced in other fields be systematically applied to politics and that the relationships to existing political science concepts be treated seriously.

As one possibility, note that the first volume under the current editor will appear in 1992, which is the five-hundredth anniversary of Columbus's voyages. The occasion may call for a retrospective application of political science concepts to Columbus's voyages, decision making about them, and their consequences for human society, both on this side the Atlantic and in Europe and Africa. In the same spirit, the editor would particularly welcome attempts to explore the later transformation of European imperial ventures into a self-conscious "white supremacy."

The global politics of white supremacy in the second half of the nineteenth century and the first third (more or less) of the twentieth century deserves attention. In this last decade of the twentieth century political scientists may also wish to consider the new politics that should be associated with a Europe that tends to be both unified and powerful, in a way that Europe never was before, as well as to other power shifts in the world.

General Comment

The special emphasis in the previous discussion must also not obscure the fundamental point. The NPSR is a journal of political science, as its first volumes have shown, and is open to inquiry on any subject. The present editor will receive not only papers within the scope indicated, but also papers on the politics of economic and financial change, on "globalization," and on the political consequences of technological change. The editor will, moreover, welcome direct inquiries on any other subject.

A word may be in order about the receipt of submissions. We are wide open to all scholars. Some highly regarded journals have deemed it worthwhile to restrict publication to authors chosen on extrinsic criteria, such as location. The *National Political Science Review*, though sponsored by the National Conference of Black Political Scientists, adopts no such extrinsic criterion. The editor looks forward to the receipt of submissions from scholarly colleagues on the widest possible basis, both in the United States and elsewhere in the world. The editor also looks forward to communications from any scholar of politics discussing subjects related to the welfare of the journal or the study of politics.

MATTHEW HOLDEN, JR.
EDITOR, VOLUMES 4 AND BEYOND

Notes

1. In my view, the premier figure in this regard was Harold F. Gosnell, whose *Negro Politicians* (1935) was far ahead of the curve. Gosnell deserves our respect, as well, as one of the earliest political scientists to take seriously to quantitative methodological innovation, in his other works.
2. The premise appears to have been even stronger in sociology, psychology, and philosophy, as one infers from Mecklin, 1914, especially Chapter 2 on "Race Traits." The notes in that chapter are particularly instructive.

References

Bobo, Lawrence, and Frank D. Gilliam, Jr. 1990. "Race, Sociopolitical Participation, and Black Empowerment." *American Political Science Review*, 84, no. 2 (June): 377–93.

Gosnell, Harold F. 1935. *Negro Politicians*. Chicago: University of Chicago Press.

Herskovits, Melville J., ed., 1941. *Interdisciplinary Aspects of Negro Studies*. Washington, DC: American Council of Learned Societies, Bulletin no. 12.

McClain, Paula, and Albert K. Karnig. 1990. "Black and Hispanic Socioeconomic and Political Competition." *American Political Science Review*, 84, no. 2 (June): 535–45.

Mecklin, John. 1914. *Democracy and Race Friction*. New York: Macmillan.

Persons, Georgia. 1987. "Blacks in State and Local Government: Progress and Constraints." Pp. 167–92 in *The State of Black America*. New York: National Urban League.

Walton, Hanes, Jr., Leslie Burl McLemore, and C. Vernon Gray. 1990. "The Pioneering Books on Black Politics and the Political Science Community, 1903–1965." *National Political Science Review*, 2 (1990): 196–218.

Reconceptualizing Urban Violence: A Policy Analytic Approach

Paula D. McClain*

University of Virginia

Much debate has occurred within the National Conference of Black Political Scientists over the years concerning the importance of work done by black political scientists to the development of the discipline. As political scientists, we argue about the importance of particular policies and policy areas. However, rarely do we examine the more mundane, yet critically important, topic of issue definition and problem structuring related to particular policy areas. The discourse centers around the policies that have been or should be developed, but rarely do we question whether the underlying theoretical framework or causal theory is the correct conceptualization of the problem. It is important that black political scientists enter into the debate on issue definition and problem structuring in policy areas that are of importance to black America.

This article is an attempt to initiate discussion around the conceptualization of urban violence, particularly homicide, for policy formulation purposes. Several aspects of urban violence are explored. First, what is the nature and structure of black urban violence? Second, given the nature and structure of urban violence, is the present conceptualization of the problem for policy purposes the most appropriate or correct conceptualization? Finally, an argument is developed to reconceptualize urban vio-

Presidential address delivered at the Business Meeting of the National Conference of Black Political Scientists, 15 March 1990.

*I must thank my research colleague of 14 years, Harold M. Rose, for his contributions to my thinking about issues of urban violence. Thanks are also due to Theodore J. Lowi and Matthew Holden, Jr. for comments on this proposed reconceptualization. I also owe a debt to my colleagues N. Joseph Cayer and Kathy J. Boyd for helpful comments on earlier drafts of this article.

lence for purposes of policy development that, hopefully, will move us in a direction to begin to reduce the levels of violence present in a large number of urban black communities.

The first section discusses urban areas and violent crime; it is followed by an examination of the urban environment and dangerous places. The third section explores the nature and structure of urban black homicide as identified through my research on the subject with Harold M. Rose. An argument for the reconceptualization of urban violence is advanced in the fourth section. Finally, the importance of black political scientists to policy research is raised in the last section.

Cities and Violent Crime

Throughout the last three decades, it has been common to refer to the business of urban government and life in large urban centers by prefacing statements with the word "crisis"—the crisis of civil disorders, crisis of urbanization, fiscal crisis. Each event has pushed and pulled local governmental machinery in attempts to ameliorate the problem, and each "solution" has altered the scope and purview of local government authority in many aspects. Some suggest that the cumulative effect of these urban crises has been to transform the city "from a formidable engine of growth to a federal and state client dependent on a form of municipal welfare" (Gottdiener, 1987:16). Whereas once political scientists spoke of the unbounded abilities of urban government, they now speak in terms of the "limits of the city" (Peterson, 1981; Bookchin, 1974; Elkins, 1987).

The urban crisis of the latter 1980s and the 1990s is urban violence. Many cities are overwhelmed by the extent and increasing frequency of the violence. Washington, D.C., experienced its most violent year in history in 1989 with 437 reported homicides, 60 percent of which were drug related. Furthermore, there was a doubling in the number of juveniles wounded by gunfire: from fifty to one hundred juveniles injured (*Washington Post*, 1 January 1990). In 1988 the city recorded 368 reported homicides, more than half of which were gang related. The city also had the highest homicide rate in the country in 1988: 59.2 murders per 100,000 persons (*Washington Post*, 7 January 1989).

In both 1988 and 1989 Washington, D.C., had the dubious distinction of being the "homicide capital" of the United States. The city may retain the title in 1990 as well, having had 188 homicides through the end of May of 1990. If this trend continues the city could reach an all-time high of over 450 homicides in 1990.

In the City of Los Angeles, while overall murders declined from 832 in 1987 to 734 in 1988, gang killings rose to 257 from 205 the previous year. Moreover, overall gang-related crimes rose to 5,371 from 5,129 in 1987 (*New York Times*, 11 January 1989). Additionally, the number of gang-related homicides in Los Angeles County rose to 432, a 67 percent increase in three years (*Los Angeles Times*, 30 January 1989). Although the number of homicides dropped in 1988, homicides began to spiral upward again in

Table 1. Total Homicide Risk and Black Homicide Risk
in Major Urban cities, 1980
(per 100,000 persons in the population)

City	Total Risk	Black Risk
New York	23.9	46.8
Philadelphia	26.4	51.8
Baltimore	28.6	40.6
Washington	36.1	39.9
Atlanta	38.6	46.3
Memphis	24.2	37.7
New Orleans	37.5	56.8
Dallas	33.6	55.3
Houston	37.1	45.9
Cleveland	45.7	76.8
Detroit	45.7	59.3
Chicago	28.6	45.1
St. Louis	48.8	91.6
Los Angeles	33.8	87.3

Source: Rose, Harold M., "Can We Substantially Lower Homicide Risk in the Nation's Larger Black Communities," *Secretary's Task Force on Black and Minority Mental Health* (Washington, D.C.: U.S. Department of Health and Human Services, 1986).

1989, with the number of reported homicides reaching 802 through 30 November 1989 (*Los Angeles Times*, 16 January 1990). Although the final figures are not yet available, the Los Angeles Police Department estimates that the final count for 1989 will be slightly higher than the figures reported in 1987.

Violent crime and fear of victimization were central themes in the 1988 presidential election, with George Bush using the furlough of Willie Horton in Massachusetts as a symbol of the risk of criminal victimization to which citizens are exposed. Although his tactic struck a responsive chord among a large segment of the electorate and proved successful in helping to elect George Bush, the reality is that the risk of criminal victimization is race specific, with the risk to blacks, who principally reside in urban centers, being substantially higher than the risk to whites. Table 1 shows the black homicide risk in fourteen major urban cities in 1980, compared to the homicide risk for the total population. In all fourteen cities, the black homicide risk is higher than the homicide risk to the total population.

Blacks are six times more likely than whites to be victims of homicide (Rose and McClain, 1990) and two-and-one-half times more likely than whites to be victims of rape. For robbery, the black victimization rate is three times that of the white race, and the black rate for aggravated assault is one-and-one-half times that of the white rate (Rose, 1981; Silberman, 1978). The Federal Bureau of Investigation (FBI) recently indicated, based on 1987 data, that a nonwhite male born today has a 1 in 38 chance of being murdered, while the risk to the aggregate population is 1 in 177 chances. For men already 20 years of age, nonwhites have a 1 in 41 chance of being murdered, while whites have a 1 in 224 chance (*Washington Post*, 13 January 1989). In 1987, there were an estimated 20,096 murders. Of that figure, 45 percent of the victims were black (FBI, 1987:9).

On the other side, in 1987, blacks represented slightly more than one-half, 52 percent, of those arrested for murder and non-negligent man-slaughter (FBI, 1987:12); yet they were only 12 percent of the population. Moreover, the FBI data state that, based on incidents involving one victim and one offender, 94 percent of the black murder victims were slain by black offenders.

As suggested earlier, anxiety over urban violence is present in most elections; violent crime is a salient campaign issue. Scheingold (1984, 1988) purports that politicization of crime seems to occur when political leaders, in part taking their cues from the media, choose to play upon public anxieties, which are themselves inflamed by media imagery and vicarious victimization rather than by crime as such. This process invariably leads to the development of proposals that assuage the public's anxiousness about crime and victimization, but do not address the problem as its exists or help the people who are the real victims of violent crimes—urban black residents.

Urban Environment and Dangerous Places

Considerable scholarly research has been undertaken in the field of urbanism and urbanization and their impacts on the behavior patterns of individuals. These studies have developed a variety of findings and con-clusions that are helpful to the understanding of patterns of urban vio-lence. This section will review the literature on the effects of urbanism on behavior, particularly as it relates to criminal behavior.

Urban areas are characterized as being more prone to violence and less safe than either suburban or rural areas. The question of what makes some neighborhoods more dangerous places to live is difficult to answer, but several attempts have been made. The classic works of Wirth (1938) and Simmel (1951) suggests that certain aspects of the urban environment promote social disorganization and individual alienation. These two con-ditions may lead to deviant social behavior, which could result in urban areas being more dangerous places to live than less urban environments. Included among the elements that contribute to deviant behavior are the size, density, and heterogeneity of the urban environment.

While taking issue with the contention that urbanism results in isolation and anonymity, Fischer (1976a,b) argues that the concentration of large numbers of people who share the same attitudes, including the acceptance of illegal activity, contributes to the development of subcultures that sanc-tion many types of deviant behavior. Fischer argues that the "deviance and disorganization" found in urban areas are the result of the develop-ment of distinctive subcultures that encourage or tolerate behaviors that the broader society considers to be deviant, rather than the result of individual alienation. However, Fischer does emphasize that ecological variables—population density, heterogeneity, and size—have great influence on social life.

A body of literature has examined the consequences of urbanism on crime and criminal victimization. Cohen and Felson (1979) view an individual's susceptibility to criminal victimization as stemming both from the victim's characteristics and behaviors and from the context in which they are located. It has also been suggested that neighborhoods (communities) are not random aggregates of individuals, but are "collective representations" of people and environment (Hunter, 1974:178; Rees, 1970). In support of this position, Kornhauser (1978) specifies that the reasons why some areas are more violence prone than others may depend on the sociological characteristics of communities, or on the characteristics of individuals selectively aggregated into communities; in effect, the reasons may be contextual. In the same vein, Roncek (1981) concluded that environmental factors of residential areas are important to explaining where crimes occur, suggesting that changes in the environments of residential areas can affect crime. Overall, these studies suggest that there are elements of urban environments that may promote criminal behavior among individual residents.

Subculture of Violence

What have been the past explanations of the high rates of homicide among urban blacks? The most often cited explanations are those proposed by Wolfgang and Ferracuti (1967) and Gastil (1971). Wolfgang and Ferracuti espoused the subculture-of-violence thesis, while Gastil proposed a theory of a regional culture of violence. Each is firmly grounded in the culture-of-poverty theory originated by Oscar Lewis (1959).

Wolfgang and Ferracuti stated that an ethnic or racial group that had high homicide rates would possess a specific set of characteristics, for example, a response to particular gestures, or a weapon, that would identify them as members of a subculture of violence. Blacks had high homicide rates and possessed these sets of characteristics; thus black violence was the result of their membership in a subculture of violence. Wolfgang and Ferracuti emphasized the role of the internalization of social norms of violence and the sanctioning of violent behavior by one's peers. They viewed blacks as a product of the ghetto tradition, which tends to sanction violence under particular circumstances. Blacks were more or less viewed as passive actors in the subcultures they fashioned, or as the product of a regional culture that increased their vulnerability to involvement in situations requiring a violent solution. Although Wolfgang and Ferracuti drew these sweeping conclusions about black violence, they did not specifically study blacks.

Gastil, on the other hand, emphasized the importance of learned traditions in combination with a biosocial response to one's position at the bottom of the status hierarchy. In Gastil's view blacks were disproportionately a product of a regional culture of violence—rural and southern.

These explanations made several major assumptions. First, the violence that occurred among blacks was the result of what occurred within their own communities. There was no acknowledgment that violence could be influenced by factors and events occurring outside the boundaries of the ghetto. This assumption parallels James J. Wilson's notion in *Negro Politics* (1960) that the ghetto had a life and logic of its own, apart from what the larger society did. There was no recognition of how external forces shape and influence politics.

Second, these explanations assume that a ghetto is a ghetto is a ghetto. The assumption is made that urban environments are all the same and do not differ in any significant way—at least the black communities do not differ. Therefore, if one studied homicide in one ghetto, one could generalize to another. Black homicide in a Detroit ghetto would be the same as black homicide in a St. Louis ghetto.

Finally, the subculture-of-violence explanation also assumes that urban black communities are static entities. It assumes that the values, culture, mores, and traditions are fixed and unchanging and are passed unchanged from one generation to the next. Thus, although these existing explanations were widely accepted as plausible, some scholars feel that they were not adequate for explaining black homicide because they dismissed the notion that societal events and values have an impact on lethal violence (Rose and McClain, 1990). Moreover, these explanations do not deal with the issue of the interaction of race, class, and violence in an urban setting.

Although blacks are the predominant victims and perpetrators of homicide, most previous homicide research lacked specific attention to blacks (Wolfgang, 1958; Lunndsgaard, 1977). If blacks were mentioned, it was usually as an afterthought, or as a chapter in a work that principally concentrated on white homicide. Furthermore, most previous studies have concentrated on only one city rather than on several urban environments.

Nature and Structure of Urban Black Homicide

Recognizing the woeful lack of research in the area of black urban violence, in 1977, Harold M. Rose and I undertook a major study of black-on-black homicide. The study is unique in a number of ways. First, it takes the position that what is important to study to gain an understanding of the factors that contribute to the high incidence of black-on-black homicide is not the homicide event itself, which is an isolated point in time and has been the focal point of previous homicide studies, but the environmental backgrounds the victim and offender brought with them to the situation that resulted in death. We utilized the concept of environment at several levels—macro- , meso- , and micro-environmental—and utilized an ecological approach. Second, black homicide is studied in several urban environments—Atlanta, St. Louis, Houston, Pittsburgh, Detroit, and Los Angeles. Third, the time frame for the study was from 1960 to 1985. A brief summary of our findings is presented in the following section.

One thing is clear from the multicity approach to the study of homicide: homicide is a complex phenomenon; cities differ in their inhabitants' risk of victimization (likelihood of death) and the structure of victimization (relationship of victim to offender and whether single or multiple offenders and victims). The six cities studied were found to occupy different points on a continuum between traditional violence (motivated by anger) and nontraditional violence (motivated by gain). At the beginning of the time period (1960), Atlanta, Houston, and Los Angeles anchored the traditional-violence end of the continuum, while Detroit, Pittsburgh, and St. Louis were on the nontraditional-violence end. By the end of the period (1985), Los Angeles had changed categories and joined Detroit, Pittsburgh, and St. Louis as centers where acts of nontraditional violence predominated.

The risk of black male victimization is strongly associated with age. Traditionally, the age structure of victimization peaked in the 30s. However, we observed a decrease in the point at which risk peaked—to 15–24 years of age. In 1970 black males 15–24 were the most vulnerable to homicide, but the risk of victimization varied substantially among our sample. Black males in St. Louis were off the chart relative to risk (1 in 200). Compared to national figures for black males in this cohort, those in St. Louis, Detroit, and Houston were at least twice as likely to become homicide victims. The Atlanta and Los Angeles groups were only somewhat less likely to become victims. By 1980, the risk for this age cohort in three cities had continued to climb—St. Louis (303 per 100,000), Detroit (227 per 100,000), and Los Angeles (252 per 100,000). These individuals also appear to be increasingly involved as victims and offenders in instrumental violence.

We also observed a shift in the structure of victimization in some cities (structure of victimization refers to the relationship between the victim and offender and whether there were single or multiple offenders and single or multiple victims). In traditional violence, the victims have commonly been family members and acquaintances; in nontraditional violence victims are primarily strangers or of unknown relationships. But we observed a shift in the structure of victimization that implied that those who are victims of instrumental violence are increasingly acquaintances. For example, in Detroit there was no substantial change over the study period in stranger victimizations (robbery-homicide), but there was a major change in the number of victimizations in which victims and offenders were acquaintances. The largest number of these individuals were under 25, which may be attributed to the increased use of teenagers in drug distribution and to random shootings. In Detroit, as well as in other northern urban centers, we are witnessing the coming-of-age of a cohort socialized in an environment where instrumental violence has become entrenched; as a result, gratuitous, violent confrontations have become more commonplace. This situation is fueled by the changing demands of the mainstream economy, the lure of the irregular economy (i.e., drug trafficking), the strengthening of secular values, and the growing attractiveness of the street hustler as a role model.

Los Angeles, over the period of a single decade became a dominant center for risk of violent victimization, and acquaintances were increasingly the victims. It began the period (1960) with risk levels that were unusually low and with mostly traditional forms of violence when compared to each of the other sample cities, with the exception of Pittsburgh. But since the late 1970s, risk levels have remained high and Los Angeles has moved from traditional to nontraditional forms of violence. The growing problem of gang violence in the city probably represents the prime element in the transition from low risk to high risk. The gang activity in Los Angeles is radically different from that of gangs in New York in the 1950s. Present-day gangs are involved in a number of criminal enterprises (e.g., crack cocaine distribution) and maintain an arsenal of weapons, including automatic weapons, making them a greater threat to community safety than earlier gangs. The rise of gangs and their growing involvement in drug trafficking is creating havoc in previously quiet, middle-class neighborhoods in Los Angeles, as drive-by shootings become more commonplace.

In our sample generally, in those communities where young blacks had experienced less success in sustaining themselves in the regular economy, nontraditional patterns of victimization were most in evidence. Houston, which had experienced few negative consequences as an outgrowth of economic transformation, had moved much less slowly away from the traditional end of the structural spectrum than had those communities that experienced many negative consequences. Therefore it appears that the continuing examples of elevated risk are indirectly dependent upon urban growth and the ability of young adult males to successfully find a satisfactory niche for themselves in the growth section of the economy.

The economic and subsequent cultural changes have had an impact on the structure of victimization, thereby altering patterns of risk. We contend that blacks residing in large manufacturing-belt cities prior to 1940 were still strongly bound by aspects of southern culture. Most violent altercations during this earlier period were basically associated with individuals engaged in a primary relationship.

During the years following World War II, southern migration to northern urban centers continued to escalate, but at the same time a large base population of northern origin was being formed. In this situation one would anticipate a weakening of selected elements of the traditional culture and the adoption of values prevalent in the environment in which individuals were socialized. Values and lifestyle practices vary through space and over time, and account for subsequent differences in the modal pattern of victimization. It is also clear these two sets of influences operate in tandem and ultimately influence the magnitude as well as the character of victimization. Several generational cohorts are present in large nonsouthern cities, each having encountered varying social experiences in a range of environments. The complexity of those groups' experiences, in terms of time spent in varying environments, should serve to distinguish initially between the prevailing structure in southern and nonsouthern urban environments, as well as within individual nonsouthern neighborhoods. Therefore, the very general concept of the existence of a subculture of violence, as developed by Wolfgang and Ferracuti (1967), is inadequate to explain levels of risk we identified as being supported by etiological differences based partially on location.

Location is simply a surrogate for a stage in the economy's developmental sequence and the manner in which identifiable subpopulations adapt to changing sets of circumstances. Thus, we labeled the subculture that originated in the rural South, largely involving primary relationships, as a *subculture of defensive violence*. Yet in the latter third of the twentieth century, we find that young adult blacks have been exposed to a substantially different set of environmental pressures and have consequently adopted a different worldview. This alternative worldview, initially manifested in manufacturing-belt cities, has now begun to spread across the landscape at varying speeds. This different worldview has led to the evolution of another subculture in which the resort to violence is commonplace. We have labeled this the *subculture of materialistic aggression*. In most locations, robbery-homicide tends to be the situation in which materialistic aggression is principally manifested, but there is growing evidence that as this subculture matures it expresses itself in a growing variety of ways.

What happens in the future relative to levels of risk most likely will be influenced by the emerging status of individuals born since 1970. The extent to which these individuals successfully negotiate the economy will play a critical role in risk abatement, but certainly not the only one. The broader question is, What do we, as a society, do to restore what Holden (1969) refers to as "public order" to the urban black communities that have become debilitated and ravaged by the violence? Why have not the plethora of "crime control" policies interdicted or ameliorated the problems?

Reconceptualizing Urban Violence

Policy analysts continually argue that one crucial aspect of policy formation, which is often not given adequate consideration, is problem structuring and problem identification (Dunn, 1981). If one conceptualizes the problem incorrectly then one falls into the error, which Raiffa (1968) refers to as a Type III error, of constructing a solution for the wrong problem. Consequently, the solution fails to address the problem because it was incorrectly structured and identified. Such is the case, I suggest, with urban violence. It is possible that the reason why policies aimed at curbing the rise of violent crime, particularly homicide, have not had an effect is that the situation has been conceptualized incorrectly. The American polity, as well as our policymakers, have conceptualized the issue of urban violence (homicide) in a way that ensures that whatever policy initiatives are developed will not address the problem as it exists.

Our current approach to homicide and violent crime uses the legal definition as the basic conceptualization of the problem for policy-formation purposes. Homicide is defined as a criminal act; therefore it is deemed a criminal justice problem. From this perspective, the emphasis is placed on the perpetrator, and the institutions involved in solving the problem are the police, prosecutors, prisons, and parole systems. Thus the policy recommendations call for the death sentence, more police, longer jail terms, mandatory sentencing for firearms crimes, and stricter furlough and parole standards. The emphasis is on punishment, and the assumption is made that if the individuals who perpetrate these crimes are locked up, the crimes will not reoccur. Unfortunately, given the structure of the problem, there are others already in the queue ready to replace those who are arrested and incarcerated. Moreover, the policies only take effect *after* someone or a number of someones have been murdered. This narrow definition of urban violence as a criminal-justice problem ensures that the situation will only get worse in our urban centers, and many more years of black citizens' lives will be lost.

During my spring 1989 sabbatical, I spent five months with the Homicide Division of the Phoenix Police Department. Long hours, mostly in the wee hours of the morning, were spent at homicide scenes—on a street, in a nightclub, or in a vacant lot. Regardless of the circumstances and location of the homicide, the variable that was constant across homicide events was the presence of the victim's body. Moreover, the tagging and removal of the victim's body was the last task after all the investigative work was completed. It was painfully clear, and frustratingly expressed by the detectives, that by the time the Homicide Division is called, someone is already dead. Moreover, by the time the police catch the offender (if they do given the changing nature of the victim-offender relationship), two or three additional people may also have been murdered or assaulted. One faces a very grim reality investigating homicides, and these criminal justice officers want something to be done *before* the event, so that it becomes unnecessary for them to respond.

Another painful reality was that many of the black victims were people who were minding their own business and were not involved in any criminal activity. They simply had the misfortune of sharing the same geographical space with individuals for whom human life meant nothing. They were in the proverbial "wrong place at the wrong time." As discussed earlier, the predominant victims of urban homicide are blacks, and they are murdered by other blacks.

The only way we as a society are going to begin to ameliorate the situation is to reconceptualize the problem so that the policies developed address the risk of victimization that confronts urban black residents. The present conceptualization places the emphasis on the offender after a homicide has occurred. This particular orientation to the problem makes it virtually impossible to discuss or develop homicide-prevention strategies. If homicide prevention and the preservation of the lives of urban black citizens is a reasonable policy goal, then an alternative conceptualization is in order.

The proposed reconceptualization views homicide not as a criminal act but as a cause of death (O'Carroll and Mercy, 1986). The term "homicide" in this context refers to victimization, rather than perpetration. Additionally, this reconceptualization places homicide within the framework of a public health response, rather than a criminal justice response. The emphasis, therefore, is on prevention and interdiction rather than on punishment. And the time frame is before the event, rather than after.

Mercy and O'Carroll (1988) argue that violence in general, and homicide in particular, have enormous public health implications. Several factors imply that homicide should be viewed from a public health perspective. First, as other causes of death decline in importance as a result of innovations in medical treatment, homicide is becoming more prominent as a leading cause of death. In fact, in 1985 the Centers for Disease Control listed homicide as the number one cause of death of black males 15 to 34 years of age (O'Carroll and Mercy, 1986). Second, there is the increasing recognition within the public health field of the importance of behavioral factors in the etiology and prevention of disease. For example, prevention of the three leading causes of death in the United States—heart disease, cancer, and stroke—has been attributed to behavioral modifications such as exercise, changes in diet, and nonsmoking (Mercy and O'Carroll, 1988). Public health perspectives and practices hold promise for beginning to address the seriousness of the problem of urban violence.

The principle goal of public health is to preserve, promote, and correct (i.e., improve) health (Last, 1980:3). Several dimensions of the public health philosophy are devoted to attaining this goal (Mercy and O'Carroll, 1988). First, public health emphasizes prevention of disease or injury from occurring or recurring. This parallels nicely the differences between homicide defined as a cause of death (preventable) and homicide defined as a criminal act (after the fact). Second, public health interventions are concentrated on those at greatest risk of disease or injury—those in greatest need of intervention (Mercy and O'Carroll, 1988). This implies that homicide policies would focus on those at greatest risk of victimization—urban black residents—rather than exclusively on those who are the victimizers (as in the criminal-justice approach).

An integral part of the problem of interdicting homicide risk among blacks is the question of where policy issues originate and gain attention, particularly when issues of concern to black communities are at stake. Elder and Cobb (1984:115) stress that policy problems are not a priori givens, but rather are matters of definition. Whether or not a certain situation constitutes a policy problem worthy of governmental attention depends not just upon facts, but upon beliefs and values. There may be a core set of values that undergird the U.S. governmental structure evolving from the Constitution; however, the importance of one set of issues in relation to another is subject to interpretation by the various segments of the American polity. More often than not problems that are viewed as important only to black citizens are not viewed with the same degree of importance by the dominant community (Wilson, 1987).

Furthermore, interdicting homicide risk among black Americans will require a set of long-term strategies. The U.S. governmental system and its citizens are not excited about long-term strategies; the system is only geared to accommodate short-run solutions. The polity wants to see results from its policies and programs, and if things do not change quickly, the commitment begins to wane. Any set of strategies devised will have marginal utility in the short run, but in the long run they may do some good. The desire for short-run results pushes the punishment (criminal-justice) response to the problem. It is only in the area of public health problems (e.g., cancer and AIDS) that the political system is inclined to make long-term policy commitments, realizing that results will occur for and benefits will be reaped by future generations.

If homicide is reconceptualized within the context of a public health model, our policy options for attacking, and hopefully interdicting, the problem are substantially broadened. The current stream of criminal justice approaches is nicely subsumed under the public health approach as part of an overarching solution to urban violence, but it is not seen as the only approach. Moreover, in this proposed framework the criminal justice machinery can become an active participant in the development of prevention strategies, because the broadened definition of the problem allows these agencies to move beyond their arrest and punishment responsibilities, which a few agencies (e.g., the Phoenix Police Department) are beginning to see as essential to reducing levels of urban violence.

By adopting this conceptualization of homicide, we begin to focus on interdicting the development of behavior patterns and worldviews in at-risk children that put them in danger in later years of becoming victims of lethal violence. As Allen (1981) has argued, potential victims can be made aware of their own dangerous behavior patterns that make them susceptible to being murdered. The concern, therefore, is with helping people learn and practice alternative behavior patterns (Spivak, Hausman, and Prothrow-Stith, 1989). Furthermore, it means that we begin to recognize that other social problems, (e.g., black teenage pregnancy) are connected to the issue of lethal violence. Homicide is a very complex phenomenon that will require a complex set of solutions. The public health model offers us a vastly superior policy framework for tackling the issue than does the narrowly focused criminal-justice model.

Civil Liberties and Civil Rights Issues

Even though the public health model is infinitely better for devising policy solutions for interdicting urban homicide, it, like the criminal justice model is not without its potential problems. As a political scientist, one must be concerned with issues of individual rights. As the debate swirls around issues such as preventive detention in the criminal justice model, some elements of the public health approach may also give one reason to pause. The overriding concern will be issues of civil liberties and civil rights.

A threat that is present within the public health model is the question of quarantine or removal from society (i.e., public health surveillance). This issue was raised decades ago in the debate surrounding cancer patients and has been raised more recently with AIDS patients. A related controversy, also raised in the AIDS debate, is whether files or lists ought to be maintained of individuals with high-risk characteristics.

An argument can be made that urban black communities are already "quarantined" from the larger society. While the health and welfare of these communities is directly affected by changes in the external environment, the world of many of the residents of urban black communities may not extend beyond the boundaries of their neighborhoods. Moreover, in cities like Los Angeles and Washington, D.C., the police have, for all intents and purposes, isolated certain communities from the remainder of the city in efforts to contain the violence.

The problem with public health surveillance is one of definition, rather than substance. Public health surveillance is the ongoing and systematic collection, analysis, and interpretation of health data (Mercy and O'Carroll, 1988). Surveillance systems are used extensively in criminal justice areas, e.g., the FBI's Uniform Crime Reporting Program, the Bureau of Justice Statistics National Crime Survey, and data systems maintained by state and local criminal justice agencies. The problem will arise, as it has in the AIDS area, over the issue of the maintenance of files or lists of individuals with high-risk characteristics.

The question of risk-group identification is potentially the more dangerous threat to civil liberties and civil rights. One could envision hordes of public health "detectives" invading urban black communities, going door-to-door with clipboards asking for names and encouraging people to turn in neighbors with high-risk characteristics. Risk-group identification has already been accomplished, however, through the work of many social scientists as well as in data compiled by the Centers for Disease Control and the U.S. Census Bureau. We *know* the categories of individuals at greatest risk to homicide victimization, and we also have the ability to identify risk to the smallest aggregate unit—the neighborhood. Moreover, we have done this at an aggregate rather than an individual level. In fact, it is not necessary to specifically identify individuals in order to develop prevention strategies. The problem will be to make sure that risk-group identification is kept at the aggregate level and not reduced to the level of the individual. In spite of these problems, a public health conceptualization appears to be the only viable approach to addressing a problem that is growing daily.

Black Political Scientists and Policy Research

As mentioned earlier, a continuing debate within the National Conference of Black Political Scientists surrounds the question of the role of research done by black political scientists within the discipline. Holden (1983:1) observes that "it has long been conceived that the Black Scholar has some affirmative responsibility to participate in the collective search for freedom" for blacks in North America. Dianne M. Pinderhughes, in her 1989 Presidential Address to the National Conference of Black Political Scientists, suggested that one role played by black political scientists in the discipline is to "press for the accurate, complex representation of politics in the black community" (Pinderhughes, 1990:14).

Black political scientists also have an important role to play in the identification of the problem and the structuring of the debate on policy issues of concern to the black community. Kingdon (1984) notes that the treatment of a policy issue on the agenda will be affected by the way in which a problem is recognized and defined and by the category in which it is placed. Thus, in this instance, defining urban violence as a criminal justice problem narrows the scope of the debate and limits the range of potential policy options, while defining urban violence as a public health issue broadens the scope of the debate and expands the range of potential policy options. Black political scientists need to direct more attention in public policy research to issue identification and problem structuring with the hope that future policies of concern to black America will address problems as they exist, not as they have been politicized.

References

Allen, Nancy H. 1981. "Homicide Prevention and Intervention." *Suicide and Life Threatening Behavior*, 11 (Fall): 167–79.

Bookchin, Murray. 1974. *The Limits of the City*. New York: Harper and Row.

Cohen, Lawrence E., and Marcus Felson. 1979. "Social Change and Crime Rate Trends: A Routine Activity Approach." *American Sociological Review*, 44:588–608.

Dunn, William N. 1981. *Public Policy Analysis*. Englewood Cliffs, NJ: Prentice-Hall, Inc.

Elder, Charles W., and Roger W. Cobb. 1984. "Agenda Building and the Politics of Aging." *Policy Studies Journal*, 13:115–29.

Elkins, Stephen L. 1987. *City and Regime in the American Republic*. Chicago: University of Chicago Press.

Federal Bureau of Investigation. 1987. *Uniform Crime Reports*. Washington, DC: Government Printing Office.

Fischer, Claude S. 1976a. "Toward a Subcultural Theory of Urbanism." *American Journal of Sociology*, 80:1,319–1,340.

_____. 1976b. *The Urban Experience*. New York: Harcourt, Brace, Javanovich, Inc.

Gastil, R. D. 1971. "Homicide and a Regional Culture of Violence." *American Sociological Review*, 36:412–26.

Gottdiener, M. 1987. *The Decline of Urban Politics: Political Theory and the Crisis of the Local State*. Newbury Park, CA: Sage Publications.

Holden, Matthew, Jr. 1969. "The Quality of Urban Order." In Henry L. Schmandt, ed., *The Quality of Urban Life*. Los Angeles: Sage Publications, Inc.

_____. 1983. *Moral Engagement and Combat Scholarship: Contemporary Notes on a Black Scholarly Tradition*. McClean, VA: Court Square Institute.

Hunter, A. 1974. *Symbolic Communities*. Chicago: University of Chicago Press.

Kingdon, John W. 1984. *Agendas, Alternatives and Public Policies*. Boston: Little, Brown, and Co.

Kornhauser, Ruth. 1978. *Social Sources of Delinquency*. Chicago: University of Chicago Press.

Last, John M. 1980. "Scope and Methods of Prevention." In John M. Last, ed., *Public Health and Preventive Medicine*. 11th ed. New York: Appleton-Century-Crofts.

Lewis, Oscar. 1959. *Five Families: Mexican Case Studies in Culture of Poverty* (New York: Basic Books). "Culture of Poverty." In Daniel P. Moynihan, ed., *On Understanding Poverty: Perspectives from the Social Sciences*. New York: Basic Books, 1968.

Los Angeles Times, 30 January 1989.

Los Angeles Times, 16 January 1990.

Luundsgaard, H. P. 1977. *Murder in Space City*. New York: Oxford University Press.

Mercy, James A., and Patrick W. O'Carroll. 1988. "New Directions in Violence Prediction: The Public Health Arena." *Violence and Victims*, 3:285–301.

New York Times, 11 January 1989.

O'Carroll, Patrick W., and James A. Mercy. 1986. "Homicide Trends in the United States." In Darnell F. Hawkins, ed., *Homicide among Black Americans*. Lanham: University Press of America.

Peterson, Paul. 1981. *City Limits*. Chicago: University of Chicago Press.

Pinderhughes, Dianne M. 1990. "NCOPBS: Observations on the State of the Organization." *National Political Science Review*, 2:13–21.

Raiffa, Howard. 1968. *Decision Analysis*. Reading, MA: Addison-Wesley.

Rees, P. H. 1970. "Concepts on Social Space." In Brian J. Berry and Frank C. Horton, eds., *Geographic Perspectives on Urban Systems*. Englewood Cliffs, NJ: Prentice-Hall.

Roncek, Dennis W. 1981. "Dangerous Places: Crime and Residential Environment." *Social Forces*, 60:74–98.

Rose, Harold M. 1981. "The Changing Spatial Dimensions of Black Homicide in Selected American Cities." *Journal of Environmental Systems*, 11:57–80.

Rose, Harold M., and Paula D. McClain. 1990. *Race, Place, and Risk: Black Homicide in Urban America*. Albany, NY: State University of New York Press.

Scheingold, Stuart A. 1984. *The Politics of Law and Order*. New York: Longman.

_____. 1988. "The Politicization of Crime." Paper delivered at the 1988 meeting of the American Political Science Association.

Silberman, Charles. 1978. *Criminal Violence, Criminal Justice*. New York: Random House.

Simmel, George. 1951. "Metropolis and Mental Life." In Kurt H. Wolff, ed., *The Society of George Simmel*. New York: Free Press.

Spivak, Howard, Alice J. Hausman, and Deborah Prothrow-Stith. 1989. "Practitioners' Forum: Public Health and the Primary Prevention of Adolescent Violence—the Violence Prevention Project." *Violence and Victims*, 4:203–12.

Wilson, James Q. 1960. *Negro Politics: The Search for Leadership*. New York: Free Press.

Wilson, William Julius. 1987. *The Truly Disadvantaged: The Inner city, the Underclass and Public Policy*. Chicago: University of Chicago Press.

Wirth, Louis. 1938. "Urbanism as a Way of Life." *American Journal of Sociology,* 64:1–24.

Wolfgang, Marvin E. 1958. *Patterns in Criminal Homicide.* Philadelphia: University of Pennsylvania.

Wolfgang, Marvin E., and Franco Ferracuti. 1967. *The Subculture of Violence.* London: Tavistock-Social Science Paperbacks.

Political Science and the Black Political Experience: Issues in Epistemology and Relevance

Mack H. Jones

Prairie View A & M University

This heuristic essay argues that the worldview of a people conditions the nature and content of its social science knowledge and that two peoples' or cultures' social sciences will differ to the extent that they have different worldviews. However, when there is an adversarial relationship between two peoples' who share a common territory, as is the case with white and black Americans, the worldview of the dominant group will be used to give meaning to social reality and to generate social science knowledge. Knowledge so generated conveys only a caricature of the oppressed or dominated people and hence has little prescriptive utility for their struggle to end their domination.
This article relies on formal but not empirical proof of assertions intended to stimulate discussion and research.

The 1960s and 1970s were years of challenge and upheaval in the United States, politically, economically, socially, and culturally. Proponents of conventional wisdom and orthodox practices in almost all sectors of society were called upon to demonstrate their relevance and efficacy in the face of changing circumstances. The challenge was especially pronounced in academia, particularly in the social sciences. The failure of the latter to anticipate the turbulence of the period made them especially vulnerable to charges of irrelevance and demands for fundamental change. David Easton dubbed this call for relevance in political science the New Revolution, a revolution that promised to produce a more relevant political science with enhanced utility for those seeking a more just American society

(Easton, 1969). The prospect for such a political science was eagerly ap-
plauded by those with a special interest in improving the political circumstances of black Americans.

However, approximately a decade-and-a-half later the New Revolution
has become the New Orthodoxy, and the relevance and utility of American political science for understanding and ameliorating the problems of
black Americans remain in question. In 1985, in a thoughtful essay in *PS*
(the newsletter of the American Political Science Association), Ernest Wilson, in trying to explain the continued limited utility of U.S. political
science toward the understanding of black life in the United States, argued
that the contribution of political science has been considerably less impressive than that of allied disciplines such as history and sociology because of a "'mismatch' between the central substantive concerns and current
methodological orientations of the discipline, and the most salient and
interesting features of Afro-American life." (Wilson, 1985:600). According
to Wilson, political science typically studies elites and the processes and
channels through which decisions are made, and, given the fact that blacks
have been deprived historically of elite status, it follows syllogistically that
political science would give only limited attention to political activity and
developments central to black political life.

For those concerned with the utility of political science for understanding the black political condition, Wilson's observations are insightful as far
as they go; but they are not exhaustive. As he acknowledges in his essay,
they were offered as stimuli for other questions rather than as definitive
answers. This essay is a continuation of the discussion of the limitations
of political science for understanding black political life in the United
States. However, the focus is less on why so little attention is given to
black politics qua black politics than on the broader question of why political science as a discipline has such a limited relevance and utility for
describing and explaining political life in the United States in a way that
would yield prescriptive insights for those interested in developing programs for black advancement.

This then is meant to be a theoretical essay in the general area of the
philosophy of science. The overriding purposes are, in general, to stimulate reflections on and debate about the impact that worldviews have on
the nature and content of social science knowledge, and, in particular, to
explore the consequences of using the dominant white American worldview to develop social science knowledge about black Americans and
other dominated groups. In the course of developing my thesis, I make
assertions that rely on formal but not empirical proof. I can only beg the
indulgence of readers who may be reluctant to take such a flight.

The cause of the limited relevance and marginal utility of U.S. political
science goes much deeper than problems associated with its narrow focus
on elites. Rather, the explanation lies in much more basic epistemological
and paradigmatic assumptions of American political science. The essential
argument below is that the irrelevance and disutility of U.S. political science for those concerned with black advancement are explained by the
fact that in the United States black and white societies are adversaries with

conflicting goals, and that American political science grows out of, and in turn serves the needs of, white society. As a consequence, American political science cannot simultaneously serve the needs of its antagonist, the black society seeking to overturn white dominance. Further, social science knowledge is generated to serve a people's anticipation and control needs, and to the extent that two societies are adversaries and thus have conflicting anticipation and control needs, the social science knowledge that serves the interest of one cannot serve the interest of the other.

The terms "anticipation" and "control needs" are borrowed from Eugene Meehan, who defines them as "the need to anticipate future events so that behavior can be adapted to them . . . [and] the need to be able to control future events (the past is beyond control) so that man can become something more than a servile prisoner of natural forces." (Meehan, 1968:19). In short, anticipation and control needs refer to a people's need for information that is useful for understanding their circumstances and developing prescriptions for moving toward their goals as posited in their worldview. As Meehan argues, "the quality of knowledge depends upon the purpose it will serve." (1968:18).

This argument will be constructed by first discussing the purpose and nature of social science inquiry and then showing how the worldview and the derivative normative assumptions of a people structure the content of the paradigms used to give meaning to social reality and serve to determine what circumstances constitute problems. This will be followed by an attempt to demonstrate how and why the social science of one people necessarily creates a self-serving caricature of their adversaries. This analysis of some of the major assumptions of the paradigm that now governs American political science will reveal why these assumptions give rise to a political science of only marginal utility for those interested in understanding and transforming the conditions of blacks in the United States.

The argument being advanced here runs counter to the commonly accepted notion that social sciences in general and American political science in particular have universal validity and utility because they are allegedly generated through systematic intersubjective procedures and hence are amenable to public validation. This idea that objective procedures yield knowledge with universal utility is untenable. Social science inquiry, indeed all scientific inquiry, has two distinct dimensions: a consciously normative dimension and a scientific or objective dimension. The substantive content of a people's social science is determined by the consciously normative assumptions with which the process of knowing begins rather than by the science.

The schematic diagram in Figure 1 summarizes and depicts the operations involved in the process of social science inquiry. It shows that social science inquiry begins with and issues from the worldview of the society or people in question, and that inquiry is undertaken to serve their anticipation and control needs as determined by those who have the power to influence the content of a society's social science. All societies develop processes for the social generation of information, which helps them anticipate factors that might compromise their ability to achieve their objec-

Figure 1. Schematic Diagram of the Process of Intellectual Inquiry through Which People A Develop Caricature of People B

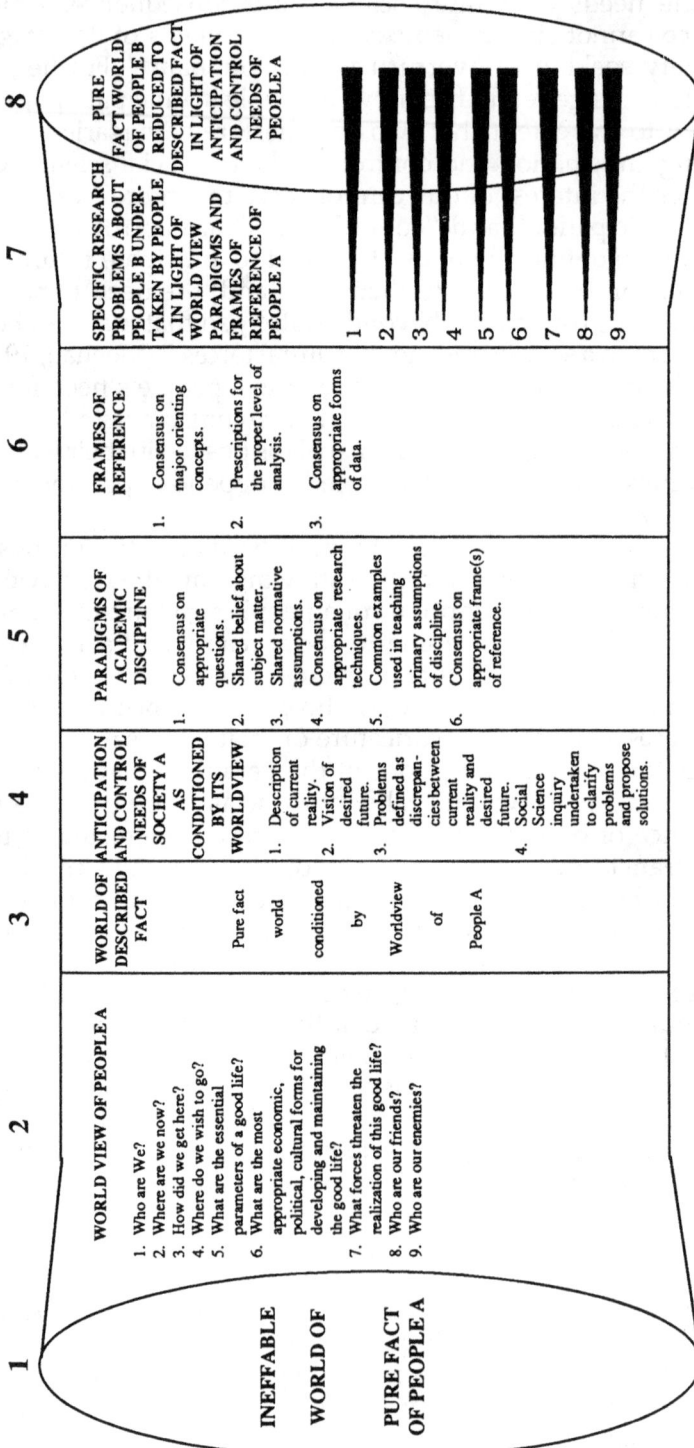

The diagram shows how a people reduce the world of pure fact sense data to researchable problems. Using their world view as the primary lens through which they view the world, people develop a description of existing reality and a vision of the desired future. Problems are discrepancies between existing reality and a vision of the desired future. The dominant paradigm and prevailing frames-of-reference determine the nature and content of the problems to be addressed. Blocks 7 and 8 show that the process of inquiry of People A illuminates developments of People B only to the extent that the problems as defined by People A require such illumination. The sum of information generated about People B by People A becomes a caricature of People B which is accepted by People A as adequate depiction of People B.

tives, and which also facilitates the development of strategies for controlling these factors or, if control is not possible, adapting their behavior accordingly.

For example, societies develop new academic disciplines or new subfields within existing disciplines as societal circumstances change and as there is a resulting felt need for new or different information to understand, control, or adapt to the changing circumstances. The rise of "politics in developing states" in the 1950s and "urban politics" in the 1960s as subfields in political science are cases in point. The need for the former was occasioned by the rise of the United States as the new custodian of Western interest in Africa, Asia, and the Americas; the growing urbanization in the United States and attendant sociocultural and political problems accounted for the development of urban politics as a subfield. The basic underlying assumptions upon which both subfields rest come from the prevailing U.S. worldview, and the frames of references adopted in the two subfields were compatible with the normative concerns that stimulated their development.

Structural functionalism and modernization theory used in explaining the politics of developing states reflect the Eurocentric bias of the American worldview and serve the interest of those seeking to maintain Western dominance of developing states. They do so by suggesting that Western societies represent the ideal state of development, and that for the poorer countries to reach a similar state they must adopt not only the values of the West but their economic and political institutions as well. As Claude Ake points out, this "encourages dependence and inculcates a sense of inferiority in Third World peoples" (Ake, 1982:140).

In the urban politics subfield both pluralism and community power orientations are consistent with the idea that the United States is a system of diffused and countervailing power that maximizes human growth and liberty through enlightened competition. Both foci left undisturbed and unilluminated the question of the relationship between the distribution of power and the pattern of urban ills, and as a result research and scholarship serve the interest of those who now hold power, rather than of those seeking fundamental change (for further discussion of the argument that these mainstream approaches are biased in favor of the status quo see Bachrach and Baratz, 1982; Ricci, 1984; Parenti, 1983).

As mentioned earlier, the process of social science inquiry may be divided into two distinct dimensions: the consciously normative and the objective or scientific dimension. The consciously normative includes (1) the process in which we confront the world of sense perceptions of what is external to us as observers, which F. S. C. Northrop has labeled the world of pure fact (Northrop, 1969: 35–58);[1] (2) the normative rules prescribed by the culture of the people in question for giving meaning to sense perceptions; or, to put it differently, the societally sanctioned rules for converting the world of pure fact into described fact; (3) the development of social science disciplines in response to the anticipation and control needs of the people in question; (4) the development of paradigms within which communities of scholars work; (5) the construction of frames-of-reference to guide problem formulation, prescribe the level of analysis, determine the criteria of evidence, and stipulate the appropriate methods and techniques to be used; and (6) the determination of which regularities constitute "problems." All of these operations are purposive and normative.

The scientific phase of social science inquiry, which gets underway within boundaries established by the consciously normative operations, involves (1) the development of descriptions, classifications, and taxonomies as preconditioned by the normative phase; (2) the identification and validation of interrelationships; and (3) the development and elaboration of explanations and theories to explain and resolve normatively determined problems.

Although most discussions and descriptions of the process of scientific inquiry, particularly in the social sciences, focus on the scientific or objective phase, the consciously normative phase merits equal if not greater attention and understanding, because it is the consciously normative operations that render all social science inquiry parochial and idiosyncratic to the culture from which it emanates. The central role that the worldview plays in ascribing meaning accounts for the inherent parochialism of social science inquiry.

Every people has a worldview that is a product of its lived experience and that constitutes the lens through which the world of sense perceptions is reduced to described fact. The worldview answers these kinds of questions: Who are we? From where did we come? How did we get here? Where do we wish to go? What are the appropriate agencies for transformation, reformation, and conservation? Who are our friends? Our enemies? The Worldview also summarizes the societal perception of the nature of the good life and the appropriate political, economic, and cultural forms necessary for its realization. Academic discipline, especially social science disciplines, are developed within the constraints of worldviews.

The establishment of academic disciplines and the determination of their substantive content, then, is a purposive, normative exercise that is necessarily parochial. It is parochial because a people's need to know is a function of their anticipation and control needs, and because the latter can be determined only by juxtaposing a society's perception of where it stands in a given historical moment with its vision of the future that it is pursuing. Information is generated to describe, clarify, and explain the difference between current reality and the desired future, as well as impediments that threaten the conversion of current reality into the desired future. Problems are framed in this context, and the nature and content of academic disciplines are driven by the society's definition of its problems.

The Paradigm as the Source of Parochialism

The centrality of the consciously normative dimension of inquiry in determining the content of social science may be demonstrated by focusing on the role of the paradigm in social science inquiry. The paradigm comprises those assumptions that a community of scholars share and that guide their work. In the social sciences the paradigm includes, inter alia, (1) shared normative assumptions on basic ideological issues, (2) shared beliefs about the subject matter, (3) consensus on the range of appropriate questions to be raised, (4) shared examples in teaching the primary assumptions of the discipline, and (5) consensus on appropriate frames of reference.

This list of the elements of a paradigm was adapted from the postscript of the second edition of Thomas Kuhns' celebrated work *The Structure of Scientific Revolution* (Kuhn, 1972).[2] Kuhn, of course, had in mind the physical sciences when he delineated the elements of a paradigm. Thus when he spoke of shared beliefs about the subject matter, consensus on appropriate questions, and common examples used in teaching, it did not necessarily imply anything about the ideological character or cultural specificity of the work of those sharing the paradigm. This is not true, however, in the case of the social sciences, particularly political science.

When applied to political science, these assumptions are more than disciplinary guideposts, because they determine to a great extent the substantive core of the inquiry. Shared beliefs about the subject matter are common beliefs about the nature of political authority; about governing, the governed, and governors; and about various political institutions, conventions, and practices. Regarding black politics, these shared beliefs include predispositions about race and racial differences and about the role of government in promoting equal opportunity. Consensus on frames of reference involves, as an example, choosing as an orienting device structural-functionalism, with its emphasis on consensus, stability, and equilibrium, over class analysis, with its concern with conflict and change; or choosing pluralism over power theory as a device for understanding black political life. In a similar vein, a consensus on shared examples used in teaching the primary assumptions of the field entails using the evolution of the United States (or perhaps Great Britain) to convey what is meant by the process of development or political integration. It also means using the history of Irish Catholics or American Jews to demonstrate the presumed utility of the pluralist model for understanding the politics of groups labeled as disadvantaged.

The mere listing of the categories of beliefs that comprise the paradigm conveys unmistakably the ideological character and cultural specificity of the normative dimension of American political science. The beliefs that are dominant among political scientists are derived from the prevailing American worldview, and these beliefs serve to legitimize and sustain the existing order. For those who are content with the prevailing order, that does not constitute a problem.

However, for those who are dispossessed or oppressed by the prevailing order, it is a different matter. Their experiences have been different, they view the prevailing order in a different light, and these differences are reflected in their worldview. For example, the worldview of white Americans explains the continuing domination by whites and the concomitant continuing inequality of blacks in a manner decidedly different from the explanation derived from the worldview of black Americans. Polling data show that blacks assign primacy to racism and systemic structural impediments as causes of the unequal position of blacks in American life, while whites place greater weight on presumed shortcomings of blacks themselves. A political science grounded in the black definition of reality would of necessity raise different questions from those that emanate from the prevailing paradigm.

It is not only through its culturally specific definition of problems, however, that the paradigm generates parochialism. The fact that the scholarship of one group in an adversarial relationship is likely to focus on its antagonist only insofar as the latter's presence impinges upon the former's anticipation and control needs also contributes to the parochial character of the scholarship. That is, the paradigm leads the practitioner to study the adversary community only to the extent that the adversary constitutes a problem. This explains why in American social science for the most part, blacks are simply discussed as problems. In the United States, the black presence is a problem that compromises the dominant forces' ability to realize the future envisioned in their worldview. Hence, black life is studied with a view to obviating the problem that the black presence causes for the dominant interest. In urban politics, criminal justice, sociology, etc., blacks are discussed merely as problems. Such scholarship focuses disproportionately upon the negative aspects of black life and culture and presents correspondingly negative caricatures. These caricatures are in due course synthesized and offered as an empirically valid description and explanation of black life. Such caricatures may have utility for those only interested in finding ways of circumventing the problems that the black presence is presumed to cause them, but they have neither descriptive nor prescriptive utility for those interested in transforming the inequitable conditions under which blacks live. An analysis of the dominant paradigm in contemporary political science will demonstrate why this is so.

The Dominant Paradigm and Black Political Life

The irrelevance and limited utility of mainstream political science do not result from a conspiracy among scholars to produce misleading caricatures of black life. Rather, they are predictable results of scholars doing precisely what they are trained to do, that is, define and research problems within the context of the prevailing worldview. The assumptions of the paradigm that are derived from the worldview explain the irrelevance. Identification and analysis of some of the critical assumptions of the dominant paradigm will dramatize this point. Some of the major assumptions in the paradigm that guides political science inquiry in the United States are these:

I. Shared Normative Assumptions
    A. Euro-American nations represent the apex of civilization and development.

   B. The presumed gap between Euro-American peoples and others
       in terms of civilization and development is a function of certain
       virtues unique to western European peoples.
   C. There is a natural hierarchical ordering of people, with Euro-
       American people at one pole and African people at the other.
   D. The capitalist economic arrangement is the most efficient one,
       and it is more compatible with individual liberty than other eco-
       nomic arrangements.
   E. The dire socioeconomic conditions of non-Western peoples are
       the result of their own inappropriate behavior.
   F. Government should facilitate the development of privately owned
       and controlled businesses.
   G. Economic worth is a justification and important criterion for de-
       termining political participation and political authority.
   H. The continued dominance of the market economies, led by the
       United States and Western Europe, in the world economy is es-
       sential for human progress.

 II. Beliefs about the Subject Matter
   A. The best government is the one that governs least.
   B. Political participation is a privilege rather than a right.
   C. A republican form of government is superior to either direct de-
       mocracy or democratic centralism.
   D. Political structures alone determine whether or not a political
       system is democratic, and "one person—one vote" is a necessary
       and sufficient condition for democratic government.

III. The Frames of Reference
   A. The idea of system, functionalism
   B. Major orienting concepts-systems, equilibrium, tension manage-
       ment, categories of functional analysis
   C. Level of analysis-system, with some focus on individuals and
       reified groups but not on social classes
   D. Types of data—psychological and situational, with the latter be-
       ing accorded primacy; scant attention given to reflections about
       values and the relationship between them and empiricism

IV. Consensus on Appropriate Questions
   A. How do systems maintain stability in the face of competing and
       contradictory interests?
   B. How do political systems adapt to environmental changes with-
       out altering significantly the substantive outcomes of the political
       process?

 V. Shared Examples Used in Teaching
   A. The political development of the United States is used as the
       example of the optimum evolution of political systems.
   B. The sequential inclusion of ethnic immigrants in the United States

political culture is used to demonstrate the presumed-inexorable process of development and progress in the United States.

This list of the elements that comprise the dominant paradigm in American political science is meant to be suggestive rather than definitive or exhaustive. Others might draw up quite a different set of assumptions. Some might challenge the appropriateness of some of the elements listed. However, adding to or subtracting from this list only serves to reinforce the point that the prior normative assumptions that comprise the paradigm establish the parameters within which problems are conceptualized, conventional interpretations are made, and solutions are prescribed.

Having outlined salient assumptions of the existing paradigms, the remaining task is to demonstrate what picture of reality arises from them, what anticipation and control needs follow, how, in turn, these needs determine what the important problems are, and, finally, to demonstrate the implications of all of this for those interested in understanding black political life in the United States.

The dominant paradigm, based on what Ake has called Eurocentric teleologism, assumes that human societies evolve inexorably toward some predetermined end (Ake, 1982: 125–43). Euro-American cultures, especially the United States, are assumed to have reached or are approaching that end: the good society has been developed; the end of ideology and the end of history are upon us. Armed with these and related paradigmatic assumptions, the American political scientist begins with an image of the United States as the most advanced human society, a society not simply committed to developing an egalitarian order, but one that has developed the optimum economic and political structures that can bring such a human community into being.

The American politico-economic system is seen by those working within the dominant paradigm as one without fundamental or systemic flaws. It is thought to provide near-optimum arrangements for the allocation of societal resources, both human and nonhuman. Given this perception of near perfection, the need to preserve the existing institutional arrangements are taken for granted. The structural arrangements are not analyzed or evaluated as historically determined and historically conditioned agencies or as structures designed to facilitate the pursuit of certain ends to the exclusion of others, but rather, the structural arrangements are presented as ends in and of themselves. Consequently, those working within the dominant paradigm assume that all problems can and should be resolved within the existing structural arrangements. As a consequence, the existing institutional arrangements become self-justifying, ideological precepts. The existence of certain structural arrangements is taken as evidence that the ends they were initially designed to facilitate are being attained. Thus democracy, for example, becomes simply the presence of certain structures and procedures. Substantive outcomes become immaterial; only the procedures matter.

Starting from the assumption that the system is near perfect, with optimum institutional arrangements, political scientists are predisposed to

view most problems as transient, resulting from routine societal maturation and amenable to solutions through existing arrangements. The system, by definition, is sound. Persistent and recurring problems that defy
such solutions are not perceived to be systemic. Instead they are viewed
as accidents of history, as the result of deficiencies of those in whom the
problems are manifested, or as some combination of the two. Since the
paradigm defines them as nonsystemic, such problems are also to be
resolved without systemic change.

In this context, the primary focus of American political science centers
around how to maintain a stable commonwealth, that is, how to maintain
the existing order, in the face of systemic stress. The configuration of
regularities that threaten existing institutional arrangements is defined as
problems.

The concern with maintaining stability through existing institutional
arrangements significantly conditions the handling of black political life in
American political science, but it is not the only assumption that does so:
the paradigmatic assumption of Euro-American supremacy and the cor-
relative belief that the lagging position of non-European people is the
result of their own inappropriate behavior also come to bear. Taken together, these three sets of normative assumptions dissuade scholars from
even considering whether the enduring inequality of blacks is a function
of systemic imperatives of the United States politico-economic system.
However, inasmuch as the persistent and enduring black inequality ren-
ders indefensible any attempt to define it as transitory, those working
within the existing paradigm are obliged to explain it as an accident of
history going back to the days of chattel slavery on the one hand, or as the
result of the inappropriate behavior of blacks themselves, on the other.
This yields a scholarship and body of information with little descriptive
relevance and even less prescriptive utility for those committed to the
fundamental transformation of the conditions under which blacks live.

The descriptive irrelevance flows from the fact that the definition of
problems does not issue from a concern with what impediments stand
between blacks and their efforts toward self-realization. Rather, the initial
concern is the potential impact of the black presence and their efforts
toward self-realization on the capacity of existing institutional arrangements to maintain a stable commonwealth. Studies undertaken in this
context yield only information that may be useful in determining how the
black presence may be managed to minimize stress on the system, and not
information about how the system might be transformed to serve black
interest.

Driven by the dictates of the dominant paradigm, such studies necessarily view black life through the eyes of its adversaries. These adversarial
studies are taken as authentic and universally useful descriptions of black
political life, when in fact they are only caricatures by those for whom the
black presence is a problem. The caricatures are built around the presumed pathologies of black life. Such scholarship is bereft of prescriptive
insights.

Toward a More Useful Paradigm

The move toward a political science with descriptive relevance and pre-scriptive utility for black Americans can be undertaken only by those who see the full liberation of black Americans as the ultimate objective to be served by their work. Scholars so committed would not begin their cri-tique of mainstream political science simply looking for procedural errors, biases, misplaced emphases, ulterior motives, or similar academic trans-gressions. Instead they would begin by challenging the existing corpus of political science literature in its entirety. The quest for relevance would begin with a systematic examination of the consciously normative assump-tions upon which American political science rests. This would allow one to determine the nature of the relationship between societal forces, dom-inant values, and discrete political interests on the one hand, and the nature and content of political science on the other. Such an examination would demonstrate how discrete interests give rise to and are served by conventional scholarship, and in doing so it would confirm the limited scope and parochial nature of American political science.

With that accomplished, the next task would be to develop a political science that grows out of and serves the anticipation and control needs of black Americans. The first stage in such a process would be the develop-ment of an appropriate paradigm. Paradigms, of course, are not born whole, nor are they created by fiat. They evolve over time and in the context of a worldview that is in itself the product of an even more pro-tracted historical process. Thus no effort will be made here to develop a paradigm. Commenting on some of the assumptions that such a paradigm might comprise will have to suffice.

A paradigm for a more useful political science for black interests would reflect the worldview of black Americans. Some might argue that there is no black American worldview, but only a synthetic American worldview that reflects the racial and ethnic diversity that characterize the United States. Although it is consistent with the Great American Myth, that po-sition is a bit fanciful. All people who perceive themselves as a distinct, historically determined people and who are perceived by others to be so have a corresponding worldview. The fact that there may be considerable similarities in the worldviews of proximate peoples indicates nothing more than that there is a certain correspondence between worldview and lived experience, and that consequently people whose experiences overlap and are intertwined will manifest equally complementary worldviews. How-ever, when proximate peoples are also adversaries, their worldviews will reflect the adversarial character of their relationship. The worldview of each adversary explains, among other things, its perception of its position in the adversarial relationship, how the adversarial relationship came about, and what forces are responsible for maintaining it. It also conveys the collective perception of the desired futures and the preferred strategies for pursuing alternative futures.

Dominant and subordinate communities who are parties to a given adversarial relationship have different interpretations of the nature and causes of the relationship, and their visions of the desired futures also differ. This is certainly true of the black and white communities in the United States. For example, as alluded to earlier, polling data show that black Americans assign primacy to the ideology of white supremacy and the institutional practices driven by that ideology as the cause of persistent black inequality.[3] Black respondents reject the conventional notion of the United States as a benign pluralist society in which there is an inexorable peristaltic progression of all racial and ethnic groups toward equal status, and in its stead substitute the view that white Americans are determined to maintain their dominant position at all cost. Blacks are more cynical and less trusting of American political and economic institutions, while at the same time being much more positively disposed toward state intervention in the economy. Finally, blacks are much less sanguine than whites about the role of the United States in world politics, especially in its relationship with the impoverished nations of Africa, Asia, and the Americas.

Operating from the worldview of black Americans, political scientists would perceive the United States as hierarchically ordered society with whites at the top and blacks at the bottom. The black condition would be viewed as a systemic outcome of the American political economy rather than as a historical accident or aberration. Scholarship that began from such normative assumptions would produce a world of described fact decidedly different from that found in mainstream political science. First of all, blacks would not be perceived merely as problems; rather, those values in the broader American culture that thwart black efforts effect change and the institutions to which they give rise would constitute the problems around which scholarly works would cohere. Such a scholarship would not take for granted the benevolent character of the basic values of the American political culture, nor would it assume that the existing political institutions and practices are appropriate forms for political struggle.

The structural-functional systems, and pluralist frames of reference would have no place in such a paradigm. Their focus on consensus and stability, gradualism and incremental change, and accommodation and automaticity would render them suspect. Conceptual schemes such as Donald Harris's alternative formulation (Harris, 1972) and my dominant-submissive group model (Jones, 1972:10) would command greater attention.

Harris postulates that the various debilities that have always characterized black life in the United States (for example, high unemployment, high poverty levels, inadequate health care, inadequate educational preparation) are all logical, systemic outcomes of the American politico-economic system. Racism, according to the Harris frame of reference, serves as a device for rationing these systemic debilities so that a disproportionately high share is visited upon black Americans.

Black-white politics may be best understood as a power struggle in which whites, as the superordinate group, act toward blacks in a manner designed to maintain whites' dominant position, whereas blacks seek to eradicate whites' dominance. The politics of this conflictual relationship takes the form of a struggle between the two communities to influence public policy, one seeking to maintain and the other to overturn the existing power relationship. Conflict and collaboration within and across community lines are viewed and interpreted in light of the broader power struggle.

A political science starting from such assumptions would produce a picture of the world radically different from the one that grows out of the dominant paradigm. It would highlight exactly how power is exercised, by whom and in whose interest. The new paradigm would facilitate our understanding of the American system not simply as a set of procedures with positive systemic outcomes as is the case with the dominant paradigm, but as a set of procedures whose systemic outcomes are both positive and negative. The dialectical and reciprocal relationship between affluence and poverty, power and powerlessness, privilege and deprivation, development and underdevelopment, and white progress and black stagnation would be made clear. From such an understanding, empirically useful descriptions could be developed and more promising prescriptions for action could be fashioned.

Notes

1. Northrop's use of the term "pure fact" can be a source of confusion for those who assume that the word "pure" is being used to convey the notion of "true" or "absolute." That is not the intended meaning however. The term "pure fact" is counterpoised with the term "described fact" to convey the idea that there is a world external to the observer, but that the meaning given to it depends upon the rules that the observer follows in describing it. Thus the reduction of pure fact to described fact is the process of moving from being aware to giving meaning to that of which we are aware. The argument that the act of becoming aware is a part of the process of determining meaning, in my view, does not lessen the heuristic value of the concepts of pure and described fact in helping us understand the idiosyncratic and parochial nature of all social science scholarship.

2. Kuhn's seminal ideas have been used to support such a disparate collection of ideas that to invoke them once again requires special justification, if not an apology. The most insightful aspects of Kuhn's notion of a paradigm have not been explored by social scientists. The constituent elements of the Kuhnian paradigm are for the most part normative assumptions about the nature of the reality being studied. These assumptions govern the conceptualization of what is experienced, and hence the identification of "problems" and the range of possible solutions. Kuhn's observations have much more profound implications for the social sciences than for the natural or physical sciences because all social scientists develop emotional and ideological attachments to certain beliefs about the political world, which is their subject matter, even before they become social scientists.

3. See for example, "Polls Find Black-White Gap on Variety of Issues," *The New York Times* (August 26, 1981): 10. Also Kluegel and Smith, 1986; and Joint Center for Political Studies, 1986.

References

Ake, Claude. 1982. *Social Science as Imperialism*. 2nd ed. Ibadan, Nigeria: Ibadan University Press.

Bachrach, Peter, and Morton Baratz. 1982. "Two Faces of Power." *American Political Science Review*, 58 (December): 947–52.

Easton, David. 1969. "The New Revolution in Political Science." Presidential address delivered at the sixty-fifth annual meeting of the American Political Science Association. New York, NY, September.

Harris, Donald. 1972. "Black Ghetto as Internal Colony: A Theoretical Critique and Alternative Formulation." *The Review of Black Political Economy*, Summer: 3–33.

Joint Center for Political Studies. 1986. *1986 JCPS Gallup Survey*. Washington, DC: Joint Center for Political Studies.

Jones, Mack H. 1972. "A Frame of Reference for Black Politics." In Lenneal Henderson, ed., *Black Political Life in the U.S.* San Francisco: Chandler.

Kluegel, James, and Eliot Smith. 1986. *Beliefs about Inequality*. New York: Aldine.

Kuhn, Thomas. 1972. *The Structure of Scientific Revolution*. 2nd ed. Chicago: University of Chicago Press.

Meehan, Eugene. 1968. *Explanation in Social Science: A System Paradigm*. Homewood, IL: Dorsey Press.

Northrop, F. S. C. 1969. *The Logic of the Science and Humanities*. New York: World Publishing.

Parenti, Michael. 1983. "The State of the Discipline: One Interpretation of Everyone's Favorite Controversy." *PS*, Spring: 189–204.

Ricci, David. 1984. *The Tragedy of Political Science*. New Haven: Yale University Press.

Wilson, Ernest. 1985. "Why Political Scientists Don't Study Black Politics, but Historians and Sociologists Do." *PS*, Summer: 600–606.

State Responses to Richmond v. Croson: A Survey of Equal Employment Opportunity Officers

Augustus J. Jones, Jr.
Clyde Brown

Miami University

Using the findings of a survey, this exploratory study examines how state governments and Equal Employment Opportunity (EEO) officials, as implementing agents, have responded to the U.S. Supreme Court decision in City of Richmond v. J. A. Croson Company *(1989), in which the Court invalidated a minority business enterprise (MBE) program's set-aside provision; a provision modeled on a congressionally approved program that had been previously judged constitutionally acceptable. The survey documents that, while most states have not reacted, a majority of states with MBE programs have responded. In general, EEO officials were highly conscious of the decision, active in initiating state response, opposed to the Court's opinion, and troubled by the perceived negative impact of the decision on affirmative action programs. While it is clear that the decision will discourage efforts to aid minority businesses generally, it is also clear that, at least in the short run, many states with such programs are determined to keep their programs in essence if not in name.*

U sing the findings of a survey, this exploratory study examines how state governments have responded to the 1989 U.S. Supreme Court decision in *City of Richmond v. J. A. Croson Company.*[1] Specifically, focusing on the role of implementors, this study investigates the opinions, perceptions, and reactions of state Equal Employment Opportunity (EEO) officers to the *Croson* decree.

In *Croson,* the Court invalidated a minority business enterprise (MBE) program's set-aside provision established by the City of Richmond, Virginia; reaffirmed support for a congressionally approved set-aside program; and emphasized that state and local jurisdictions using racial classifications must meet a new, stringent legal standard if their programs are to be judged constitutionally acceptable. When the decision was announced, it was widely perceived as threatening the legality of set-aside programs across the country. How state EEO officials reacted to this decision is a major focus of this study.

In conducting our investigation, we had a set of general questions in mind:

1.   What was the response of state governments to the *Croson* decision? In the states that did respond, how did they react? Is there any connection between the existence of an MBE program in a state and the likelihood that it reacted?
2.   Were EEO officials aware of the case and its details? What sources or channels did they utilize to learn about the decision?
3.   Did the respondents agree or disagree with the Court's position; that is, what was their opinion of the decision? What was the reasoning of proponents on both sides of this question? Is there a relationship between the respondent's view and whether his or her state has an MBE program?
4.   What is the prospect for future minority business set-asides? Given *Croson*, do EEO directors think it is more likely or less likely that their states will adopt statutes with specific numerical set-asides?
5.   What was the role of EEO offices in responding to this important court case central to their functions? Did the EEO offices perform a leadership role on this issue in their states? Is there a connection between agency response and the existence of MBE programs in the states?
6.   In the states with set-aside programs, how do EEO officials perceive the impact of *Croson* in terms of their ability to achieve their goals as an agency?

Theoretical Perspectives on Judicial Impact and Implementation

Scholars who have studied the implementation and impact of judicial decisions (including Peltason, 1961; Wasby, 1970; Baum, 1977; Gruhl, 1980; Johnson and Canon, 1984; Stumpf, 1988, and Songer and Sheehan, 1990) have made the point that, while the Supreme Court makes determinative decisions, it must rely on others (lower courts, executives, legislators, and bureaucrats) to carry them out. Furthermore, the policy setting in which implementation occurs is influenced by all these political actors, the media, affected interest groups, the attentive and mass publics. Because the courts are limited in their ability to enforce decisions, the implementation of decisions should never be considered automatic.

With these theoretical considerations in mind, this study focuses on state EEO directors as key members of the implementing population for a particular affirmative action policy, set-aside provisions. Normally, implementing agents carry out court decisions (Gruhl, 1980; Johnson and Canon, 1984), but this should not be assumed and there have been instances when court decisions have not been implemented (Peltason, 1961; Becker and Feeley, 1973; Songer and Sheehan, 1990). Explaining the varied responses of implementing agents to Supreme Court decisions is complex: factors accounting for psychological reactions and behavior responses of implementors include the nature and clarity of decisions (Wasby, 1970; Baum, 1981; Johnson and Canon, 1984), the intensity of attitudes regarding decisions, perceptions of the Court's legitimacy, perceptions of the consequences (desirability versus undesirability) of the decisions, and implementers' self-interest (Peltason, 1961; Becker and Feeley, 1973; Stumpf, 1988; Johnson and Canon, 1984). If the courts do not communicate clearly and persuasively what they expect of enforcers, implementing agents are likely to capitalize on the ambiguity and use their discretion in interpreting and carrying out the courts' decision. Furthermore, if the court's decisions are highly controversial to implementing agents and affected publics, that is, if they are outside their "zone of indifference," implementing agents may attempt and succeed in ignoring or evading the courts' commands. Finally, if implementing agents disagree or feel their personal and/or institutional interests are threatened because of commitments to existing arrangements, they may narrowly construe the courts' pronouncements, search for less disruptive alternatives, or disregard the pronouncements completely.

Given the different propositions identified in the literature for explaining the enforcement of court decisions, we developed several expectations regarding how states would respond to *Croson*. First, we expected to find considerable variation in state reaction to *Croson* because the Court offered complex, conflicting, confusing, controversial, and ambiguous guidelines and directives to states with set-aside programs or states considering the adoption of MBE programs. This expectation was based on a general finding in the implementation literature that if policymakers offer implementors complex, confusing, or nebulous directions, then implementors have latitude in responding to the policymakers, at least in the short run (Edwards, 1980; Nakamura, 1980). Given that in *Croson* six justices offered contrasting assessments regarding the legality and standards for set-aside programs in general and Richmond's plan in particular, it is unlikely that implementors would perceive a "finality of decision" (Tarr, 1977) and, as a result, we expected states to react in different ways.

In addition, we postulated that there would be a high level of consciousness among EEO officers regarding the legality of race-conscious set-asides as addressed in *Croson*. Obviously, this is a highly controversial issue central to their jurisdictions in state government, and this case directly impinges on their duties. Given this, we expected state EEO coordinators to have paid close attention to the ruling in this case.

We also expected EEO respondents in general to disagree with the Court's ruling, to see the decision as negatively impacting the future prospects for set-aside programs, and to see the case as restricting their ability to accomplish their mission goals. Given this, we also expected that EEO officials would take leadership roles in defining state responses to *Croson*. Given these officers' career choices, their commitment to equal opportunity, and their perceptions that *Croson* would adversely affect their interests we posited that they would narrowly construe *Croson* and would find ways to preserve their set-aside programs.

Finally, we expected differences to exist on many of the above items between states with MBE programs and states without MBE programs. For example, we expected greater state and agency response from states with MBE programs than from states without such programs.

In testing these hypotheses, we are aware of the complexity of assessing the implementation of Supreme Court decisions. For the Supreme Court is only one, albeit an important one, of the many policymakers in the policy process. Because of its limited enforcement powers and the interests of many other political actors, the implementation and ultimate impact of judicial decisions will always remain problematic. As such, it is worthy of scholarly investigation.

Justification of the Analysis

Focusing on state EEO directors' enforcement of *Croson* is appropriate for several reasons. We have found no other study that has systematically tracked how the fifty states have responded to *Croson*. The decision is less than two years old and perhaps many policy analysts have decided that it is premature to investigate its implementation.[2] But lower court rulings,[3] press reports,[4] and analyses[5] reveal that state and local governments' reaction to the *Croson* decision has been swift.[6] In states across the country governmental bodies responded to *Croson* by revoking, revamping, or reexamining their minority set-aside programs, but there has been no careful examination of how states have been reacting to or of implementors' opinions of the Supreme Court's *Croson* decision. This study fills that void by providing an initial analysis of the short-term response to *Croson*.

Concentrating on EEO officers' enforcement of *Croson* is important because limited scholarly attention has been paid to the implementation of the Supreme Court's affirmative action decrees. With one or two exceptions (Simmons, 1982; Days, 1984), a review of the literature shows most studies regarding the Supreme Court's affirmative action decrees—*Bakke* (1978), *Weber* (1979), *Stotts* (1984), *Paradise* (1982), *Johnson* (1987), and *Croson* (1989)—have concentrated on the legal or moral argument in the cases (Spiegelman, 1985) or have attempted to track new or consensus standards emerging in the different decrees (Belton, 1988; Brown, 1987; Fried, 1989).

Few studies have focused on the enforcement of the Supreme Court's controversial affirmative action cases. To be sure, a number of studies have examined the implementation of Supreme Court decisions. However, for the most part these studies have concentrated on five subject areas: (1) school desegregation (Cooper, 1988; Schwartz, 1986; Crain, 1968;

Peltason, 1961), (2) the rights of the accused (Wasby, 1970; Cannon, 1977), (3) school prayer (Dolbeare and Hammond, 1971; Birkby, 1966), (4) reapportionment (Dodge and McCauley 1982), and (5) abortion (Hansen, 1980). It is appropriate to add affirmative action to this implementation literature by this study of the enforcement within the federal system of the Supreme Court's *Croson* ruling.

The aftermath of *Croson* provides an opportunity to examine the general proposition that implementing agents, when confronted with a complex adverse opinion, will react in ways that protect and preserve their policy preferences. Studying EEO directors is appropriate in this regard given their official duties, their commitment to affirmative action, and the general interpretation that the Court's intent in *Croson* was anti–affirmative action.

A final reason for studying how EEO officers responded to *Croson* is that the Court mandated that state and local officers alter the legal foundations upon which their minority set-aside programs rested. Prior to *Croson*, practically all local and state governments justified their set-aside schemes on the grounds that they were necessary to combat widespread or societal discrimination in the construction industry, without documenting that identifiable discrimination existed in their particular jurisdictions.[7] With *Croson*, the Supreme Court has now signaled that justifying these particular schemes on this basis is unacceptable. In fact, the Court requires state and local governments to predicate their programs on actual findings of past discrimination in their jurisdictions. Given this, and given that the EEO officers are generally charged with carrying out their state set-aside programs, it is important to ask them about the response of their respective states to *Croson*.

From Fullilove *to* Croson: *Changing Standards?*

Richmond v. Croson was not the first time that the Supreme Court addressed the legality of minority business set-asides. In *Fullilove v. Klutnick* 448 U.S. 448 (1980), the Supreme Court weighed whether it was constitutionally permissible for Congress under the Public Works Act of 1977 to adopt a race-conscious program mandating that 10 percent of the then four billion dollars for public works be used by state and local grantees to obtain services and supplies from minority businesses. By a vote of 6 to 3, the Supreme Court, citing the equal protection component of the due process clause of the Fifth Amendment, upheld congressional use of a racial quota for minority business on the grounds that such a quota was designed to rectify past discrimination, was narrowly tailored, and was flexible. Speaking for the Court, Chief Justice Burger acknowledged that although Congress had made no preliminary finding of illegal discrimination against minorities under the federal contracts and public works program, it had abundant historical basis from which it could conclude that minority businesses had been denied effective participation in public contracting opportunities at the federal, state, and local levels by procurement practices that perpetuated the effect of past discrimination.[8]

Burger also found Congress's set-aside program valid because it was narrowly tailored and flexible. Its benefits were limited to specified minority groups that had been the victims of past discrimination under the federal procurement program. And he pointed out that the 10 percent program was flexible in that state and local contractors who attempted in good faith to meet set-aside goals but failed would not be penalized, because they could be granted a waiver.

Dissenting Justices Steward, Rehnquist, and Stevens opposed the majority ruling because they claimed it allowed Congress to establish a race-conscious set-aside program without any prior finding that Congress itself has engaged in discrimination against minorities.

While the Court first examined whether a congressionally mandated set-aside program was legal in *Fullilove*, it deliberated whether a similar municipal program was constitutionally permissible in *Richmond v. Croson*. In this instance, the Supreme Court addressed the issue of whether the city of Richmond had violated the Equal Protection clause of the Fourteenth Amendment by requiring prime contractors to whom the city awarded construction contracts to subcontract at least 30 percent of the dollar amount to minority businesses.

By a vote of 6 to 3, the Supreme Court declared that the Richmond program was constitutionally invalid, because it was not designed to remedy past discrimination and was not narrowly tailored. Before amplifying the Court's argument, it is important to note that Justice O'Connor, who wrote the principal opinion for the majority, announced for the first time that all racial classifications (whether designed to end past discrimination or current bias) would be subjected to the Court's most rigorous equal protection test—strict scrutiny.[9] To satisfy the requirements of this test, (1) governmental bodies must have a compelling reason for using a racial classification, and (2) the classification must be narrowly tailored.

O'Connor found that Richmond's plan failed both prongs of the strict scrutiny test. According to O'Connor, Richmond's minority set-aside program was constitutionally impermissible because city officials offered no convincing evidence of past or present discrimination in the city's contracting practices. Richmond city officials had cited various indicators of racial discrimination: minorities received a very small number of city contracts, local contracting agencies had few or no minority members, Congress and other governmental agencies had found that past discrimination stifled minority participation in the contracting industry locally and nationally, and city officers had asserted that there was discrimination in Richmond's contracting programs. Justice O'Connor found these indicators unpersuasive.

Justice O'Connor also found that the Richmond program was invalid because it was not narrowly tailored. Speaking for the majority, she concluded that Richmond's use of 30 percent goals was not limited to specific groups that had been victims of prior discrimination.

Still, the majority in *Croson* did express support for the federal set-aside upheld in *Fullilove*. It was congruent with the Constitution, because it was designed to remedy past discrimination in federal procurement and was narrowly tailored to rectify this bias. At the same time, O'Connor emphasized that where Congress could adopt a minority set-aside program based on societal discrimination, the states could not. According to Justice O'Connor, Congress has unique remedial powers under Section Five of the Fourteenth Amendment that states do not possess. Hence the congressional set-aside program could be based on societal discrimination, but state set-aside programs required a particular finding that states or recipients of state funds had actively or passively engaged in past discrimination.

Justice O'Connor also made it plain that *Croson* does not prevent state or local governments from adopting race-conscious programs. Instructing the states, she observed that "if the city had evidence before it that majority contractors were systematically excluding minority businesses from the subcontracting opportunities, it could take action to end the discrimination."[10] She wrote that some racial preference might be permissible in certain cases to break down the patterns of exclusion.

While Justice O'Connor wrote the principal opinion in *Croson*, six other justices also authored opinions. Justices Stevens, Kennedy, and Scalia agreed with that portion of O'Connor's opinion that stressed that the *Croson* program was illegal but disagreed with other portions. Justice Stevens took issue with the premise that a government decision that rests on a racial classification is never permissible except as a remedy for a past wrong. Like Stevens, Kennedy agreed that the Richmond plan was deficient. Unlike Stevens, he did not favor relaxing equal protection standards for racial classifications. Justice Kennedy indicated that he was tempted to join Justice Scalia, who would strike down all racial preferences, but opted not to because "narrowly drawn racial preferences might be appropriate as a last resort to eliminate bias."[11]

Justices Marshall, Brennan, and Blackmun dissented, labeling the majority opinion a giant step backward. Marshall attacked the majority opinion on several grounds, but two will be highlighted here. First, Marshall took issue with O'Connor's contention that Richmond had failed to catalog adequate findings of past discrimination, stressing that federal courts had uncovered widespread discrimination in Richmond on previous occasions in education and voting. Second, Marshall criticized the part of O'Connor's opinion that dealt with different standards for justifying race-conscious measures at the federal and state levels. He felt that this portion of her opinion, plus adoption of the strict scrutiny test, "would inevitably discourage or prevent government entities, particularly states and localities, from acting to rectify the scourge of racial discrimination."[12] Marshall believed that these standards would make it more difficult to justify race-conscious measures and would foster confusion and possible litigation, and that in response the states would not act.

Like Justice Marshall, Justice Blackmun also dissented. He joined Marshall in holding that Richmond's set-aside plan was valid and went beyond that, charging that the majority, in striking down Richmond's plan, had acted "as if discrimination had never existed or was not demonstrated in this case."[13]

When *Fullilove* and *Croson* are jointly considered, it becomes apparent that the Court has concluded that the federal set-aside program is constitutionally permissible, but that Richmond's program was not. In doing so, the Supreme Court has promulgated one set of rules for gauging the legality of federal set-aside programs and another set for appraising the validity of local and state programs.[14] According to the Court, Congress is not obligated to demonstrate that it has discriminated against minorities before adopting a set-aside program, but localities and states must do so. Congress, the Court has said, can justify set-aside programs on findings that there has been nationwide discrimination against minority contractors, but local and state governments cannot. Congress is empowered to act this way, but the states are not, because Congress has unique powers under Section Five of the Fourteenth Amendment. These disparate standards are significant because they call into question the validity of practically all local and state set-aside programs, which, prior to *Croson*, were based on national findings of widespread discrimination in the construction industry and not on findings within individual jurisdictions that they had discriminated against minority contractors. That the Court has ruled that states cannot justify their programs on the same grounds as Congress poses a number of questions: How will the states respond to the new standards in *Croson*? Have the states revised or revoked their set-aside programs in response to this case? Or are they seeking to distinguish their particular program from Richmond's program and do nothing, on the grounds that *Croson* does not apply to them? These are issues that will be taken up in the course of this study.[15]

Data Collection

To test our hypotheses a mail survey was sent to the fifty state EEO directors as identified by the Council of State Governments.[16] These officers "enforce laws promoting equal employment opportunities" and they are intimately involved on a day-to-day basis with affirmative action issues. An initial and two follow-up mailings, in November and December 1989 and February 1990, with supporting telephone calls on the third mailing, resulted in a response rate of 72 percent. Data was collected on thirty-six of the fifty states.[17]

Because of the survey's timing (about one year after the *Croson* decision) and subsequent higher and lower court rulings regarding set-aside provisions, this study should be viewed as an *initial analysis* of the response to *Croson* at the state level. Our intent was to conduct an exploratory study of judicial implementation politics in the months immediately following an important and highly controversial decision.

It is not our purpose to generalize from the states in the survey to the others, but the responding states seem to be a good cross section of Amer-

Table 1. Type and Frequency of Program ($N = 36$)

	Frequency	Percent
MBE program	24	66.7
Statute with specific %	8	22.2
Statute without specific %	6	16.7
Executive order with specific %	4	11.1
Executive order without specific %	4	11.1
Program, no details	2	6.6
No MBE program	12	33.3
No program (other)	2	5.6
No program	10	27.8
Total	36	100.0

ican states.[18] The State and Local Legal Center in Washington, D.C., has reviewed state statutes and executive orders and surveyed state governments to collect information about state MBE programs; it has reported that thirty-three states have MBE programs, and that three other states have other provisions that are beneficial to MBEs.[19] We have identified two additional states on the basis of our survey as having MBE programs, so our respondents represent twenty-four of the thirty-five states with MBE programs. We count twelve states without MBE-type programs in our survey. Our percentage of states with MBE programs (twenty-four of thirty-six: 67 percent) is essentially identical to that identified by the State and Local Legal Center (thirty-three of fifty: 66 percent).

State programs can be classified as being established by legislative statute or by executive order, and by whether the authorization states specific numerical percentages as goals for MBE programs. Table 1 lists the frequency of MBE program types contained in the survey.[20]

Because we were interesting in collecting basic factual information about state responses and the opinions and perceptions of implementors, a survey instrument was ideally suited for our purposes. In addition to documenting what is going on at the state level, we are interested in discovering the reasoning behind the opinions expressed by EEO coordinators.

Findings

This section reports on EEO officials' responses to our survey conducted in the late 1989 and early 1990.

State Response

Did individual states respond (file lawsuits, enact legislation, initiate studies, etc.) to the *Croson* decision in the subsequent months? As reported by the EEO directors, more than 60 percent of the states ($N = 22$) in our study have not responded in any way. More than one-third ($N =$

Table 2. State Response (N = 35)

Type of Program	No	Yes
MBE program	11	12
Statute with specific %	2	6
Statute without specific %	3	2
Executive order with specific %	2	2
Executive order without specific %	3	1
Program, no details	1	1
No MBE program	11	1
No program (other)	2	0
No program	9	1
Total	22	13

13) of the states have responded in some way to the situation created by *Croson*.[21] Five states (Florida, Maryland, Washington, Nevada, and Wisconsin) initiated disparity studies focusing on contract practices either on a statewide basis or for selected state agencies. Five states changed laws or programs (Illinois amended its law to require a finding of discrimination; Iowa temporarily suspended its program pending review and recommendations for revision; Pennsylvania revised its programs in light of the *Croson* decision by the Court of Appeals; Colorado eliminated its Department of Transportation (DOT) set-aside provision; and Alaska modified its DOT and public facilities set-aside program). Legislation that would affect state MBE programs has been introduced in three states (Ohio, North Carolina, and Virginia). Four states (Florida, Maryland, Pennsylvania, and Wisconsin) are defending legal challenges to their programs. Virginia held meetings with industry groups; many other states held staff meetings.[22]

An overly simplified but reasonable expectation might be that states with MBE programs will have reacted in some way to the decision, while those states without programs will not have reacted. Table 2 summarizes state response to the Court case.

Among the twelve states without programs, eleven did not respond, and one state is engaged in a disparity study. Among states with programs, the division was essentially equal; twelve did exhibit a response, whereas eleven did not. A closer examination of Table 2 makes clear what is happening. States without MBE programs conform to expectations, while states with MBE programs divide evenly.[23] Within the MBE states, only among states with a statutory set-aside (that is, with MBE programs established by state law containing specific numerical percentages) did a majority of states respond to the Court's decision.[24] In general, states behaved in a predictable fashion.

Information Sources

We were interested in learning whether the EEO officials were acquainted with the decision. As it turns out, the EEO respondents were well aware of the *Croson* case. More than nine-tenths (94.4 percent) of the respondents were familiar with the decision, and almost as many (86.1 percent) claimed to have read it. The high level of awareness is not surprising, given the highly controversial nature of the issue and the ruling.

The survey asked EEO directors to indicate how they learned about the *Croson* decision. Respondents utilized the following sources: print media (88.9 percent cited newspapers and magazines as a source of information); electronic media (75.0 percent); professional conferences (61.1 percent); professional journals (58.3 percent); discussions with lawyers (40.0 percent); and briefings in state government (25.0 percent). Twenty-two (62.8 percent) of the thirty-five respondents indicated that they first learned of the case through the print media, with thirteen others (37.1 percent) identifying television or radio as their first source.

The high degree of consciousness of the issue reported by the EEO respondents makes sense, given the respondents' responsibilities, the controversy inherent in affirmative action programs, and the widespread publicity given the case. There is clear evidence that most respondents used a wide variety of information channels to learn about the Court's action. The "instantaneousness" of daily newspapers and the electronic media was very evident in the replies.

Opinions about the Decision

Given the saliency of the *Croson* decision to EEO officials, as well as their stated awareness and knowledge of the case, it would be interesting to know how they evaluated it. In response to an inquiry as to whether they agreed or disagreed, 68 percent of the thirty-one valid cases ($N = 21$) disagreed with the Court's decision. Slightly more than a quarter (29.0 percent, $N = 9$) of the EEO officials agreed with the decision, and one respondent (3.3 percent) both agreed and disagreed with the decision. Interestingly, among the thirty-one replies, those without MBE-type programs were much more united in their opposition (88.9 percent to 11.1 percent) to the decision than those with programs (59.1 percent to 36.4 percent). Table 3 displays the relevant details.

Respondents were provided with an open-ended opportunity to explain the reasons behind their opinion. The primary rationale expressed by those supporting the decision ($N = 9$) was the arbitrariness of the set-aside percentages in the Richmond ordinance ($N = 4$). Such sentiments were expressed by two respondents, one from the Midwest and the other from the South. Echoing Justice O'Connor's opinion the first wrote: "Set-asides should not be arbitrarily established. Adequate research and clear proof of discrimination should be documented." And the second reasoned: "Arbitrary selection of set-aside percentages is very difficult to substantiate. You should be able to justify how you arrived at a certain percentage, and it must be related to your specific population." The belief

Table 3. Opinion of the Decision ($N = 31$)

Type of Program	Agree	Disagree	Both
MBE program	8	13	1
Statute with specific %	1	6	0
Statute without specific %	1	3	1
Executive order with specific %	3	1	0
Executive order without specific %	1	2	0
Program, no details	2	0	0
No MBE program	1	8	0
No program (other)	0	2	0
No program	1	6	0
Total	9	21	1

that Richmond had not proven past discrimination in the local construction industry ($N = 2$) and the view that the Court had correctly interpreted the Fourteenth Amendment ($N = 3$) were two other reasons for approving of the decision.

Those in disagreement with the decision ($N = 21$) were more diverse in expressing their opposition. Leading the list was a general belief that remedial efforts to rectify past and current discrimination were needed ($N = 8$). One Mountain state respondent expressed the view of several others (and Justice Marshall) in writing:

Historically, minorities have been excluded from enjoying basic privileges in American society. Remedying the lingering effects of racial discrimination has long been one of the most profound moral and constitutional challenges facing our nation. Serious remedial efforts sometimes require race-conscious programs designed to incorporate members of minority groups that have too often been excluded.

Two southern respondents were more direct: "Historical discrimination makes it mandatory that some strategy be adopted to level the playing field for minorities wishing to participate in the economic arena" and "I disagree because of historical discrimination in all governmental contracting and private sector contracting."

Two types of responses tied for second most frequent among those disagreeing with the decision: a belief that *Croson* imposes a burdensome standard of proof on states ($N = 4$), and a fear that the decision creates an excuse for states to reverse or slow equal employment opportunity gains made in the past ($N = 4$). Commenting on the "standards" issue, a Great Lakes state respondent, siding with the dissenters in the case, stated:

Though I recognize that the Court was attempting to narrowly carve out a rational system within which affirmative action plans can operate, I believe the Court drew its boundaries far too restrictively and that it will be difficult for elected government officials to declare in excruciating detail how their community was guilty of past discrimination.

A survey from a Gulf Coast state contained the accusation that "The present Court is turning the clock back in favor of racism. [Recent] majority decisions are indicative of this negative attitude."

Rounding out the list was the view that MBE-type programs will be harder to justify in the future because of *Croson* ($N = 2$). One response focused on the public—"It makes EEO/AA programs harder to justify and present to the public"—while the other emphasized the impact on public officials.

Symbolic Politics and Prospects for Future Set-Aside Programs

At one point in the survey we inquired as to the existence of a set-aside program in each state (that is, programs with specific numerical percentages with or without waiver provisions). Before documenting state responses to this question, we note what we believe to be an interesting, developing instance of symbolic politics involving manipulation of language. State EEO respondents, in reacting to the positions taken by the current Court in *Croson* and other cases (such as *Bakke*), avoid using terms such as "set-aside" or "quotas" to characterize their programs. This is understandable in the current judicial climate. It is in their interest, if they wish to preserve and extend affirmative action programs that are to withstand judicial review, to speak in terms of "initiatives," "goals," "goal-driven programs," "good-faith efforts," "minimum participation standards," "outreach programs," and "race-and-gender-neutral requirements."

This phenomenon seems to have been especially present in one question. We found that EEO officials in six of the eight states with statutory set-asides correctly identified themselves. On the other hand, none of the four states listed by the State and Local Legal Center as having executively established set-asides with specific numerical percentages volunteered to classify themselves with the term. Likewise only two respondents from the other twelve MBE program states answered that he or she worked with a set-aside program. In any event, it is clear that the overwhelming majority of respondents identified the term "set-aside program" as statutorily established set-asides with specific numerical percentages rather than as less-specified MBE programs.

Examining twenty-six valid cases, we are able to inquire whether the *Croson* decision makes it more or less likely, in the opinion of the respondent, that the state will adopt a set-aside program. The answer is as one-sided as expected: twenty-three respondents (88 percent) felt the decision makes it less likely that a set-aside program will be adopted, only one respondent (4 percent) felt it more likely, and two respondents (8 percent) felt it would have neither result.

Focusing further on the valid respondents ($N = 20$) who explained in an open-ended question why they felt it was less likely that set-asides would be adopted in their states, we find one-fourth (25 percent) of them holding the view that state legislatures will not be proactive on behalf of minority

Table 4. Reasons Why Adoption of State Set-Aside Is Unlikely ($N = 20$)

	Frequency	Percent
Legislature less proactive	5	25.0
Satisfaction with status quo	5	25.0
Rationale for retreat	4	20.0
Stricter criteria	4	20.0
Fear of lawsuits	2	10.0
	20	100.0

businesses after *Croson* (that is, the legislatures will not act). A Western EEO respondent wrote: "This will give a very conservative legislature a 'legitimate' reason not to establish a set-aside program." That position was essentially repeated by a Southern respondent who stated: "Several years ago the [State] Legislature considered a minority set-aside and the bill failed to pass. Considering the Supreme Court's ruling it is impossible to believe the Legislature would change their position." Three groups of equal size divided most of the remaining respondents. One-fifth (20 percent) of the respondents saw *Croson* as providing an opportunity to retreat from affirmative action goals. "The decision has had a chilling effect on existing set-aside programs in and around the state," was the evaluation of a Southeastern respondent. An equal number felt that the stricter criteria required by *Croson* for MBE set-aside programs would make state action less likely. Like the Court's dissenters in this case, they were concerned that the uncertainty of requirements, the requirement of a "higher" standard for states, the application of a "strict scrutiny" test, and the difficulty of obtaining data would dissuade states from establishing set-asides. A third group felt that the decision would reinforce current satisfaction with the status quo in their states among both politicians and the public, thereby making change less likely. Finally, two respondents (10 percent) felt that the potential threat of litigation precludes the possibility of their states establishing set-aside programs. Table 4 summarizes responses on this topic.

Agency Response

In nearly one-third of the states ($N = 13$), staff meetings were held to discuss the case. All thirteen of these states have MBE programs. In the other twenty-three states, staff meetings were not reported. A fairly strong association exists between the two types of states and the occurrence of meetings.[25]

For twelve of these thirteen states we know who called the staff meetings. In a clear majority of instances ($N = 8$), the EEO offices took the lead in organizing state reaction to the *Croson* decision. In the other cases, meetings were organized by a variety of state agencies.

Impact on Set-Aside Goals

We were interested in whether or not *Croson* is perceived by EEO directors has having a negative impact on their ability to accomplish MBE program goals. Although the number of cases is small because the question is only relevant to those states with set-aside programs established by statute with specific numerical percentages, we did collect some information on this concern.

Nine respondents provided us with a response to our inquiry regarding this issue. None felt that *Croson* made it less difficult to achieve program goals. Six EEO respondents were of the opinion that the decision made it more difficult for them to achieve state goals for the set-aside programs. Three others did not see the impact as falling either way. Those seeing the decision as having a detrimental impact mentioned that the decision created a burdensome standard, foreshadowed litigation, and spawned confusion in government and society.

Conclusion

This study investigated how states and state EEO directors have responded to the U.S. Supreme Court decision in *Richmond v. Croson*. Acutely aware of perceptions and opinions as conditioners of human motivation and behavior and the crucial role implementors play in determining the ultimate impact of Court decrees, we also examined the opinions and motivations of the individuals who are in a pivotal position to shape state reactions to this complex and ambiguous decision.

With these points in mind, we developed several expectations. We anticipated that (1) the broad and ambiguous *Croson* ruling would result in varied state reactions; (2) there would be a high level of consciousness, as well as opposition, to the decision among state EEO officials; (3) state EEO officials would seek to maintain their set-aside programs; and (4) states with set-asides would behave differently from states without set-asides. We found general support for our propositions.

Our survey found that, while most states did not responded to *Croson*, a majority of states with MBE programs did respond. Clearly, some states have not reacted because they do not have a minority set-aside program; consequently, they view the Court's affirmative action ruling as not applying to them. Other states with race-conscious programs may not have reacted to *Croson* because they may have distinguished their program from Richmond's and concluded that the *Croson* guidelines are not applicable to them. And still other states may not have reacted by the time of our survey because the decision was fairly new then, and it may take more time before they respond. Still, we would underscore the point that an impressive amount of activity took place at the state level on this issue in the twelve to fifteen months following the Court's ruling, and it is reasonable to expect additional state response will be forthcoming.[26]

Responses from EEO officials indicate that one short-run impact of *Croson* is that states with set-aside programs are engaged in the symbolic manipulation of language. Specifically, open-ended responses show that many states with these particular programs identify themselves by terms other than "set-asides." They labeled their race-conscious efforts by a variety of other terms, such as "goals," "good-faith efforts," "outreach programs." We take this reticence to use the term "set-aside" to be a symbolic response to the fact that in *Croson* the Court had just struck down a set-aside program and to the likely perception among EEO directors that this term, like quotas, has become controversial.[27] Changing the name of such programs may make them less vulnerable to attack and more politically acceptable.

We found that state EEO coordinators possess a high level of consciousness about *Croson*. The vast majority of coordinators indicated they had read the decision and were cognizant of its particulars. Additionally, we discovered that the equal opportunity coordinators relied principally on the print media (newspapers and magazines) to acquire information about *Croson*. Their dependence on the press for information underscores the pivotal role the press plays in communicating Court decisions.

Moreover, we discovered that most EEO officials disagreed with the majority opinion in *Croson*. Three reasons were cited most frequently: (1) *Croson* may bring an end to race-conscious remedies, which are needed to eliminate past and current racial discrimination; (2) *Croson* places a cumbersome standard of proof on states to defend race-conscious programs; and (3) *Croson* may provide a convenient alibi to states to reverse, veto, or slow down equal opportunity gains.

While most respondents opposed *Croson*, a sizable minority favored the decision. Those favoring the decision did so because of the arbitrariness of the set-aside percentages in the Richmond ordinance, because they felt Richmond had not proven past discrimination, and because the Court had correctly construed the Fourteenth Amendment. It is of particular significance that most state EEO officials disagreed with *Croson*. That a policymaker, the Supreme Court, and its implementing agents, the EEO coordinators, are in sharp disagreement probably foreshadows less-than-vigorous enforcement.

Furthermore, we discovered that an overwhelming majority of respondents in states without MBE programs felt that *Croson* would make it less likely that their states would adopt such a program. Their belief was based on (1) the fact that conservative politicians, for whom civil rights is not a top priority, will use *Croson* as an excuse not to act on behalf of minorities, (2) the belief that *Croson* provides state policymakers with a rationale to retreat from affirmative action goals, (3) uncertainty about standards (such as strict scrutiny and higher requirements for states), and (4) the fear of lawsuits.

This last finding suggests that *Croson* may prevent some states from modifying their programs and may discourage others from contemplating the adoption of new minority set-asides. This is not good news for the proponents of set-asides; the evidence suggests that *Croson* put the brakes on efforts to promote or adopt race-conscious measures in states without MBE programs. Another finding contained in this study is that most equal opportunity coordinators in states with set-aside programs in place perceive *Croson* as negatively affecting their ability to accomplish their goals. In effect, *Croson* is viewed as hindering the enforcement of set-aside programs.

What does this study suggest overall about the function of the U.S. Supreme Court in the American political system? Basically, it highlights the Supreme Court's role as interpreter of the Constitution. Since the cases of *Marbury v. Madison* (1803) and *Fletcher v. Peck* (1810), the Supreme Court has defended its powers to determine whether the acts of coordinate branches and lower levels of government are consistent or inconsistent with the Constitution, claiming emphatically that is is the duty of the Court to say what the Constitution means. With respect to *Croson*, we find the Court fulfilling its duty as construer of the Constitution. In this instance, the Court exercised its immense discretion in interpreting the constitutional status of Richmond's set-aside program in light of the Equal Protection clause.

This study also illuminates the policymaking function of the U.S. Supreme Court. Though the Court's *Croson* decision pertained specifically to the city of Richmond, Virginia, the effects of this particular decision extended far beyond Virginia. States in all regions of the country responded in some way to *Croson*. That the Court's *Croson* decision affected the agendas of various states demonstrates the Court's role in the policymaking process.

A final note regarding the future prospects of race-conscious set-asides. The Supreme Court has made it more difficult for state and local governments to justify such programs and, as we found, while many states complained about this, many states have not been so discouraged that they have abrogated their programs. In *Croson*, the Court has shifted the nature of the debate regarding set-asides by promulgating stringent legal standards that future programs must meet to be judged constitutionally permissible. Opponents of set-asides can use the decision to deter and block attempts to adopt and implement affirmative action programs. Their case is made easier at the state and local levels because proponents of set-asides must now bear the evidentiary burden of the strict scrutiny test. In the future, proponents will have to develop programs that satisfy *Croson's* standards. Proponents of these programs now have standards that they can meet to justify the continuation of their particular programs. Although this will be difficult, we do not expect supporters of affirmative action measures to give up the fight.

It is unlikely that this controversy will end soon, as the actions taken by different policy actors since our survey strongly suggest. Lower federal court judges' decisions to invalidate the set-aside programs of various municipalities; the Supreme Court's decision in June 1990 upholding a federal race-conscious set-aside; the July 1990 resignation of liberal Supreme Court Justice William Brennan, a vigorous champion of affirmative action; and the nomination of seemingly conservative federal appellate court Judge David Souter to the Court signify that the policy debate on affirmative action programs, including set-asides, will continue.

Although this is an exploratory study, it documents that almost immediately after *Croson* was handed down, activity was generated at the state level. In some states officials held meetings regarding *Croson*. Others have conducted exhaustive and expensive studies to uncover past discrimination. Still others have proposed legislation, enacted laws,or revised laws to fulfill *Croson's* requirements. This suggests that many states are determined to ensure that they keep their programs. At least in the short run, actions by these states to satisfy *Croson's* standards cast significant doubt on predictions that *Croson* signifies the end of set-aside programs.

Notes

1. We would like to thank Herb Waltzer, Michael Pagano, Carl Stover and the *Review's* anonymous referees for helpful suggestions. All errors remain the authors' responsibility.
2. We are aware of one very insightful article (Drake and Holsworth, 1990), which provides historical background on Richmond politics, a summary of the legal issues involved in the case, an analysis of the implications of the decision for black economic advancement, and strategies black politicians might use to gain acceptance of set-aside programs.
3. See *Covington v. Beaumont Independent School District* 714 F. Supp. 1402 (E. D. Texas 1989); *Milwaukee County Power Association v. Fielder* 707 F. Supp. 1016 (W. D. Wisconsin 1989); and *Mann v. City of Albany* (883 F. 2nd 999 (1989). Also see "Minority Contract Nullified," *New York Times*, Friday, 1 December 1989, p. 16.
4. See *Editorials on File*, 20, no. 2 (16–31 January 1989). Editorial, *The Seattle Times*, Seattle, Washington, 25 January 1989, p. 81. Editorial, *The Indianapolis Star*, Indianapolis, Indiana, 29 January 1989, p. 81. Editorial, *The Arizona Republic*, Phoenix, Arizona, 25 January 1989. Editorial, *The Chattanooga Times*, Chattanooga, Tennessee, 30 January 1989.
5. See "A Collection of Articles by Constitutional Scholars and Economists" published by the House of Representatives Committee on the Judiciary, January 1990.
6. *Ibid.*, p. 71.
7. *Ibid.*, p. 14.
8. *Fullilove v. Klutznick*, 448 U.S. 449, (1980).
9. *City of Richmond v. J. A. Croson Company*, 57 U.S.L.W. 4133, (1989).
10. *Ibid.*, 57 U.S.L.W. 4143.
11. *Ibid.*, 57 U.S.L.W. 4134.
12. *Ibid.*, 57 U.S.L.W. 4149.
13. *Ibid.*, 57 U.S.L.W. 4155.
14. The Court reaffirmed this position in June 1990 in two companion cases (*Metro Broadcasting Inc. v. Federal Communications Commission* and *Astroline Communications Co. v. Shurberg Broadcasting of Hartford*) in which it upheld federal laws granting minority set-asides in the ownership of broadcast licenses without requiring a finding of past discrimination. Citing *Fullilove*, the 5-to-4 majority claimed that the federal government has more authority to establish set-asides than do other levels of government.

15. For an excellent journalistic review of municipal response to *Croson* see Pear (1990). He reports that lower courts are following the precedent of *Croson* in striking down set-asides (San Francisco; Atlanta; Philadelphia; Birmingham, Alabama; and Jacksonville, Florida) while some municipal authorities (Minneapolis; Columbus, Ohio; South Bend, Indiana; and King County, Washington) search for alternatives and experiment with program adjustments that they hope will withstand court scrutiny.

16. The data reported in this paper are part of a larger project we are working on, in which state EEO directors and attorneys general were surveyed to ascertain their opinions regarding the *Croson* decision, as well as to identify the responses by state governments that have occurred in each state. This paper reports only on the responses received from the state EEO offices.

    The surveys were read by the authors. Coding closed-ended items was straightforward and, where possible, checked against the surveys of attorneys general for consistency of response within a state. Interpretation and selection of open-ended materials quoted below were mutually agreed upon by the authors. Individual respondents were promised anonymity to encourage open and frank participation in the study.

17. A copy of the survey instrument is available from the authors upon request. Surveys were received from the following states: Alabama, Alaska, Arizona, Arkansas, Colorado, Florida, Georgia, Hawaii, Illinois, Indiana, Iowa, Kansas, Kentucky, Maryland, Mississippi, Missouri, Montana, Nebraska, Nevada, New Hampshire, New Mexico, North Carolina, North Dakota, Ohio, Oklahoma, Pennsylvania, South Carolina, South Dakota, Texas, Utah, Vermont, Virginia, Washington, West Virginia, Wisconsin, and Wyoming.

18. For example, in terms of geographical regions of the country, using the Interuniversity Consortium for Political and Social Research (ICPSR) regions, we find the following distribution: New England (two or six states), Middle Atlantic (one of four), East North Central (four of five), West North Central (six of seven), Solid South (nine of ten), Border States (four of five), Mountain (seven of eight), Pacific States (one of three), and External States (two of two). There might be some concern about the response rate among Northeastern and Western states. However, examination of the surveys of attorneys general collected for additional states (three New England states, two Middle Atlantic states, and one Pacific state) beyond the thirty-six states reported here shows those regions not to be atypical; their inclusion would not change any of the major findings reported.

19. It needs to be stressed that this information was collected *prior* to the Court's decision on *Croson* and is included in Appendix I of the *amici curiae* brief of the National League of Cities, the U.S. Conference of Mayors, the National Association of Counties, and the International City Management Association in support of the City of Richmond.

20. The breakdown of MBE program types for our responding states is as follows: statute with specific percentages (Florida, Illinois, Indiana, Iowa, Maryland, Ohio, Oklahoma, and Wisconsin); statute without specific percentages (Kentucky, Missouri, North Carolina, South Carolina, Texas, and Washington); executive orders with specific percentages (Arkansas, Colorado, New Mexico, and Virginia); executive orders without specific percentages (Alabama, Arizona, Nebraska, and Pennsylvania); program, no details (Alaska and West Virginia); no program, other (Georgia and Kansas); and no MBE program (Hawaii, Mississippi, Montana, Nevada, New Hampshire, North Dakota,

South Dakota, Utah, Vermont, and Wyoming). "No program, other" includes measures such as tax credits, employment preferences, and technical assistance to minority businesses.

21. Numbers reported are always for valid cases. Missing data on an item for a case results in the case being omitted for that particular operation. In this case, one respondent did not supply information on the question.

22. The list is not exhaustive, since it represents only those responses reported by the EEO directors. From our survey of attorneys general we can also report other state responses: various disparity studies (Minnesota, New Jersey, and Connecticut); legislative amendment or modification (Minnesota, New Jersey, and Oregon); and lawsuits defended (New York and Rhode Island). Michigan has had its set-aside program overturned by the courts. In addition, responses have come from counties and cities across the nation.

23. A test of independence and measures of association can be calculated on the basis of a 2×2 contingency table: existence of a MBE program ("yes" or "no") by presence of state response ("yes" or "no"). The continuity correction for χ^2 equals 4.75, with a significance level $= .03$. The strength of the relationship is fairly strong as indicated by ϕ (.43 with an approximate significance $= .01$) and Goodman and Kruskal's τ, with state response dependent (.18 with an approximate significance $= .01$).

24. This last point is not explained by the need to defend oneself in court; it is true that three of these six states have been challenged in the courts, but each of the three have also responded in other ways, which are documented in the surveys.

25. Cross-classification based on these two variables reveals a statistically significant relationship, as demonstrated in a continuity corrected χ^2 of 7.96 (significance $= .00$) ϕ of .53 (significance $= .00$), and Goodman and Kruskal's τ with meetings dependent of .28 (significance $= .00$).

26. We will not repeat specific findings about states in the conclusion in the interest of space. For a quick review of the evidence, see the subsection on "State Response" in the Findings section, note 22 for additional state response, and note 15 for municipal response.

27. This point is illustrated by the legislative debate over the 1990 Civil Rights Act, which would have reversed or modified six 1989 Supreme Court rulings and expanded punitive awards for intentional discrimination under Title VII of the 1964 Civil Rights Act. Although the act did not require quotas, Republican congressional leaders opposed and President George Bush vetoed the bill on the grounds that it was a "quotas" bill. A veto override failed in the Senate. See Greenhouse (1990) for an account of this political dispute over quotas.

References

Articles and Books

Baum, Lawrence. 1977. "Judicial Impact as a Form of Policy Implementation." In John A. Gardiner, ed., *Public Law and Public Policy*. New York: Praeger.
_____. 1980. "The Influence of Legislatures and Appellate Courts Over the Policy Implementation Process." *Policy Studies Journal*, 8 (Special issue no. 2): 560–74.

_____. *The Supreme Court*. 1981. Washington, DC: Congressional Quarterly Press.

Becker, Theodore and Malcolm Feeley, eds. 1973. *The Impact of Supreme Court Decisions*. New York: Oxford University Press.

Belton, Robert. 1988. "Reflections on Affirmative Action After Paradise and Johnson." *Harvard Civil Rights and Civil Liberties Law Review*, 23 (Winter): 115–37.

Birkby, Richard H. 1966. "The Supreme Court and the Bible Belt: Tennessee Reaction to Schempp Decision." *Midwest Journal of Political Science*, 10: 304–17.

Brown, Barbara A. 1987. "Affirmative Action: The Emerging Consensus: A Review of the Supreme Court's Decisions." *Employment Relations Today* 14 (Autumn): 225–30.

Cannon, Bradley C. 1977. "Testing the Effectiveness of Civil Liberties Policies at the State and Federal Levels: The Case of the Exclusionary Rule." *American Politics Quarterly*, 5 (January): 57–82.

"A Collection of Articles by Constitutional Scholars and Economists. Minority Business Set-Aside Programs, *The City Of Richmond V. Croson*." 1990. Committee on the Judiciary, House of Representatives, 101st Congress, January.

Cooper, Phillip J. 1988. *Hard Judicial Choices: Federal District Court Judges and State and Local Officials*. New York: Oxford University Press.

Crain, Robert. 1968. *The Politics of School Desegregation*. Chicago: Aldine.

Days, Drews S. 1984. "Minority Access to Higher Education in the Post-Bakke Era." *University of Colorado Law Review*, 55 (Summer): 491–514.

Dodge, John F. Jr. and Patrick B. McCauley. 1982. "Reapportionment: A Survey of the Practicality of Voting Equality." *University of Pittsburgh Law Review*, 43: 527–99.

Dolbeare, Kenneth M. and Phillip Hammond. 1971. *The School Prayer Decision: From Court Policy to Court Practices*. Chicago: University of Chicago Press.

Drake, W. Avon and Robert D. Holsworth. 1990. "Electoral Politics, Affirmative Action and the Supreme Court: The Case of Richmond v. Croson." *National Political Science Review*, 2: 65–91.

Edwards, George C. 1980. *Implementing Public Policy*. Washington, DC: Congressional Quarterly Press.

Fried, Charles A. 1989. "Affirmative Action after the City of Richmond v. J. A. Croson Company: A Response to the Scholar's Statement." *Yale Law Journal*, 99 (October): 155–61.

Gruhl, John. 1980. "The Supreme Court's Impact on the Law of Libel: Compliance by Lower Federal Courts." *Western Political Quarterly*, 33 (December): 502–19.

Greenhouse, Linda. 1990. "The Dispute Over Quotas." *New York Times*, 21 July, p. 1.

Hansen, Susan B. 1980. "State Implementation of Supreme Court Decisions: Abortion Rates Since Roe v. Wade." *Journal of Politics*, 42 (May): 372–95.

Johnson, Charles and Bradley C. Canon. 1984. *Judicial Politics: Implementation and Impact*. Washington, DC: Congressional Quarterly Press.

Nakamura, Robert. 1980. *The Politics of Policy Implementation*. New York: St. Martin's Press.

O'Brien, David M. 1990. *Storm Center: The Supreme Court in American Politics*. 2d ed. New York: W. W. Norton Co.

Pear, Robert. 1990. "Courts are Undoing Efforts to Aid Minority Contractors." *New York Times*, 16 July, p. 1.

Peltason, J. W. 1961. *Fifty-eight Lonely Men: Southern Federal Judges and School Desegregation*. New York: Harcourt Brace Jovanovich.

Poister, Theodore. 1978. *Policy Program Analysis: Applied Research Methods*. Baltimore: University Park Press.

Schwartz, Bernard. 1986. *Swann's Way: The School Busing Case and the Supreme Court*. New York: Oxford University Press.

Simmons, Ron. 1982. *Affirmative Action: Conflict and Change in Higher Education After Bakke*. Cambridge, MA.: Schlerkman Publishing Company, Inc.

Songer, Donald R. and Reginald S. Sheehan. 1990. "Supreme Court Impact on Compliance and Outcomes: Miranda and New York Times in the United States Courts of Appeals, 1955–1986." *Western Political Quarterly*, 43 (June): 297–316.

Spiegelman, Paul J. 1985. "Court Ordered Quotas after Stotts: A Narrative on the Role of the Moralities of the Web and the Ladder in Employment Discrimination Doctrine." *Harvard Civil Rights and Civil Liberties Law Review*, 20 (Summer): 339–424.

Stumpf, Harry. 1988. *American Judicial Politics*. New York: Harcourt Brace Jovanovich.

Tarr, G. Alan. 1977. *Judicial Impact and State Supreme Courts*. Lexington, MA: Lexington Books.

Wasby, Stephen. 1970. *The Impact of the U.S. Supreme Court: Some Perspectives*. Homewood, IL: Dorsey Press.

Cases

Astroline Communications Co. v. Sherberg Broadcasting of Hartford (1990)

Covington v. Beaumont Independent School District 714 F. Supp. 1402 (E.D. Texas 1989)

Firefighters Local Union #1784 vs. Stotts 104 S. Ct. 2576 (1984).

Fletcher v. Peck 6 Cranch 87 (1810)

Fullilove v. Klutznick 448 U.S. 448 (1980).

Johnson v. Santa Clara County Transportation Agency 107 S. Ct. 1442 (1987).

Mann v. City of Albany 883 F. 2nd 999 (1989)

Marbury v. Madison 1 Cranch 137 (1803)

Metro Broadcasting Inc. v. Federal Communications Commission (1990)

Milwaukee County Power Association v. Fielder 707 F. Supp. 1016 (W.D. Wisconsin 1989)

Regents of the University of California v. Bakke 438 U.S. 265 (1978).

City of Richmond v. J. A. Croson Company 57 U.S.L.W. 4135 (1989).

United States v. Paradise 107 S. Ct. 1053 (1987).

United Steelworkers of America v. Weber 443 U.S. 197 (1979).

The Impact of At-Large Elections on the Representation of Black and White Women

Rebekah Herrick
Susan Welch

University of Nebraska

Previous research indicates that blacks are substantially better represented when council representatives are selected by districts rather than at-large. On the other hand, women are very slightly better represented in at-large than district systems. Given these contrasting patterns, the impact of election systems on black women is of some interest. An analysis of council representation in 239 major U.S. cities whose populations are at least 5 percent black reveal that black women are not more proportionally represented in district elections, though black men are. Hence, the choice of electoral structure has much more effect on the representation of black men than of black women.

T he fact that election structures are not neutral is hardly news. Con- sequently, during the past fifteen years, students of American urban politics have been looking carefully at the impact of local election struc- tures on the representation of minorities. Though analysts are not unan- imous, the preponderance of evidence indicates that at-large elections impede the representation of blacks (Welch, 1989; Karnig and Welch, 1982; Engstrom and McDonald, 1981, 1986; Davidson and Korbel, 1981; Robin- son and England, 1981; Latimer, 1979; Taebel, 1978; Heilig, 1978; Robinson and Dye, 1978; Karnig, 1976; Jones, 1976; for dissenting views see Bullock and MacManus, 1987; MacManus, 1978, 1979; MacManus and Bullock, 1987; for reviews of this extensive research see Engstrom and McDonald, 1986; Grofman, 1982; Karnig and Welch, 1982). While the gap between the degree of black representation afforded by at-large as compared to district elections has shrunk in the past decade (Welch, 1989), differences still exist. In cities with single-member district systems, blacks have city council representation in about the same proportions as their population proportions; in cities with at-large elections, they are represented at only about 80 percent of their population proportions (Welch, 1989).[1]

Based on these sorts of findings, many observers of urban politics believed that district elections were clearly fairer to diverse demographic groups within cities. But recently, other research has indicated that women are somewhat better represented in multimember than in single-member districts (cf. Karnig and Welch, 1979; Darcy et al., 1987; Welch and Studlar, 1990). If so, this would present a conundrum to those interested in promoting equity in descriptive representation among major social and political groups. Replacing at-large elections with district elections or combinations of district and at-large systems, as many cities have done, appears to increase the representation of blacks, but may impede the representation of women.[2] Yet the evidence about the impact of at-large elections on women's representation is still tentative, and the research done on their representation in local governments is now about a decade old. Thus, the potential impact of structure on the representation of women is still an open question, albeit a very important one.

The aim of this paper is to examine whether at-large systems have equally inhibiting effects on the election of black women and black men. We will also compare black women with white women to see if patterns of the structure-representation linkage are similar for all women.[3] These analyses will use 1988 data from 239 U.S. cities of 50,000 or more population and a black population of at least 5 percent.

Previous Research

Though perhaps initially perplexing, the reasons that single-member districts help ensure proportional representation of blacks but may inhibit the representation of women are fairly straightforward. Blacks are spatially segregated in most communities, meaning that when they are not majorities of a city's population, they may still form majorities in specific areas of the city. When these black majority areas are incorporated as districts or wards, blacks are able to elect one of their own as representatives even without white support. In at-large cities, however, black minorities cannot elect blacks without white support. Thus, to the extent that voting is along lines of race, black representation is facilitated in cities employing districts.

Black women share the spatial segregation of black men, but *as women* are not spatially segregated. Women as women are not especially advantaged in district elections because district boundaries do not increase their chances of being a member of an extraordinarily large majority in the same way districts do for blacks. Several explanations for why districts may actually slightly inhibit the chances of women being elected to office have been offered. Women may feel more comfortable in running for office in multimember districts; voters may be more likely to vote for a women as one of several candidates rather than as the only candidate to be elected; or turnover (and the opportunity for new members to be elected) might be higher in multimember systems. Welch and Studlar (1990) tested these explanations and found that women are more likely to run in multimember districts and are slightly more likely to be elected there. Their study, like most other studies examining the link between structure and representation, did not examine racial differences among women candidates or office holders.

Similarly, previous research linking black representation and electoral structure has focused almost exclusively on overall black representation. We know very little about black, female office holders at the municipal level. Recent data show that although about 20 percent of all black mayors are women, only three black women serve as mayors in communities of 50,000 or more (Moore, 1988: 374). And only one study has analyzed the council election of black men and black women separately. That study, based on 1978 data from U.S. cities of 25,000 and above, showed that black men are represented in city councils at about 126 percent of their population proportions, while black women were represented at about 16 percent of their population proportions (Karnig and Welch, 1979). Comparable proportions for white men and women, respectively, were 200 and 33 percent.

The council representation of black men was larger where district elections were employed, but the representation ratios of black women were not at all affected by whether or not the city had district elections (Karnig and Welch, 1979: 475). Thus district elections appeared to have been more important in electing black men than black women. Moreover, the percentage of black men on the council was significantly related to the median income and educational level of blacks in the community, as well as to the percentage of black population. None of these relationships held for black women's council representation.

If these findings are generalized, fairer representation of blacks in district systems is largely due to the greater likelihood that black men will be elected in district elections. The election of black women may be invariant to electoral structure.

However, there is a possibility that these findings may no longer be applicable. Since 1978, black local representation has risen dramatically. For example, in 1970 there were 623 black municipal officials; by 1978 this had risen to 2,159, and by 1987, over 3,200 municipal officials were black (National Roster, 1987).[4] This increase has been paralleled by the increase in black, female municipal officials, who now total over 700, almost double that of 1978 (National Roster, 1978). These changes may reflect new patterns of representation that were not present a decade ago.

Moreover, these different rates of election of black men and women might be artifacts of city characteristics other than election structure. The

Karnig and Welch study (1979) did not control for factors such as community size or income when examining differential effects of election structures on men and women.

Thus, the datedness of the research, coupled with its bivariate nature, prompts us to look once again at the potentially differential impact of political structure on the election of black men and black women.

Data and Methods

Our study is based on a survey of every U.S. city that had a 1984 population of at least 50,000 and whose population was at least 5 percent black or Hispanic 1980. Data were collected in May and June, 1988, by a two-page mail questionnaire to city clerks, with follow-up phone calls to the 10 percent of the initial respondents who did not return the mailed questionnaire.[5] In all, 100 percent of the clerks surveyed did respond, yielding an N of 314. In this analysis we include only those cities with 5 percent black population.[6]

This group of cities provides considerable variation in electoral type. In the early 1970s, 63 percent of city councils elected their members solely at-large, and another 15 percent used mixed systems, including both at-large and district methods (Svara, 1977). Over the years, however, more and more cities have dropped the at-large feature entirely, or combined it with district elections. Renner (1988) reported that by 1986, while at-large systems were still the dominant form in cities with populations below 50,000, only about half of the cities with populations between 50,000 and 100,000 and less than half of all cities with populations over 100,000 use them. Reflecting the fact that cities with significant minority populations have been most likely to have at-large election systems challenged, in our 239 cities, only 35 percent held purely at-large elections, 43 percent had mixed elections, 16 percent held single-member district elections only, 2 percent had multimember district elections, and the remaining 4 percent had other combinations of single-, multi-, and at-large elections.[7] Thus, all of the major types, and some other combinations too, remain alive and well in these medium and large cities.[8]

We asked each clerk to provide us with data on the number of council members elected at-large, the number elected in single-member districts or wards, and the number chosen in districts or ward selecting more than one member. For each set of members, for example those elected at-large, we asked the race or ethnicity and gender of each member. The categories included black men and women, Hispanic men and women, non-Hispanic white men and women, and "other" men and women.

Two different analyses are done. We first examine the proportionality of representation in cities employing at-large, single-member district, and mixed systems using a ratio measure, whereby the percentage of black men and women on the council is divided by the percentage of black men and women in the city population. Similar calculations are done for whites.

This ratio measure was used by Heilig and Mundt (1983), Karnig (1976), Karnig and Welch (1980, 1982), and Robinson and Dye (1978); it yields a figure greater than 1 if the council representation proportion for a given group exceeds the population proportion for that group and less than 1 if the council proportion is less.

To calculate the population percentage of black men and women in each community, we apply the sex ratio in the U.S. (which is about 53 percent women and 47 percent men [*Statistical Abstract*, 1987: Table 18]) to the percent black in the community. A similar procedure is used for whites. Using the national male-female ratios overlooks variations from community to community, but these differences are very minor.

Because the ratio measure of black representation has methodological problems (for reviews see Engstrom and McDonald, 1981, 1986; Karnig and Welch, 1982),[9] we also employ a regression analysis technique used by Engstrom and McDonald (1981). To examine overall black representation, instead of creating a ratio measure of equity, they regressed the proportion of the city's council that is black on the proportion of the city's population that is black. This bivariate regression allows one to see the relationship between the two factors at different levels of black population proportions. To examine how different electoral structures affect that relationship, Engstrom and McDonald added dummy and interaction variables to the regression equation. To examine the conditional effect of black population proportions on black council representation in three types of electoral systems (district, at-large, and mixed), the following equation was specified (let district cities be the omitted category):

$$\text{PCblcn} = a + b_1\text{atl} + b_2\text{mixed} + b_3\text{pcblpop} + b_4\text{pcblpop} \times \text{atl} + b_5\text{pcblpop} \times \text{mixed} + e$$

where:
PCblcn = Percent of council that is black (in whole numbers)
atl = 1 if city uses only at-large elections, 0 if not
mixed = 1 if city uses both at-large and district, 0 if not
pcblpop = the percent of the city's population that is black

Note that this formulation allows three separate equations to be specified within the overall equation (cf. Friedrich, 1982). For those cities with only district elections, the at-large and mixed system variables are both equal to 0, and black representation is specified by:

$$\text{PCblcn} = a + b_3\text{pcblpop}$$

Similarly, if the city has only at-large elections, the constant becomes the sum of a and b_1, and the slope the sum of b_3 and b_4. Black council representation is thus specified by:

$$\text{Pblcn} = (a + b_1) + (b_3 + b_4) \times \text{pcblpop}$$

Table 1. The Representation of Black and White Women on City Councils among Cities with Population over 50,000

	Black Women	White Women
Mean percent on council	4.5%	16.5%
Standard deviation	7.3	13.4
Percent of councils with no black (white) women	67	23
Percent of councils with more than 5 percent black (white) women	31	75
Range of membership	0–29%	0–57%

Note: Cities of 5 percent or more black population only (N = 239). Data collected in 1988.

In a similar fashion, we see that when the city has both at-large and district elections, the constant is represented by (a + b_2) and the slope by (b_3 + b_5).

We will use this regression formulation, substituting black male and female and white male and female council and population proportions in the equation. We also add to this equation several variables designed to control for city demographic and structural characteristics that could account for black representation and that of women. One is the total membership on the city council, shown to be positively related to black council representation (Taebel, 1978). A second is the ratio between black and white median family income. Engstrom and MacDonald (1981) have shown that the black-white ratio is positively related to black council representation. The third control is the education level of the city's population, which has been shown to be related to the election of women to councils (Karnig and Welch, 1979). We also control for the city's population size, largely because our sample of cities varies considerably in that dimension.

While using both the ratio and regression techniques may seem redundant, we believe it is important to show how each measure and type of analysis describes the underlying relationship. Because of the controversy over the issue of electoral structure and minority representation, we want to demonstrate that our conclusions represent the reality of this relationship and are not an artifact of the methods we use.

Findings

In Table 1 we present some basic descriptive data on the council representation of both black and white women. We see that, overall, black women comprise somewhat less than 5 percent of council membership in these cities. Sixty-seven percent of all councils have no black women on them, while 31 percent have over 5 percent. White women are better represented in absolute terms. Over 16 percent of the council membership are white women, and only 23 percent of the councils have no white women on them. The range of membership comprised by white women (0 to 57) is about twice the range of black women's membership (0 to 29 percent).

In Table 2, we present the ratio measures comparing the mean percent

Table 2. Rations of Representation to Population by Election Type, Sex, and Race

	District	Mixed	At-Large	MMD[a]	All Types
Black women	.25	.30	.35	.87	.33
White women	.44	.45	.58	.69	.50
Black men	1.96	1.32	1.37	.95	1.42[b]
White men	1.72	1.80	1.73	1.68	1.77

[a]Multimember districts. There are only five of these.
[b]Intra-election type differences significant at .05.

of black men and women and white men and women on the councils to the mean percent of these four gender-racial groups in the cities' populations. Recalling that the ratio equals 1 where the proportions of the council and in the population are equal, black women are represented at only about one-third their population proportions, while white women are represented at one-half theirs.[10]

Black women are substantially underrepresented in all three of the major systems, though their representation approaches parity in the five multimember district cities. Interestingly, they are slightly better represented in at-large then in mixed, and in mixed than in single-member district cities, but they are severely underrepresented in all three. Moreover, the differences are not statistically significant even though the district systems provide only about two-thirds the representation that the at-large systems do.[11]

White women also are somewhat more likely to be members of councils elected at-large, compared to those elected by district or in mixed systems. Again, the differences are not large, but are consistent with the pattern found for black women. White men, overrepresented in all system types, are very slightly more likely to be elected in mixed systems, by a very small margin.

Election structures have by far the greatest effect on the representation of black men, who are overrepresented in all three systems, but the most overrepresented in single-member districts. Unlike for the other groups, differences in representation among the election types are significant at the .05 level for black men.

On the whole, then, based on these simple ratio measures, women, both black and white, are slightly more likely to be represented in at-large systems than in district ones, but these differences are not statistically significant. Structure makes far less difference to their representation than to that of black men. Thus, the much greater black representation afforded in single-member district systems is due to the much larger probability that black men will be elected there; the election of black women is unaffected by this distinction. This finding is similar to the patterns found a decade ago by Karnig and Welch (1979), although both black and white women and black men have substantially increased their levels of representation.

Replicating this analysis for the 83 cities of the South shows similar patterns: black men are most affected by the different electoral structures and their representation is most facilitated by single-member districts. Electoral systems do not substantially affect black women's representation.[12]

In a regression analysis, using the proportion of black women on the council as a dependent variable, the proportion of black women in the population as an independent variable, and interaction terms representing the type of election times the black female population proportion, as described earlier, we again see that black women are not assisted by district elections. We can present the single equation as three separate ones, reflecting the impact of black female population in the presence of at-large, mixed, and district systems (standard errors are shown in parentheses under each coefficient):

% black women councillors =

$$-.34 + .33 \times \text{\% black women in population (district systems)}$$
(1.85) (.10)

$$-1.04 + .48 \times \text{\% black women in population (at-large systems)}$$
(1.27) (.10)

$$.21 + .31 \times \text{\% black women in population (mixed systems)}$$
(1.12) (.08)

These equations indicate that the council representation of black women is not extremely responsive to their population proportions, though it is most responsive in at-large systems. As the black female population proportion increases by 1 percent, the percent of black women on councils increases by about .33 percent in district systems, .31 percent in mixed systems, and .48 percent in at-large systems. Plotting each equation indicates that (because of the negative constants for the at-large systems) black women are more likely to be elected in district than in at-large elections when the black female population is fairly small, less than 5 percent (see Figure 1).[13] Above that, more black women are likely to be elected in at-large systems (a black female population of 5 percent translated into a total black population of about 9 percent). However, the maximum relative advantage of the at-large systems for black women is only about 4 percent, even at 35 percent black female population.

These findings can be contrasted with those for black men. No matter what the black male population proportion, more black men are elected in district than in at-large elections. (For both black men and black women, mixed systems generally provide the least black representation except in cities with the smallest black populations.) This is also illustrated in Figure 1, showing the predicted proportions of black male councillors at each level of the black male population. These slopes are based on the following equations:

Figure 1. District and At-Large Representation
of Blacks by Population Percent

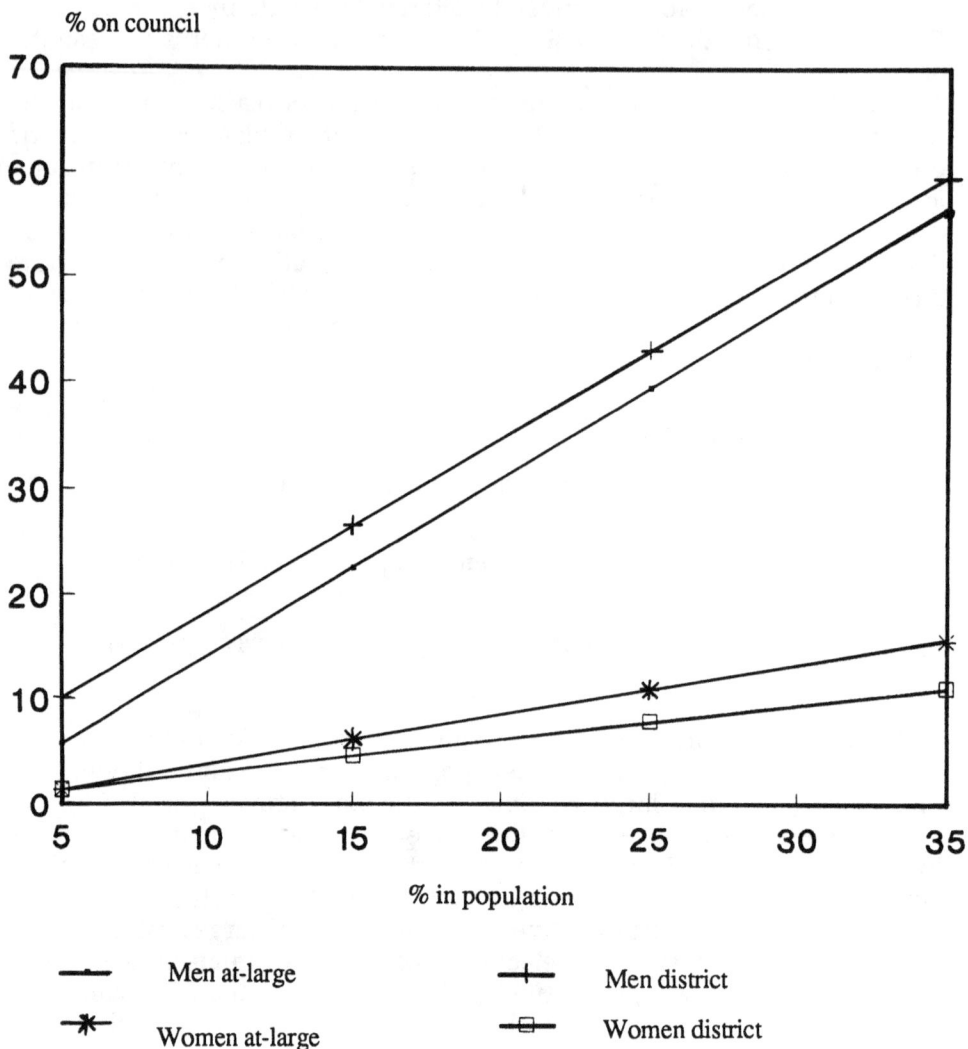

% on council

% in population

—•— Men at-large   —+— Men district

—*— Women at-large   —▫— Women district

Population percent is black male or female population percent

% black men councillors =

　　　　1.86 + 1.65 × % black men in population (district systems)
　　　　(2.98) (.19)

　　　　−2.74 + 1.69 × % black men in population (at-large systems)
　　　　(1.84) (.16)

　　　　−3.16 + 1.72 × % black men in population (mixed systems)
　　　　(1.61) (.12)

The next two sets of equations illustrate the impact of the three election types on white men and women. It is necessary to keep in mind, however, that in most of the cities, the white population was more than 50 percent, so the estimates of white council representation for small white populations are outside the range of the data. Nonetheless, the findings for white women are straightforward. Only in at-large systems are the proportion of white women on councils at all responsive to their population proportions. In district systems, the standard error of the white female population proportion exceeds the regression coefficient, and for mixed systems, the two are nearly equal.

9.94 + .14 × % white women in population (district systems)
(9.35) (.27)

8.31 + .25 × % white women in population (at-large systems)
(5.91) (.15)

9.95 + .17 × % white women in population (mixed systems)
(5.58) (.15)

For white men, the pattern is quite different. The coefficients in all equations were highly significant and indicate that within the range of the white population proportions in the data, white men are about equally overrepresented no matter what the electoral form.

−8.14 + 2.03 × % white men in population (district systems)
(11.72) (.30)

.50 + 1.72 × % white men in population (at-large systems)
(8.92) (.26)

−1.80 + 1.86 × % white men in population (mixed systems)
(7.02) (.21)

A Multivariate Analysis

In a final analysis, we used regression to examine several predictors of representation of each race-gender group. In addition to the population proportions of the group and the type of election, these predictors included the population of the city, the ratio of black to white income, the proportion of people in the city who graduated from high school, and the total size of the council.

Only the black female population proportion and the council size are related to black female representation at a level that would be statistically significant at the .05 level if we were analyzing a sample (Table 3).[14] None of the election type variables nor their interactions with black female population percent are significant, nor do any have standard errors less than

Table 3. Predictors of Representation of Each Gender-Racial Group

Variable	Black Women Beta	t	Black Men Beta	t	White Women Beta	t	White Men Beta	t
Sex-race pop. %	.49	4.19	.67	8.75	.02	.13	.70	6.06
Council size	.12	1.75	−.09	−1.91	.10	1.36	−.04	−.73
% high school grad.	.04	.53	−.53	−1.04	.43	6.01	−.23	−4.06
Bl-Wh income ratio	−.06	−.97	.13	3.12	.08	1.17	−.12	−2.28
Population size	−.04	−.56	.02	.54	.04	.51	−.00	−.04
At-large dummy	−.01	−.06	−.19	−2.03	.19	.60	−.02	−.07
Mixed dummy	−.01	−.06	−.19	−1.99	.30	.95	−.16	−.62
Sex-race % x mixed	−.11	−.82	.13	1.46	−.24	−.69	.15	.55
Sex-race % x atl	.07	.58	.08	.99	−.07	−.24	−.02	−.09
R^2	.22		.66		.18		.47	
N = 239								

the regression coefficient. Thus, other things being equal, black female representation seems little affected by election type. The black-white income ratio and educational levels of the community are also unrelated to the representation of black women.

The story is different for black men. The equation explains three times more variance in male than female representation, largely because of the strong relationship between black male population and representation. Black male representation is negatively affected in at-large and mixed elections, as we have previously noted. Black men are also slightly less likely to be found on larger councils and in cities with larger proportions of residents who have graduated from high school, though the relationships are not significant.[15] Similar to Karnig and Welch (1979), we also found that black community resources, at least as measured by the black-white income ratio, are positively related to the presence of black male council members.

White women are the only group whose population proportions are unrelated to their council representation. White women are significantly more likely to be found on councils in communities of higher education levels. They are also slightly more likely to be found when the black-white family income ratio is higher and, like black women, on larger councils, but only in at-large systems.[16]

As one might expect, there are more white men on councils whose characteristics depress the proportions of blacks and white female councillors. The more white men in the population, the more white male council members. White men are also more likely to be elected in cities with low black-white income ratios and low proportions of high school graduates. Council size does not appear to affect the election of white men.

Election type does not affect the election of either white men or white women, reaffirming our conclusion that election type is mostly significant because of its effect on the election of black men.

Conclusions

There are some limitations to the generalizability of our study. We examined only cities with populations of 50,000 or more. Population size was totally unrelated to council representation for these groups in these cities, so it is likely that our conclusions could be generalized to somewhat smaller cities than those we examined. However, there is no doubt a point at which the generalizations do not hold, since the dynamics of elections in very small communities are quite different from those in large ones.

Moreover, we excluded from our analysis cities whose populations were less than 5 percent black. Our findings probably would not apply in cities with much smaller black communities, since black representation in those cities is likely to be very idiosyncratic.

Our most important finding is that electoral structure matters most to the election of black men. In proportion to their population, they are overrepresented in all election types, but most overrepresented in district elections. However, black women are about equally underrepresented in all systems, though slightly more so in district systems. Black women are the least equitably represented of the four groups examined here, having about 23 percent the representational equity of black men and 67 percent of the equity of white women (calculated from Table 2). However, the combination of low representation of black women in all electoral systems combined with much better black male representation in district elections leads to the overall conclusion that district elections provide a considerably more equitable representation for blacks as a group than do at-large elections.

A potentially important finding is that cities that have multimember districts have the most equitable representation of all groups. Cities with multimember districts have been completely ignored in previous research (undoubtedly being combined with single-member district cities in a "district" category), though conceptually they are distinct from single-member district cities. In these cities, election district are used, but more than one person is elected from each. Though the fact that we have only five such cities in our sample mitigates our ability to draw solid generalizations, in those multimember districts, black and white women are represented at levels much closer to parity than they are in any of the other systems. White men remain considerably overrepresented, but less so than in the other systems. Black men are slightly underrepresented, but their representation is closer to parity than in the other systems. It would be useful to investigate smaller communities to see if these findings hold true with a larger number of cities.

Though all systems greatly underrepresent black women on local councils, the answer to the question of which electoral system is fairer to black women depends on which set of issues and identity is more important to them. This brings us to the question of substantive representation offered to black women. Obtaining adequate descriptive representation is an important step in and of itself, and a step that has been shown to lead to at least certain kinds of substantive policy shifts (cf. Eisinger, 1982; Karnig and Welch, 1980; Mladenka, 1989; Steward, England, and Meier, 1988). However, it seems clear that at present, as in the past, racial issues and identity are much more germane than gender (cf. Marshall, 1990; Welch and Sigelman, 1989), though women's issues are far from irrelevant to black women. To the extent that racial issues are more important, district elections will allow better substantive representation of black women. If, in the future, women's issues become more germane, then one could not automatically say that district elections allow for the fairer representation of blacks as a group. For the moment, however, our conclusions do not suggest that current conclusions about the effect of at-large systems in diminishing black representation need revision. They do suggest the complexities of achieving fair descriptive, let alone substantive, representation of every significant racial and gender group.

Notes

1. In the early 1970s, black council representation in at-large systems was only about 40 percent of what one would expect based on black population proportions (Robinson and Dye, 1978). This parity ratio rose to 50 to 60 percent by the late 1970s (Engstrom and McDonald, 1981); Karnig and Welch, 1982). These same studies found that black council representation in district systems increased from about 85 percent in the middle 1970s to over 90 percent later in that decade.
2. Although only by a small margin.
3. In this paper we exclude from consideration the representation of Hispanic women, though that is also a topic deserving attention.
4. Though these figures include municipal officials in addition to council members, most are council members.
5. The mailing procedure, suggested by Dillman (1978), consisted of an initial mailing followed three weeks later by a postcard reminder thanking those who had responded for their cooperation and urging nonrespondents to complete the questionnaire. Two weeks later a second copy of the questionnaire was sent. Phoning was begun three weeks after the mailing of the second copy. Partly due to the brevity of the questionnaire, response rate was incredibly high, exceeding even that of International City Manager's Association's 1986 survey of cities. They reported a 66 percent response rate (Renner, 1988).
6. This is about 88 percent of the 356 U.S. cities with population over 50,000. Our findings remain the same if we also exclude cities where the majority of the population is black. In our analyses, we eliminated cities with black populations so small that proportional representation would be difficult to achieve given the normal size (five to fifteen members) of most city councils. The specific cutoff used does not affect the substantive findings here. We have also examined these data using a population floor of 10 percent black and using a variable population floor in each city of $F = .5$ percent $\times$ (100/N), where F is the black population percentage floor in whole numbers and N is the number of council seats. Using this formulation includes only those cities where the proportion of black population is equal to at least one-half the population necessary to elect one council member if all seats had been by

district. For example, in cities with five member council, $F = .5(100/5) = 10$, or a 10 percent floor. But in a city with 10 council seats, $F = .5(100/10)$, or a 5 percent population floor. In reality, most councils have five to nine seats.

7. Some urban scholars have expressed surprise that, given the amount of litigation over election structures, any communities with sizable minority populations have at-large structures. However, even in the South, over one-third of these cities still have purely at-large systems.

8. Though multimember district systems provide an interesting contrast to purely at-large elections on the one hand and single-member district systems on the other, only some basic descriptive data will be provided on multimember district systems since there are so few of them.

9. The ratio measure yields the same zero value if there are no blacks on the council, no matter what their proportion in the population. Thus, cities with councils containing no blacks would have the same zero score regardless of whether their black population proportions were 5 percent or 75 percent.

10. Replicating the analysis using a 10 percent black population floor yields very similar findings, though the representation gap is not as great between single-member districts and at-large systems for black women (.31 in at-large, .28 in single member districts), while for white women the gap is slightly larger than in the 5 percent floor cities. Using a black percentage floor equal to $.5 \times (100/\text{council size})$ again yields similar results, except that the at-large–single-member district gap is fairly large for black women (.43 compared to .26 respectively).

11. This is a situation where there is disagreement about the appropriateness of tests of statistical significance. Our units of analysis represent a universe, so such tests are not absolutely necessary. They do, however, give the reader a sense of how stable such differences are likely to be.

12. Contrary to findings for the nation as a whole, more white women are elected in district than in at-large systems in the South. This may be a result of district systems allowing less traditional segments of southern populations, those more likely to elect women, to form majorities in subcity areas. White men have higher representation ratios in the South than elsewhere.

13. Readers should note that the constants are not statistically different from 0. Yet, this is not a sample, but a universe, and the constant term is the best estimate of the true intercept.

14. Here we used a one-tailed test, as we expected a positive relationship for these two variables. An analysis of the council size variable reveals that it only affects the proportion of black women on the council in at-large systems.

15. We use a two-tailed test with council size, since the direction of the relationship is opposite to that expected.

16. This relationship supports previous findings of weak positive associations between the number of seats and women's representation (Welch and Studlar, 1990).

References

Bullock, Charles, and Susan MacManus. 1987. "Staggered Terms and Black Representation." *Journal of Politics*, 49 (May): 543–52.

Cole, Leonard. 1976. *Blacks in Power*. Princeton: Princeton University Press.

Cottrell, Charles, and Arnold Fleischman. 1979. "The Change from At-Large to District Representation and Political Participation of Minority Groups in Fort Worth and San Antonio, Texas." *Urban Affairs Quarterly*, 10 (September): 17–39.

Darey, Robert, Susan Welch and Janet Clark. 1987. *Women, Elections, and Representation*. New York: Longman.

Davidson, Chandler, and George Korbel 1981. "At Large Elections and Minority Group Representation: A Re-Examination of Historical and Contemporary Representation on City Councils." *Social Science Quarterly*, 63 (March): 99–114.

Dillman, Donald. 1978. *Mail and Telephone Surveys: The Total Design Method*. New York: Wiley.

Eisinger, Peter. 1982. "Black Employment in Municipal Jobs: The Impact of Black Political Power." *American Political Science Review*, 76:380–92.

Engstrom, Richard, and Michael McDonald. 1981. "The Election of Blacks to City Councils." *American Political Science Review*, 75 (June): 344–55.

_____. 1986. "The Effect of At-Large versus District Elections on Racial Representation in U.S. Municipalities." In Bernard Grofman and Arend Lijphart, eds. *Electoral Laws and Their Political Consequences*. New York: Agathon Press.

Friedrich, Robert. 1982. "In Defense of Multiplicative Terms in Multiple Regression Equations." *American Journal of Political Science*, 26 (November): 797–833.

Grofman, Bernard. 1982. "Alternatives to Single Member Plurality Districts: Legal and Empirical Issues." In Bernard Grofman, A. Lijphart, R. McKay, and H. Scarrow, eds. *Representation and Redistricting Issues*. Lexington, Mass: Lexington Books.

Heilig, Peggy. 1978. "The Abandonment of Reform in a Southern City: Outcomes of a Return to District Politics." Paper presented at the Midwest Political Science Association Meetings, Chicago.

Heilig, Peggy, and Robert Mundt. 1983. "Changes in Representational Equity: The Effect of Adopting Districts." *Social Science Quarterly*, 64 (June): 393–97.

Heilig, Peggy, and Robert Mundt. 1984. *Your Voice at City Hall*. Albany, New York: State University of New York Press.

Jones, Clinton. 1976. "The Impact of Local Election Systems on Black Representation." *Urban Affairs Quarterly*, 11 (March): 345–56.

Karnig, Albert. 1976. "Black Representation on City Councils: The Impact of District Elections and Socioeconomic Factors." *Urban Affairs Quarterly*, 12 (December): 223–42.

Karnig, Albert, and Susan Welch. 1979. "Sex and Ethnic Differences in Municipal Representation." *Social Science Quarterly*, 60 (December): 465–81.

_____. 1980. *Black Representation and Urban Policy*. Chicago: University of Chicago Press.

_____. 1982. "Electoral Structure and Black Representation on City Councils." *Social Science Quarterly*, 63 (March): 99–114.

Latimer, Margaret. 1979. "Black Political Representation in Southern Cities: Election Systems and Their Causal Variables." *Urban Affairs Quarterly*, 15 (September): 65–86.

MacManus, Susan. 1979. "At Large Elections and Minority Representation: An Adversarial Critique." *Social Science Quarterly*, 60 (November): 338–40.

_____. 1978. "City Council Election Procedures and Minority Representation." *Social Science Quarterly*, 59 (June): 153–61.

MacManus, Susan, and Charles S. Bullock. 1987. "Race, Ethnicity, and Ancestry as Voting Cues in City Council Elections." Paper presented at the Conference on Ethnic and Racial Minorities in Advanced Industrial Democracies, University of Notre Dame, December.

Marshall, Susan. 1990. "Equity Issues and Black-White Differences in Women's ERA Support." *Social Science Quarterly* (June): 299–314.

Mladenka, Kenneth. 1989. "Does the Local Political Process Work for Blacks and Hispanics." *American Political Science Review*, 83 (March): 165–92.

Moore, W. John. 1988. "From Dreamers to Doers." *National Journal*, 13 February: 372–77.

Mundt, Robert. 1979. "Referenda in Charlotte and Raleigh, and Court Action in Richmond: Comparative Studies on the Revival of District Representation." Paper presented at the American Political Science Association Meeting, Chicago.

National Roster of Black Elected Officials. 1987. Washington, DC: Joint Center for Political Studies.

Renner Tari. 1988. "Municipal Election Processes: The Impact on Minority Representation." *Municipal Yearbook.* Washington, DC: International City Manager's Association, pp. 13–22.

Robinson, Theodore, and Thomas Dye. 1978. "Reformism and Representation on City Councils." *Social Science Quarterly*, 59 (June): 133–41.

Robinson, Theodore, and Robert England. 1981. "Black Representation on Central City School Boards Revisited." *Social Science Quarterly*, 62: 495–501.

Statistical Abstract of the U.S. 1987. 1987. Washington, DC: U.S. Government Printing Office.

Stewart, Joseph, Robert England, and Kenneth J. Meier. 1988. "Black Representation in Urban School Districts: From School Board to Office to Classroom." Paper presented at the 1988 Annual Meeting of the Western Political Science Association.

Svara, James. 1977. "Unwrapping Institutional Packages in Municipal Government." *Journal of Politics*, 39:166–75.

Taebel, Delbert. 1978. "Minority Representation on City Councils." *Social Science Quarterly*, 59 (June): 142–52.

Welch, Susan. 1989. "The Impact of At-Large Elections on the Representation of Blacks and Hispanics." *Journal of Politics* 52 (November): 1050–1076.

Welch, Susan, and Albert Karnig. 1978. "Representation of Blacks on Big City School Boards." *Social Science Quarterly*, 59 (June): 162–72.

Welch, Susan, and Lee Sigelman. 1989. "Is There a Gender Gap Among Blacks." *Social Science Quarterly*, 70 (Mach): 120–33.

Welch, Susan, and Donley Studlar. 1990. "The Impact of Multi Member Districts on the Representation of Women in Britain and the U.S." *Journal of Politics*, 52 (May): 391–412.

Media in Warsaw Pact States: Explanations of Crisis Coverage

Kathie Stromile Golden

University of Colorado at Colorado Springs

Researchers focusing on political communications in the Warsaw Pact employed wide-ranging theoretical approaches, but relatively few attempted to provide empirical (and comparative) analyses to substantiate underlying theoretical arguments. This article provides a comparative quantitative analysis of Warsaw Pact member states' dissemination of information with political content via print and broadcast media. Guiding this research is the argument that Warsaw Pact states' media coverage of crisis events varied in terms of the amounts and kinds of information distributed to citizens, and that this in turn provides clues about alliance cohesion at critical junctures. Utilizing the Foreign Broadcast Information Service's Daily Reports *and the Central Intelligence Agency's* Directories of Officials *for the Soviet Union and East European countries, my findings reveal that Warsaw Pact countries' media provided differential coverage for domestic, systemic, and international crises. Cross-national variations in the duration, extent, and intensity of member states' coverage of specific crises were found to be related to national differences in linkages between journalists and part elites and to type of crisis. The findings also provide clues about the order in which Warsaw Pact member states adopted Soviet liberalization policies.*

The rapidity with which the recent sweeping political, economic, and social changes occurred in the Soviet Union and Eastern Europe were viewed by Western as well as non-Western scholars with much surprise. Although scholars are cautious in making predictions about the ramifications of these changes, there is much speculation revolving around implications for domestic and international politics. Among the first major changes initiated under the leadership of Soviet president Mikhail Gorbachev is glasnost, which allows for more open dialogue throughout So-

78

viet society. Glasnost has been especially instrumental in bringing about more candid media reports concerning both domestic and international politics. Political regimes throughout Eastern Europe did not, however, immediately (nor all at once) take the Soviet lead. Initially, there were substantial variations in the degree of openness accorded Eastern European media.[1]

That openness in Warsaw Pact members' media reports varied in spite of Soviet support for more liberal policies regarding media institutions suggests that (WTO) media operations were differentially censored and controlled. Prior to Soviet initiatives, media in the Warsaw Pact states were institutions that supported each regime and thereby constituted a tool by which the Warsaw Treaty Organization (WTO) could ensure popular support for its collective action. But when crisis occurred, inside the WTO or elsewhere, how did these media perform? Were the states of the WTO speaking with one voice? And, to the degree that they did not, what might explain such differences across the alliance?

For a number of years, scholars of Soviet and Eastern European politics devoted considerable attention to political communications. Some researchers, for example, focused on the role of the mass media in the political socialization process, while others examined foreign news coverage patterns. Still others assessed the relationship between government and the mass media in communist systems. Scholarly endeavors in these areas encompassed a wide range of theoretical approaches, but provided few empirical tests for the underlying theoretical arguments. The paucity of studies devoted to empirical analysis of political communications in the Soviet Union and Eastern Europe suggests that potentially interesting explanations of these states' political behavior were not examined.

Although previous research on states in the Warsaw Pact focused on media coverage of various events, such research most often used qualitative case studies. The failure to study empirically (and comparatively) the Warsaw Pact member states' media coverage of strikes, protests, military interventions, military conflicts between nations, severe economic crises, and natural disasters is, perhaps, an indication that such crises were expected to receive almost identical coverage across communist systems. This paper, therefore, challenges what appear to have been prevalent assumptions about media behavior in the Warsaw Pact countries.

Beyond merely challenging assumptions, however, assessment of crisis reporting among WTO states can indicate the extent to which member states differed in the amounts and kinds of information about crises distributed to citizens. Such differences would provide clues about the degree to which member states deviated from expected patterns of political behavior, that is, from Soviet behavior. Additionally, variations in crisis reporting among WTO states will provide clues about the order in which those states adopted the Soviet liberalization policies.

Research on political communications in communist systems suggested that mass media were crucial to the political regimes' ability to legitimate their rule.[2] The "proper" socialization of journalists was viewed as an important aspect of the regimes' efforts to obtain legitimacy. Journalists were seen as agents of the state and party, and party membership among media personnel was maintained at high levels.[3] Government ownership and control of media institutions facilitated party elites' desire to ensure that the opinions and values expressed through the media would coincide with their own. Implicit, then, was the expectation that integration of media personnel into party organs would affect media performance.

There were few attempts, however, to measure the degree of interaction between journalists and party or state officials. Further, we have no empirical studies of WTO states' media performance—especially of differences among media of WTO states. This study, then, examines the relationship between the integration of media personnel and political elites and Warsaw Pact states' media coverage of crises.

Issues and Expectations

Crises are the foci for this study for two reasons: first, to the extent that one finds variations in WTO states' media coverage of crises, one may have an interesting indicator of alliance cohesion at such critical junctures.[4] Second, a crisis may have heightened the probability of coverage by all Warsaw Pact countries' media, and thereby enhanced comparability of data.

Space considerations preclude a full elaboration of the definitional issue of what constitutes a "crisis." Other efforts to derive such a definition have encountered difficulty (Hermann, 1963:36). Yet, three generalizable characteristics—uncertainty, discontent, and hostility—tend to be exhibited by people during crises. More important, crises are conflictual occurrences in which those involved (citizens and/or government officials) are unsure of the outcomes; crises do not occur when the outcomes are known. A crisis almost always involves the evidence of discontent among citizens or leaders (or both) in one or more political systems. Hostility on the part of government officials and citizens can be the trigger for the crisis, or a consequence of it—but violence or the threat of violence will always be present.

There are, of course, substantive differences among crises that are likely to alter the degree of variation in coverage by alliance members. However, in my data collection efforts, crises are sampled from among three categories: "international crises," where the issue at hand does not directly involve any WTO member or other communist state; "systemic crises," which involve relations between or among communist states; and "domestic crises," which are contained within one nation-state insofar as no Soviet or collective action is threatened or affected, and effects of the crisis are domestic in scope. The crises examined occurred during the 1970s and 1980s.

In order to discern variation in WTO states' media coverage of crises, four dimensions—duration, extent, intensity, and salience—are examined. These four dimensions, although not mutually exclusive, offer different notions of the importance communist regimes attach to crises.

Duration is the uninterrupted time period in which a crisis is reported in a major daily or weekly newspaper or major journal or featured as a principal radio report. As such, duration tells one about the degree to which communist regimes were following the development and subsequent outcomes of crisis events.

Extent of coverage refers to the frequency with which a crisis is mentioned in a newspaper or journal or on the radio. It is one way of assessing the breadth of the regime's concern about crisis events and their outcomes.

Intensity, the third dimension of crisis coverage, refers to the proportion of front-page and/or lead-story radio coverage received by a particular crisis times the total number of words devoted to the crisis. Intensity is an assessment of the prominence and thoroughness of crisis reporting. It depends, in part, on the duration and extent of coverage, but it can be determined for any length of time and for any frequency with which a given crisis received attention.

Finally, *salience* refers to the frequency with which party leaders are quoted in the coverage and/or the frequency with which they sign editorial comments about a particular crisis. Salience has relevance for each of the other three dimensions and was, perhaps, the key to media coverage of crises. That is, the amount of attention given by media reports to party leaders' comments regarding crises would have had significance for the duration, extent, and intensity of such reports. Of course, the frequency with which party leaders addressed crises would vary with the types of crises the media were covering.

Research on political communications in communist societies argued frequently that ideology affected communist news coverage (Katz, 1978; Gerbner, 1961; Galtung and Ruge, 1965:64–89; Gerbner and Marvanyi, 1984; Pisarek, 1984:114–19). Previous studies also implied that several other factors impinged upon crisis coverage by communist states' media. One had to consider, for example, (1) the nature of the crisis, (2) the parties involved and their relationship with countries providing coverage, and (3) the significance of the crisis for countries' reporting of the events (see Simon, 1979:6). Of course, the degree to which these factors affected crisis coverage might also vary.[5]

Government control of the media in the Soviet Union and Eastern Europe obviously enhanced the state's and party's efforts to socialize citizens "properly" (see Hollander, 1972; Kaplan, 1977; Dzirkles, 1982:85–103; Curry 1982:102–8). But when was such control used to maximize the socialization role of media? The answer, I think, is clear: when there was a domestic crisis, regimes would have been most desirous of affecting citizens' behavior, necessitating an expanded media activity. Curry (1982: 122), for example, noted that Polish workers' demands in August 1980 included an emphasis on free information concerning Poland's situation—a demand that forced the Polish communist leadership to reveal past failures and to allow unorchestrated discussion of the future. The Polish experience suggests that distorting domestic realities by state-controlled media was even more difficult than was manipulating images of external events.

Citizens were, in fact, aware of existing problems and the regimes'

failure or inability to provide necessary correctives. Further distortion or
limits on information probably exacerbated citizens' discontent. Communist party regimes, of course, possibly responded in such circumstances
with heightened flows of information, albeit information useful to the
regimes' efforts to maintain their political rule.

Based upon previous research (Kaplan, 1977; Curry, 1982), one can
reasonably expect that the four dimensions of media activity introduced
earlier—duration, extent,intensity, and salience—were greater for coverage of domestic crises than for systemic and international crises. In other
words, one can expect the dimensions of crisis coverage to have been
greater in the country experiencing the crisis than in other countries.
Further, WTO states' media reports would have reflected more immediate
concern for conflictual events transpiring in another member state than
for conflictual events in other arenas. These expectations also stem from
the argument that communist governments had vested interests in the
manner in which conflictual events were reported. That is, the reporting
of such events had consequences for citizens' perceptions about the adequacy and efficiency of the political regimes (see Kaplan, 1972:126–28).
That a particular regime would be motivated to orchestrate more media
reports on domestic conflict might expand crisis coverage. The regime's
efforts to influence citizens' perceptions could result in greater coverage
and more news stories about the conflict and its ultimate resolution. This,
however, would depend on the severity of the crisis. One would expect
the duration and extent of media reports to be minimized in cases where
the regime was able to resolve the conflict relatively quickly; the regime's
ability to resolve conflict would reduce the need to call attention to the
situation. One might also expect diminished media coverage during early
stages of domestic conflicts, but this too would depend on the regime's
perception of its ability to resolve the conflict without substantial proportions of the population becoming involved in or aware of the conflict.

When the magnitude of the crisis heightened and the regime was unable to resolve the conflict in a timely and effective manner, the need to
devote substantial attention to the conflict would have increased propor-
tionately. This need would also prompt the regime to become more vo-
ciferous in proclaiming its plans for bringing the situation under control,
which, in turn, would result in greater intensity; that is, in more reports
on front pages and more lead radio stories.

Research focused on the media as a primary agent of socialization (Pisarek,
1984; Gerbner and Marvanyi, 1984; also suggests that turmoil within one
communist state was probably more heavily reported by media of other
communist states in which similar unrest had once occurred. Specifically,
the coverage of crises generated by sociopolitical turmoil was possibly
affected by a country's prior experience with civic unrest (such as protest
demonstrations, work stoppages, or riots); such an effect would be evident in media coverage and would have high levels of duration, extent,
intensity, and salience.

A communist regime might have used higher levels of media attention
to crises in other communist states to illustrate the pitfalls of challenges to

the party's authority. Given that communist states engage in a variety of activities directed at shaping citizens' perceptions of both internal and external events, devoting attention to problems faced by other societies would be used to discourage similar (or repeated) occurrences of conflict in one's own society. For that reason, Hungary and Czechoslovakia may have devoted substantial attention to domestic crises in other communist states.

Countries that had not undergone similar domestic unrest were not likely to dwell on external domestic conflict, unless the events had substantial significance for them. The Soviet Union, for example, would be more likely than Bulgaria or Romania to have expressed concern about conflictual situations in any of the Eastern European countries. In fact, the Soviet leadership probably interpreted conflict in these societies as possible threats to the security of the region. Consequently, the extent and salience of Soviet media coverage of such events are likely to have approximated the extent and salience of coverage by the media indigenous to the country experiencing turmoil. It is also plausible to expect states to have devoted increased attention to crisis situations in neighboring states. Each communist regime was likely to consider the probability that conflict in a neighboring state would disrupt the maintenance of order in its own society. Therefore, such regimes would pay close attention to events, and possibly they verbalized their positions concerning a neighboring conflict.

These expectations all illustrate possible relationships between media coverage and types of crises. The few cases examined here, of course, are insufficient for an analysis of such relationships across all crises; nevertheless, one can begin to examine the range of differences that existed in media coverage across crises and across nations. Because media institutions in communist societies were crucial to the maintenance of the regimes' political-rule, it became imperative that journalists adhered to party directives. Such adherence was sought by the integration of journalists into party structures (that is, the Communist party and adjunct affiliations). Some journalists, of course, were more thoroughly integrated than others, differing in their rate of participation in party organizations. Thus, "journalistic integration" here refers to the degree to which media personnel held memberships in party organizations or institutions.

Communist parties used several mechanisms for ensuring that media personnel adhered to party directives concerning media coverage. Curry (1982:106) notes that, although lower-level journalists and those with special talents who outwardly supported the basic ideology of the regime did not always belong to the Communist party, membership *was* expected of prominent journalists and their editors. Editorial positions, foreign correspondents, and commentators were a part of the party's nomenklatura (Curry, 1982:106); aspirants for these positions had to be party members *and* well-connected with party leaders. Journalists were required to move up through the party ranks if they were to attain editorial, commentator, or foreign correspondent positions. In the process of such advancement, prominent media personnel—the media elites—would amass membership in numerous party organizations.

A second mechanism for facilitating party goals was censorship, of which there were many forms (see Curry, 1982:106). The form of censorship used in any given country could change over time (see Buzek, 1964; Kaplan, 1977; Curry, 1982; 106—7). Censorship, for example, could be *directed*, which refers to the channeling of government directives through various press committees and agencies or through general party statements. Other forms of censorship included *external monitoring* and *self-monitoring*[6] While changes in the forms of censorship might have resulted, in part, from technological advancements in communications and from changes in organizational structures and procedures, they were also related to the party's concern about journalists' adherence to party directives. Failure to submit to the prevailing form of censorship was an indication that journalists had not been "properly" socialized.

One might, therefore, posit that coverage of crises was affected by prominent journalists' involvement in the party. More specifically, as a country's media elites' membership in party organs increased, duration, extent, intensity, and salience increased as well.

Intensity of coverage was likely to increase, in part, because editors would devote front-page and lead-story radio time to political leaders more during crises than at other times. Intensity of coverage would also increase because media personnel desired to enhance their positions in the party. In other words, stroking political leaders' egos would improve one's chances for moving up socially and politically. Salience of coverage would increase as well, because media attention would be directed in crises toward espousing the government's position regarding the meaning and consequences of particular conflicts.

Duration and extent of crisis coverage may also be related positively with journalists' integration into party structures. The nature of crisis might, however, have been equally significant. Depending on the type of crisis and the actors involved, political officials may have wanted to limit coverage; that is, the less said about the crisis, the easier it would have been to keep most people uninvolved and uninformed. Media personnel, aware of the desires of political elites, would respond accordingly. Simply put, both the period of time an event was focused on and the scope of such coverage would be limited.

Data and Methodology

This paper focuses on Warsaw Pact countries' media coverage of four crises—the October 1973 Arab Israeli War, the 1979 China-Vietnam War, the 1979–1980 Soviet intervention in Afghanistan (denoted here as a crisis through all of 1980), and the 1980–1981 Polish conflict (examined from August 1980 through December 1981). These crises represent international, systemic, and domestic crises and are geographically distant from one another. Further, examination of these four crises makes it possible to discern variation in media reports across time. Admittedly, the time periods during which the four crises occurred limit our ability to ascertain the degree to which changes in the duration, extent, intensity, and salience of media reports were incremental. These crises do, however allow for the identification of patterns of change. The closeness in time for three of the four crises suggests that interaction effects might have significance for the amount of media attention received. Interaction effects, however, are not expected because each of the three crises—the 1979 China-Vietnam War, the 1979–1980 Soviet intervention in Afghanistan, and the 1980–1981 Polish conflict—represents a different type of crisis.

Coverage by WTO members' media of these four crises has been coded from the *Daily Reports* of the Foreign Broadcast Information Service (FBIS). These daily publications present transcriptions of other states' English-language broadcasts and wire-service stories as well as translations of national printed and broadcast media. FBIS does not, of course, provide exhaustive reporting of every major publication for all of Eastern Europe and the Soviet Union, but these publications are thought to be representative of these states' media. While it is legitimate to question biases inherent in a data source such as the FBIS, due to the selective basis of translations, the FBIS is particularly attentive to Warsaw Pact members' references to crises. In that sense, the FBIS works to the advantage of my analysis, enhancing the comparability of samples. The advantage of coding from the FBIS also extends to its cross-national and longitudinal sampling of media in these countries. That is, the FBIS, since 1973, has provided extensive daily media reports from each of the countries included in this study.

Aside from the question of biases, the FBIS is the most comprehensive publication of its kind. The only other alternative would be to sample media reports, in the original languages, from the daily publications or broadcasts themselves. Such an exercise is not feasible, because few will have command of all the region's languages, sufficient financial resources, or unlimited time. Even were these conditions met, the researcher would have access only to printed media reports. There are, then, methodological (comparative and longitudinal) and pragmatic reasons for using the FBIS *Daily Reports*.

The four structural dimensions of crisis coverage were coded as follows.

Duration, which is the length of time over which a crisis was mentioned, is measured in weeks. In two of the cases, the crisis per se lasted only for brief periods. The Arab-Israeli War broke out on 6 October 1973, and fighting lasted until 25 October. The sample of media coverage was taken from 1 October 1973 through 1 November 1973 (five weeks). Fighting between China and Vietnam, although skirmishes took place over a lengthy period in previous years, began in earnest on 17 February 1979 (the day Chinese forces crossed the border in strength). Fighting continued for approximately five weeks, until the Chinese withdrew. The sample of media coverage for this crisis covers eight weeks, from 30 January 1979 through 31 March 1979. The Soviet Union began to send its combat units into Afghanistan on 27 December 1979. Although Soviet troops were only withdrawn from Afghanistan in 1989, the dependent variable was coded for the last week of 1979 and all of 1980, that is, for fifty-three weeks of coverage. The domestic problems in Poland were evident as early as the spring of 1980, and were not on the way to being resolved completely until 1989. For this case, the four dependent variables have been coded from 1 August 1980 through 31 December 1981 (martial law was declared in December 1981), that is, for seventy-five weeks of coverage. The four crises for all countries equal 987 weeks of coverage (114 weeks for each of the seven countries whose media were examined).

Extent, the number of times a crisis was reported in a country's media per week of coverage, was determined by adding the number of radio, newspaper, and news agency reports for each day of the week.

Intensity was calculated by dividing the number of times a crisis received front-page or lead-story radio coverage by the number of reports for a given week and by multiplying the result by the number or words devoted to that crisis per week, ranked on a 1–5 scale, where the content of the scale changed for each crisis. (Table 1 shows the content of the scale for each crisis.) Five categories were used because it was important to exhibit the variance in intensity across crises and countries while creating a small number of categories that could be assigned ordinal values (such as high, moderately high, low, etc.). Later, when discussing "aggregated crisis coverage" (that is, all countries' coverage combined), intensity was measured using the content of the 1–5 scale for the Polish crisis, which subsumes that for all crises.

Salience is another way of gauging how important a particular crisis was to the political leadership. Here the data were coded in terms of the number of times, for each week of coverage a party leader (Politburo or equivalent) was quoted or signed an editorial comment about the crisis *or* gave a speech concerning the crisis that was broadcast or reprinted. The importance of such a measure is exemplified by a hypothetical case in which one Eastern European country would report on a crisis only twice, but in both instances the party leaders would be quoted, whereas, in another country the crisis would be often covered, but the leadership would make no remarks or commentaries by the leadership. Salience, measured in this manner, is anticipated to be an important determinant of other dimensions of crisis reporting because of the centralized control that was evident in Leninist party systems.

Ordinarily, examining media coverage involves measuring printed media in terms of column inches and broadcast media in minutes. Since the FBIS *Daily Reports* do not permit this type of measurement, counting the number of words devoted to both print and broadcast media was used as an alternative measure. By counting the number of words per report per week of coverage, an indication of the importance of a crisis is provided.

The independent variable, journalists' integration into party structures, is derived from information on the party membership and the organizational affiliation of journalists contained in the CIA's *Directories of Officials* for the Soviet Union and Eastern European countries. These publications list all of the national and regional officials for each country: the Communist party Central Committee membership and candidate membership, positions held in each organization or government position, and dates of

Table 1. Scale for Intensity of Crisis Coverage

Rank	Number of Words			
	1973 Mid East	1979 S.E. Asia	1979–1980 Afghanistan	1980–1981 Poland
1	0–2,201	0–5,146	0–6,229	0–13,457
2	2,201–4,0400	5,147–10,292	6,230–12,458	13,476–26,950
3	4,401–6,600	10,293–15,438	12,459–18,687	26,950–40,425
4	6,601–8,800	15,439–20,584	18,688–24,915	40,426–53,900
5	8,801–11,000	20,585–25,734	24,916–31,146	53,901–67,378

elections or appointments. Using this information, a scale was created based upon the total number of membership affiliations, government positions, and party membership for journalists who contributed stories for communist news reports for each week of coverage. The total number of affiliations and memberships is then divided by the total number of journalists, for a mean integration score by country. This is, of course, but a crude measure of journalistic integration into party structures, due to unavailable or incomplete biographical data. Nevertheless, the measure offers an estimate of the extent to which media personnel were responsive to the wishes of political leaders.

In the following discussion, the data for the four cases are examined in two ways. First, Warsaw Pact member states' media coverage of crisis is described. Second cross-crises and cross-national explanations of differential media emphases are offered. The descriptive part of the analysis employs a means and standard deviations, while the explanatory analysis utilizes simple bivariate regression analysis.

Cross-National Description of Crisis Coverage

As mentioned earlier, a major premise of this work is that crisis coverage varied across communist systems. But how is such variation evident?

Tables 2 through 5 display each country's aggregate crisis coverage; that is, each country's per-week average for *each* dimension of coverage for *all* crises. Also included in these tables are mean levels for dimensions of coverage for each country's coverage of two of the four crises. During the October War in 1973, cross-national comparisons of Soviet block states' coverage reveal few differences that are important enough to mention. The Eastern European states only published reports during the week of intense fighting between the Arab states and Israel. Consequently, intensity and salience of coverage have scores of 0, while there are no standard deviations for extent and duration of coverage. The Soviet Union appears to have been dominant in providing coverage of the 1973 October War.

When the Chinese attacked Vietnam in February 1979, Eastern European states generally were more active in their media coverage of this crisis. Although fighting lasted longer in this crisis than during the Middle East conflict, coverage was not significantly different. In neither case did

Table 2. National Means and Standard Deviations
for Duration of Crisis Coverage

	All Crises	1979–1980 Afghanistan	1980–1981 Poland
Bulgaria	.411 (.439)	.300 (.463)	.480 (.503)
Czechoslovakia	.730 (.455)	.528 (.504)	.920 (.273)
G.D.R	.397 (.491)	.339 (.478)	.453 (.501)
Hungary	.496 (.501)	.264 (.445)	.653 (.479)
Poland	.645 (.480)	.188 (.395)	1.0 (0.0)
Romania	.134 (.342)	.056 (.233)	.133 (.342)
U.S.S.R.	.950 (.218)	1.0 (.040)	.920 (.273)
	N = 141	N = 53	N = 75

Notes: Entries are mean duration scores for each country. Numbers in parentheses represent standard deviations.
Duration is the percent of the total crisis timespan during which a country's media provided reports or commentaries about the crisis, ranging from 0–100 percent.

Table 3. National Means and Standard Deviations
for Intensity of Crisis Coverage

	All Crises	1979–1980 Afghanistan	1980–1981 Poland
Bulgaria	.015 (.0633)	.013 (.050)	.020 (.073)
Czechoslovakia	.050 (.141)	.110 (.186)	.020 (.055)
G.D.R	.040 (.267)	—	.060 (.343)
Hungary	.016 (.119)	.071 (.267)	—
Poland	.064 (.072)	.011 (.035)	.077 (.073)
Romania	—	—	—
U.S.S.R.	.070 (.054)[a]	.020 (.054)	.022 (1.0)

Notes: Entries are mean levels for each country. Numbers in parentheses represent standard deviations.
Intensity is the proportion of front-page and lead-story radio coverage, ranging from 0–100 percent for each week of coverage examined.
[a]This entry is high because of intense coverage of the other two crises.

Eastern European media provide noticeable front-page or lead-story coverage. The mean scores for intensity were found to be 0 in all cases, while the salience scores (the quotation of party leaders) were less than 1.

The aggregate crisis coverage for each country as well as national coverage of the 1979–1980 crisis in Afghanistan and the 1980–1981 Polish conflict reveal dissimilarities in Eastern European and Soviet media reports. It was predicted that the duration, intensity, salience, and extent would be greater for the country experiencing a crisis. Tables 2 through 5 support this expectation.

Polish media, as might be expected, covered the crisis of 1980–1981 fully. The Polish media provided reports 100 percent of the time for which

Table 4. National Means and Standard Deviations
for Salience of Crisis Coverage

	All Crises	1979–1980 Afghanistan	1980–1981 Poland
Bulgaria	.138 (.347)	.126 (.341)	.053 (.226)
Czechoslovakia	.166 (.378)	.250 (.585)	.058 (.235)
G.D.R	.412 (1.53)	.500 (1.20)	.294 (1.52)
Hungary	.060 (.289)	—	.041 (.199)
Poland	4.74 (4.42)	.100 (.316)	5.71 (4.28)
Romania	.211 (.713)	.333 (.577)	—
U.S.S.R.	.716 (1.46)	1.07 (1.56)	.217 (.565)

Notes: Entries are mean levels for each country. Numbers in parentheses represent standard deviations.

Salience is the frequency with which political leaders are quoted each week of crises coverage, ranging from 0–75.

Table 5. National Means and Standard Deviations
for Extent of Crisis Coverage

	All Crises	1979–1980 Afghanistan	1980–1981 Poland
Bulgaria	2.90 (3.17)	3.19 (4.43)	2.83 (1.70)
Czechoslovakia	8.32 (8.33)	3.50 (4.16)	10.78 (8.85)
G.D.R	3.23 (3.54)	3.72 (5.83)	2.85 (1.52)
Hungary	2.60 (2.92)	2.92 (2.12)	3.33 (1.62)
Poland	41.7 (47.58)	2.60 (2.62)	77.80 (38.0)
Romania	1.80 (2.07)	1.33 (.574)	2.30 (2.70)
U.S.S.R.	17.40 (17.7)	22.00 (15.7)	10.60 (9.18)

Notes: Entries are mean levels for each country. Numbers in parentheses represent standard deviations.

Extent is the average number of crisis stories published or broadcast per week of coverage, ranging from 1–120.

coverage was examined (see Table 2, row 1, column 3). No other country devoted such attention to the Polish crisis, although the Soviet Union and Czechoslovakia were close, with 92 percent. The average weekly intensity score for Polish media reports was found to be approximately .08 (see Table 3). This means that, on average, 8 percent of all weekly reports received front-page or lead-story coverage. Again, no other country gave such a degree of prominence to reports of this crisis, although the East Germans were close, at 6 percent. The average weekly salience score for Polish coverage of the Polish crisis was found to be 5.71 (see Table 4). Substantively, this means that, on average, Polish media quoted political leaders 57 times per week. The greatest frequency in any other country for quoting political leaders in the Polish crisis was only 2.9 times per week, in Germany. Here, no other country approached the Polish frequency of citing party leaders. There was also an average of approximately 78 stories per week in Poland's media coverage of the Polish crisis (see Table 5). Again, no other country revealed this extent of coverage.

The Polish media did not cover other crises as thoroughly. As Tables 2 through 5 reveal, the Polish media's average weekly levels for each dimension of coverage for all crises is lower than those for coverage of the Polish crisis. Poland's average duration of coverage for all crises is .645, which translates into coverage for 65 percent of the period examined, but that includes the 1979–1980 Afghan crisis, where Polish media covered the event only 19 percent in the time examined (see table 2). Table 3 indicates that 6.4 percent of all crisis reports were placed at the forefront of coverage in the Polish media. But for the Afghan crisis, only 1 percent of reports received such prominent coverage. On average, Polish weekly reports for all crises included forty-seven statements or commentaries attributable to top officials. By contrast only 1 commentary per week by leading party officials was recorded during the Afghan crisis. The Polish media, on average, published forty-two crisis stories per week of coverage (see Table 5). The corresponding Polish media on the Afghan crisis are substantially lower, at 2.6. The same general trend is obvious in the Soviet Union. Its coverage of the Afghan crisis generally is greater than that of other countries. Table 2 (Duration), 4 (Salience), and 5 (Extent) point to higher levels of Soviet coverage. However, the intensity of Soviet coverage of the Afghan crisis was not high (Table 3). These findings, then, support the prediction that the duration, intensity, extent, and salience of domestic crisis crisis coverage would be greater than for coverage of systemic crises.

The third hypothesis predicted that a state's prior experience with domestic crisis would affect coverage of crises generally. Two Eastern European states—Hungary in 1956 and Czechoslovakia in 1968—experienced crises similar to that of Poland. Indeed, as can be seen in Tables 2 through 5, in both Hungary and Czechoslovakia coverage of the Polish crisis exhibited greater duration and extent than did coverage in other Eastern European countries. Their reporting about Poland in 1980–1981, however, did not exceed the duration or extent of Soviet coverage. Czechoslovak media reported on the Polish crisis 92 percent of the time, while Hungarian media published reports 65 percent of the available time (see Table 2). Intensity and salience of Hungarian coverage of the Polish crisis, however, are lower than that for all other states, save Romania, which has intensity and salience of coverage scores of 0 and .333 respectively (see Tables 3 and 4). Czechoslovak media had an average weekly intensity-of-coverage level of .050 and an average weekly salience-of-coverage score of .116. These fall in the moderate-to-low range of the countries studied. Its intensity-of-coverage level for the Polish crisis is higher than that of Bulgaria, Hungary, and Romania, but lower than that of East Germany. The salience of Czechoslovakia's coverage exceeds that of Hungary and Romania, but is equal to that of Bulgaria. Thus, the findings provide partial support for the hypothesis. That is, duration and extent of media reports are expected, while intensity and salience run counter to the hypothesized relationship. Additionally, the Soviet Union belies expectation.

Taken together these findings suggest that editors and political leaders might have considered a crisis to be newsworthy but did not see the need to place coverage at the forefront of printed or broadcast media; nor did they feel compelled to comment frequently on the crisis. The duration of the Polish crisis (well over a year) perhaps contributed to the lower levels of intensity and salience exhibited by Czechoslovak and Hungarian media coverage. Stated differently, Eastern European nations continued to publish reports but became less concerned about the Polish crisis after a period of time; consequently, the physical placement of reports changed as did the frequency of leadership comments.

Data in Tables 2 through 5 suggest that Eastern European and Soviet media placed differential emphases on crises. Romanian coverage was consistently lower on all dimensions of crisis coverage, save salience during the Afghan crisis. In this instance, Romania is higher than all countries, except East Germany and the Soviet Union. The consistently low score for Romania might be an indication that it did not take cues from other communist countries or that the media were preoccupied by other events.

The discussion, thus far, has not focused on Soviet media coverage. Since Eastern European party elites and journalists were likely to use Soviet media coverage as a reference point against which Eastern European media coverage was evaluated, one intuitively would expect greater levels of duration, intensity, salience, and extent. Soviet aggregate crisis coverage *was* generally greater than that of the Eastern European states on the dimensions of duration and intensity (column 1, Tables 4 and 5). The distributions indicate that the Soviet media's intensity score was lower than that of Czechoslovakia and Hungary for coverage of the Afghan crisis (column 2, Table 3). Distributions for duration, salience, and extent, however, reveal that Soviet coverage was greater than that of all nations except Poland (Tables 2, 4, and 5). The Polish crisis simply absorbed the attention of the Polish press in a way that no other crisis affected a national media establishment. In general, however, the data conform to expectation that the Soviet media would devote much attention to crisis coverage.

There are two possible explanations for the lower intensity of Soviet reports. First, front-page coverage and lead-story radio times usually were reserved for reports on domestic events in the Soviet Union or commentaries by government officials. Second, front-page coverage is not necessarily an appropriate indicator of the importance that was attached to an event. In the Soviet Union, international or nondomestic news was routinely placed on or about page five of newspapers. An exception to this would be made if a key political official addressed or made passing reference to a particular international event.

Indeed, it can be concluded that Soviet and Eastern European media differed in the manner in which crises were reported. Such variation can partially be associated with prior experiences with domestic crises, with the nature of the conflict, and with the nation's media undertaking the coverage. The data indicate that Soviet coverage exhibited the highest or second highest distribution across all crises dimensions, principally because of Soviet interests in maintaining dominance in the region.

Focusing on Eastern European coverage provides a better picture of who covered what. Rank ordering the Eastern European states on each dimension (from highest to lowest level exhibited) suggests that Bulgaria and Romania were most consistent. That is, their media coverage remained approximately the same across crises, and they were lower on most dimensions of coverage. Czechoslovakia ranked second or third on all dimensions across crises (Tables 2–5). With the exception of salience of coverage (Table 4), Hungary consistently ranked fourth. East Germany tends to be in the middle: it ranks sixth on duration (Table 2), fifth on extent (Table 5), and third on intensity and salience (Tables 3 and 4).

Differential media emphases require explanation. More specifically, the analysis will seek to explain why some crises appeared more important than did others; why political leaders of some nations spoke out more frequently than did others; and why some nations' media provided more coverage than those of others.

Differential Media Emphasis: Cross-Crises Analysis

To what degree did the leading role of a ruling Communist party help to account for different behavior of media in Eastern Europe and the U.S.S.R.? If the Soviet Communist party's leading role in international communism influenced Soviet media's coverage of crisis, that influence was probably exerted through journalists who belonged to the party. In Eastern European countries, as well, party influence on media coverage could be expected to be channeled through journalists enrolled in the ruling Communist party. Here I explore that plausible explanation by examining the link between journalists' party roles and several dimensions of crisis coverage.

Journalists' integration into party structures is expected to be related positively to each dimension of crisis coverage. In other words, as the careers of journalists and political elites became more congruent, the characteristics of coverage would change. The extent and salience of crisis coverage would increase as integration between media personnel and party elites increased. The effect of journalists' party involvement on the duration and intensity of coverage, although expected to be positive, would not necessarily be as strong as its effects on extent and salience. That is, journalists' membership in party bodies and direct exposure to party officials may contribute slightly to prolonged and more front-page or lead-story coverage of crisis events. Journalists' integration into party structures might have a much greater effect on salience and extent of crisis coverage.

Duration of coverage obviously will depend more on the timespan of the crisis than on the similarity between the membership affiliations of prominent media personnel and political elites. Intensity of coverage, as discussed earlier, seems to have been more fully related to internal events than to international or systemic occurrences. Additionally, *where* leaders' remarks were placed in news coverage was probably not as crucial as the fact that they appeared in print. Simply put, political leaders were possibly more concerned with the media's acknowledgment of their statements than with front-page coverage.

Bivariate regression was employed to gauge the association between the extent of journalists' integration with the party and the four dimensions of crisis coverage. Before preceding with the data analysis, however, several methodological issues need clarification. First (following Achen, 1982:76), I have elected to use unstandardized coefficients because betas (standardized coefficients) are justified only if the variables have no natural scale and the researcher wishes to score them in a consistent fashion. Use of unstandardized coefficients will perserve comparability across samples and across time.

Second, regression coefficients reported here have been multiplied by 10. When employing regression analysis, one usually speaks of units of change in a dependent variable attributed to *one* unit of change in the independent variable. For this study, however, I speak of changes in the dependent variable associated with a ten-unit change in the independent variable. The decision to multiply coefficients by 10 was predicated on the expectation that the regression coefficients would be small. Use of the constant would provide a clearer picture of how changes in journalists' integration into party structures affected the duration, extent, intensity, and salience of crisis coverage without severely distorting the relationship being examined.

Effects of Predictor on Duration of Coverage

Table 6, row 1 reveals that journalistic integration into party structures has a statistically significant effect on duration of coverage for all crises together (column 1), for the 1979–1980 Afghan conflict (column 4), and for the 1980–1981 Polish crisis (column 5). The unstandardized coefficient for duration of all crises coverage is .21 (column 1), with a standard error of .019. This means that, on average, a 10 percent change in the level of journalistic integration into party structures increased crisis coverage time by a little more than 2 percent. The amount of time devoted to reporting crises partially reflects journalists' membership in the Communist party and other party-sponsored organizations. Duration of coverage may have been determined more by journalists' direct contact with government officials than by criteria determined by media institutions themselves.

Journalists' membership in party structures affected the duration of coverage for *some* crises in ways that differed from the general pattern of crisis coverage, however. As can be seen in Table 6 (row 1, columns 4 and 5), the rate of change in duration of coverage attributable to variation in journalists' party involvement does vary across crises and is different from the pattern when all crises are aggregated. More specifically, it was found that, on average, a 10 percent increase in journalists' membership affiliations increased coverage time by 4.4 percent (that is, .44 × 10) in the

Table 6. Regression of Journalistic Integration on
Dimensions of Crisis Coverage (All Countries, All Crises)

Dependent Variable	All Crises N = 531	1973 Mid. East N = 10	1979 S.E. Asia N = 37	1979–1980 Afghanistan N = 142	1980–1981 Poland N = 342
Duration	.21 (.019)[a]	—[b]	.29 (.19)	.44 (.09)[a]	.14 (.019)[a]
	[.35]	—[b]	[.21]	[.25]	[.31]
R^2	.16		.18	.25	.31
Extent	10.7 (1.21)[a]	9.4 (2.7)[a]	9.6 (3.4)[a]	6.9 (1.6)[a]	7.8 (1.5)[a]
	[.35]	[.98]	[.30]	[.56]	[.35]
R^2	.21	.94	.60	.32	.22
Intensity	− .010 (.01)	0.0 (0.0)	− .01 (.06)	.006 (.02)	− .009 (.162)
	[− .02]	[0.0]	[− .03]	[.08]	[− .05]
R^2	.01	.00	.00	.01	.03
Salience	.06 (.03)[a]	9.4 (2.7)[a]	.51 (.28)[a]	.41 (.18)[a]	.40 (.13)[a]
	[.30]	[.75]	[.65]	[.42]	[.78]
R^2	.11	.22	.26	.06	.11

Notes: Entries are unstandardized regression coefficients with standard errors in parentheses; standardized (beta) coefficients are in brackets below.
Journalistic Integration (into party structures) is the journalists' memberships in the Communist party and other party-sponsored organizations during the years in which the crises occurred. The journalistic integration score was derived by adding the total number of memberships held by prominent journalists—those to whom reports and commentaries were attributed—and then dividing that total by the number of journalists. The score can range from 1–100 percent.
[a]Significant at $P \leq .05$.
[b]Blanks = not enough information to calculate coefficients.

case of Afghanistan (column 4), and 1.4 percent (that is, .14 × 10) in the case of Poland (column 5). This is a 3 percent difference between the rate of "conversion" of affiliation into coverage for the Polish and Afghan crises. The difference between the rate of conversion for all crises and that for the Afghan and Polish crises are 2.3 and (+).07, respectively. One might argue, then, that the effect of journalistic integration into party structures did not change substantially from crisis to crisis.

Effects of Predictor on Extent of Crisis Coverage

The data displayed in Table 6 also show that journalists' involvement in party structures has a statistically significant effect on the extent of crisis coverage. As can be seen in row 2, on average a 10 percent increase in journalists' membership affiliations increased the per-week number of crisis reports by 107 for all crises combined, by 94 for the Middle East case, by 96 for the Sino-Vietnamese case, by 69 in the Afghan case, and by 78 for the Polish case. That the effects of journalistic integration into party structures on the frequency of coverage of all crises combined (increase of 107) was greater that that for any of the crises singly is possibly a function of the increase in timespan that resulted from aggregation of the data, which suggests that the timespan of a crisis might have been as important as journalists' party membership for crisis coverage.

The rate of change in extent of coverage that can be associated with change in journalistic integration into party structures is approximately equal in the Middle East and Southeast Asian cases. The rate of change in the extent of coverage in both cases approximates that for all cases. The effect of journalistic integration into party structures on the extent of coverage of the Afghanistan and Polish cases appears to have been similar but slightly lower.

Effects of Predictor on Salience of Crisis Coverage

The frequency with which key political leaders (Politburo or equivalent) were quoted or signed commentaries alluding to crises was expected to increase as the number of party affiliations held by journalists rose. The coefficients for the effect of journalistic integration into party structures not only provide support for this hypothesis, but also reveal other information. The data suggest (Table 6, row 4) that the rate of change in salience associated with change in the number of membership affiliations held by journalists is roughly equal and significant for three of the four cases studied, while the effect is dramatically higher in the fourth case. In fact, on average, a 10 percent increase in journalists' party involvement accounts for increases of 6.0 (all cases), 5.1 (Sino-Vietnamese case), 4.1 (Afghanistan case), 4.0 (Polish case), and 94 (Middle East case) in the number of times per week that political leaders were quoted in media reports or signed commentaries focusing on crises. These findings suggest that journalists' integration has a relatively weak influence on cross-national variations in salience in each crisis, save that of the Middle East. The Middle East case is, however, based on analysis of only ten observations. Thus, it should be noted that the coefficient for all crises combined must be viewed cautiously due to the effect of Middle East crisis. (See the cross-crises estimates, Table 6, row 4, column 1.)

That the rate of change for salience of coverage during the 1973 Middle East war deviates from that for other crises could be related to the international nature of the crisis. Soviet and Eastern European political leaders and media personnel might have been attracted to external conflicts that did not involve communist states. External crises that did not have immediate significance for maintaining existing communist states would have provided ruling Communist parties and media elites opportunities to illustrate how capitalism and states outside the socialist commonwealth created hostilities because of the competing interests (see Wettig, 1977; LeDuc, 1981:140; Katz, 1978:129).

Salience of coverage for the Middle East crisis may have been affected by the general political climate within Warsaw Pact members at that time. It might be that during the 1973 October War communist media relied more heavily on statements and messages provided by political leaders than during 1979–1981. In other words, Communist party directives concerning the dissemination of information about external events may have become less restrictive during 1979–1981, and the media may have been granted greater access to information regarding external events (see, for example, LeDuc, 1981:40).

Preliminary Conclusion

Not surprisingly, the presence of leading journalists in party organs (or, if one prefers, the penetration of the party into the stratum of media elites) has a substantial effect on all of the dependent variables, except for intensity of crisis coverage. If the media were to act as agents of socialization, it was crucial that media personnel be "in tune" with government officials. As a means of ensuring harmony of perceptions and values, journalists were accorded membership in state and party organizations (the party's Central Committee, the Academy of Social Sciences, and the State Propaganda Agency). These are primarily names associated with Soviet institutions. However, all seven countries have the Academy of Social Sciences, and there are agencies corresponding to the other two Soviet institutions. Membership in such organizations would increase the social and political status of journalists, making conformity with other elites more likely. This in turn had consequences for the manner in which news was reported, and is evident in the relatively strong relationship between journalists' political integration and the duration (B = .21), extent (B = 10.7), and salience (B = .60) of coverage (see Table 6).

Differential Media Emphases: Cross-National Analysis

Media behavior varied not only across crises but also across countries within the WTO. I now turn briefly to examining differences in the relationship between the independent variable and the four dimensions of crisis coverage in each country.

Disaggregating the data, to look at specific countries, of course, often resulted in coefficients that were essentially meaningless because the number of cases was too small. Nevertheless, Table 7 includes data concerning each country's media coverage of all crises. The data presented in this table point to the impact of the integration of party-media elites on dimensions of crisis coverage across seven countries. (In Table 7, once again, a constant [10] was used to make regression coefficients clearer.)

Effects of Predictor on Duration of Coverage

The party roles and positions of journalists were found to have statistical significance for each country's duration of crisis coverage. In Table 7 one can see that, on average, a 10 percent increase in the number of

Table 7. Regression of Journalistic Integration on
Dimensions of Crisis Coverage (Each County, All Crises)

Dependent Variable	BULG N = 58	CZECH N = 103	GDR N = 56	HUNG N = 70	POL N = 91	ROM N = 19	USSR N = 134
Duration	.10 (.05)** [.15]	.096 (.027)** [.27]	.54 (.25)** [.17]	.20 (.06)** [.27]	.225 (.042)** [.44]	.87 (.21)** [.30]	.085 (.029)** [.24]
R^2	.019	.13	.04	.09	.45	.26	.07
Intensity	-.010 (.007)** [-.18]	-.011 (.009) [-.06]	-.04 (.14) [-.03]	-.004 (.0016) [-.03]	.23 (.009)** [.29]	0.0 (0.0) [0]	-.094 (.004) [-.07]
R^2	.010	.06	-.05	-.08	.09	0.0	.012
Salience	.092 (.038)** [.31]	-.010 (.020) [-.03]	1.6 (.79)** [.25]	.071 (.034)** [.23]	1.0 (.49)** [.01]	-.122 (.571) [-.01]	.562 (.191)** [.23]
R^2	.05	.001	.04	.02	.30	.09	.22
Extent	.63 (.35)	1.6 (.564)	7.6 (1.5)**	.27 (.29)	18.4 (4.5)**	5.0 (1.2)**	10.0 (2.0)**
R^2	.03	-.07	.36	-.02	.46	.51	.50

Notes: Entries are unstandardized regression coefficients with standard errors in parentheses; Standardized (Betas) coefficients are in brackets below.

*Journalistic integration (into Party Structures) = the journalists' membership in the Communist Party and other Party sponsored organizations during the years in which the crises occurred. The journalistic integration score was derived by adding the total number of memberships held by prominent journalists (journalists to whom reports and commentaries were attributed) then dividing that total by the number of journalists. The score can range from 1–100 percent.

**Significant at $P < = 0.05$.

journalists' national, regional, and local party affiliations increased crisis coverage time by approximately 1 percent for the Bulgarian, Czechoslovak, and Soviet cases. Hungarian and Polish crisis coverage time increased 2 and 2.3 percent, respectively, while those for East Germany and Romania increased by 5.4 and 9 percent respectively (see row 1).

The results seem to confirm that, in each of the seven countries, the extent to which journalists interacted with government or party elites had importance for the proportion of available time that crisis events were covered by the media (Table 7, row 1, every column). More important, there are cross-national differences in the relationship between the two variables. Interestingly, the effect of the explanatory variable on duration of coverage is modest and roughly equal for Bulgaria (B = .10), Czechoslovakia (B = .10), and the Soviet Union (B = .09), while it is substantially higher in the remaining cases (G.D.R.: B = .54; Hungary: B = .20; Poland: B = .225; Romania: B = .87). Perhaps the structures of control were most effective or most needed in the latter cases. The results will be compared with subsequent findings before making such an inference.

Effect of Predictor on Intensity of Coverage

Focusing on intensity of coverage—that is, on front-page and lead-story radio time—one finds that the independent variable is not a very useful predictor. Table 7 (row 2, all columns) indicates that the presence of media personnel in party organs is not statistically significant in most cases. In fact, it is only significant in the case of Poland, in which a 10 percent increase in the membership affiliations of journalists, on average, increased the weekly proportion of front-page and lead-story radio crisis coverage by a little over 2 percent (see column 5).

Effect of Predictor on Salience of Crisis Coverage

Focusing on the frequency with which key political leaders were quoted in reports or signed commentaries, the impact of journalistic integration was found to be statistically significant for five of the seven cases. A 10 percent increase in the number of party affiliations held by journalists (Table 7, row 3) changed the per-week number of times key political leaders were quoted or signed commentaries on crisis events by approximately 1 in the case of Bulgaria, 16 for East Germany, 10 for Poland, approximately 1 for Hungary, and 6 for the Soviet Union. Thus, it seems that journalistic integration into party structures had the greatest effect on salience-of-crisis coverage for the East German case, followed by Polish and the Soviet cases.

Thus, differences in the extent to which media personnel held membership in party organizations can help predict, albeit sometimes in small ways, intra–Warsaw Pact variation in leaders' prominence during crisis reporting. Salience of crisis coverage appears to have been affected by such an independent variable.

Effect of Predictor on Extent of Crisis Coverage

Finally, Table 7 (row 4) shows a statistically significant effect of ties between media personnel and party elites on the extent of crisis coverage for six of the seven countries. The greatest effect is found in Poland, while the smallest effects are for Bulgaria and Hungary. On average, it seems that as journalists' membership affiliations increased by 10 percent, the number of crisis reports per week increased by 16 (Czechoslovakia), 76 (East Germany), 2.7 (Hungary), 184 (Poland), 50 (Romania), and 100 (Soviet Union). Dramatic cross-national variation is thus evident in the degree to which journalistic integration into party structures affected the extent of crisis coverage.

These findings indicate that cross-national differences in the number of times crisis reports were presented by the media were, to a certain degree, due to differences in the contact between media personnel and party officials. Increased association (and identification) with political elites would provide media personnel with additional (informal) information and would more fully expose them to elite pressures concerning crisis events. This additional information would serve as the basis for additional crisis reports—to inform the public of what political elites sought to convey.

Overall, these data support the expectation that differences in the crisis coverage by Warsaw Pact members' media can be explained, in part, by *national* differences in the extent to which media personnel were members of the Communist party and adjunct party-sponsored organizations.

Conclusion

The results presented in this paper suggest that Warsaw Pact members differed in the amount of emphasis placed on media coverage of crisis events. They did not speak with one voice in that regard. The differences, however, seem to be related to prior experiences with crises or direct involvement in a conflictual situation. That duration, extent, intensity, and salience of crisis coverage were likely to be greater in the country experiencing the crisis than in other countries is supported fully by this analysis. Poland's media reports on the Polish crisis were found to rank first on each dimension of crisis coverage. This finding lends support to research that posits that the socializing role of the media would be greater when there is a domestic crisis than at other times. The findings also indirectly substantiate the argument that communist leaders' desires to affect citizens' behavior during domestic crises would generate more media coverage (see Curry, 1982; Kaplan, 1977).

It was expected that duration, extent, intensity, and salience of domestic-crisis coverage would be greater in countries having had similar experiences with domestic unrest than in countries that had not undergone such experiences. The prediction was not supported strongly by the statistical findings. Focusing on the 1980–1981 Polish crisis, one finds that Hungary and Czechoslovakia—the two Eastern European countries having had experiences with domestic crises and Soviet intervention—had duration-of-coverage and extent-of-coverage levels greater than those of other Eastern European states but lower than those for the Soviet Union. This is not surprising insofar as the Soviet leadership would have perceived domestic unrest in any Eastern European state as endangering regional security. Such a perception would result in Soviet media coverage that would approximate that of the Polish media during Poland's 1980–1981 crisis. This part of the statistical analysis lends support for previous research that suggests that domestic turmoil in the "socialist commonwealth" would be more heavily reported by communist states that once went through similar experiences (see Hutchings, 1983).

Intensity and salience of media reports on the Polish crisis were not, however, as expected. In fact, the intensity and salience of Hungarian and Czechoslovak crisis reports were found to be less than that for some other Eastern European states. Obviously, this finding would also lead one to assume that the type of crisis would have had little significance for the intensity and salience of Eastern European and Soviet media coverage of such events. Only the *volume* of coverage was affected (that is, the duration and extent) by prior experience, not (apparently) the degree of front-page or lead-story radio emphasis or the frequency of quotes by leaders.

Most generally, this study indicates that party-media links effected through journalists' involvement in party structures are a relatively good predictor of all dimensions of crisis coverage, with the exception of intensity. It was found to exert the greatest amount of influence on the extent and salience of coverage. The relationship between journalistic integration into party organs and each dimension of coverage is as predicted.

Within the Warsaw Pact, we thus find that crises produced different responses in media institutions. It is clear, however, that in all WTO states the party-media linkage was strong and was used to affect coverage of threatening, uncertain situations. But it was not uniform, and changes in such intra-elite integration were found to affect media output. From our standpoint, we now know more precisely the degree to which journalists' party involvement changed media performance, and we can thus better predict the pattern of WTO members' communications efforts in the context of various crises. The Warsaw Pact did not communicate in unison, and we can now see more clearly one of the reasons why it did not—a variable rooted in differences among communist states' domestic political environments far more than in control from Moscow.

The data also offer some insights into differences in the rapidity with which Eastern European political leaders adopted Gorbachev's policy initiatives regarding more openness in all forms of communications. In fact, it appears that one can draw parallels between such differences and specific aspects of WTO member states' crisis coverage. For example, the findings reveal that three of the four Eastern European states (Romania, Bulgaria, and East Germany) that were slowest in adopting Soviet initiatives also had the lowest levels of duration and extent of aggregated crisis coverage. Additionally, results illuminating the impact of journalistic integration into party structures on duration of crisis coverage suggest that

an in-depth examination of the manner in which various communist regimes attempted to exercise control over media as well as other institutions, and the degree to which such endeavors were effective, will provide
clues about the sequential order in which such regimes adopted the Soviet
initiative.

Finally, the results of this research suggest that future research focusing
on political transition in Eastern Europe should seek to discern the relationship between the rapidity and extent to which journalists and other
media personnel seized opportunities, resulting from glasnost, to provide
scathing indictments revolving around failures of the communist system,
and the onset and persistence of massive protests and demonstrations
during 1987–1989 (that is, the role of the media in promoting the collapse
of communist regimes in the Soviet bloc). In short, research attempting to
provide explanations of recent changes in Eastern European countries
must, to some extent, reexamine past actions and behaviors.

Notes

1. For a thorough discussion of Eastern European leaders' willingness to allow
   more open and candid discussion not only by media representatives but throughout society, see Vagvolgyi, 1989; and New York Times, 13 April 1988, p. 6.
2. Several scholars have made this argument; see, for example, Buzek, 1964;
   Hollander, 1972; Dzirkles, 1982; Barghoon and Remington, 1986.
3. While researchers have not explicitly referred to journalists as agents of the
   state and party, their arguments suggest that the recruitment process and the
   achievement of upward mobility within the communist system require that
   journalists at least appear to look after party interests.
4. For a discussion of the possible impact of crises on WTO cohesion, see Simon,
   1983:6–7.
5. Numerous scholars have examined factors affecting news flow. Although such
   studies do not have communist systems as their primary focus, they do have
   implications for the study of mass media in communist systems. Included
   among this genre of research are Ostgaard, 1965; Nnaemka and Richstad, 1981;
   Gerbner, 1964; Galtung and Ruge, 1965.
6. Curry (1982:106–22) provides an extensive discussion of the various forms of
   censorship that have been used throughout Eastern Europe since 1954.

References

Achen, C. H. 1982. *Interpreting and Using Regression*. Beverly Hills: Sage Publica-
    tions.
Barghoon, F. C., and Thomas Remington. 1986. *Politics in the Soviet Union*. Boston:
    Little Brown and Co.
Buzek, A. 1964. *How the Communist Press Works*. New York: Praeger.
Central Intelligence Agency. 1973, 1979, 1980, 1983. *Directory of Officials: Soviet
    Union and Eastern Europe*. Washington, DC: Government Printing Office.
Curry, J. L. 1982. "Media Control in Eastern Europe: Holding the Tide on Op-
    position." In J. L. Curry and J. R. Dassin, eds., *Press Control around the World*.
    New York: Praeger.

Dzirkles, L. 1982. "Media Direction and Control in the USSR." Pp. 85–102 in J. L. Curry and J. R. Dassin, eds., *Press Control around the World*. New York: Praeger.

Foreign Broadcast Information Service (FBIS). 1973, 1979–1981. *Daily Reports*. Washington, DC: Government Printing Office.

Galtung, J., and M. Ruge. 1965. "The Structure of Foreign News: The Presentation of the Congo, Cuba, and Cyprus Crises in Four Norwegian Newspapers." *Journal of Peace Research*, 2:1.

Gerbner, G. A. 1964. "Ideological Perspective and Political Tendencies in News Reporting." *Journalism Quarterly*, 41:495–509.

Gerbner, G. A. and O. Marvanyi. 1984. "The Many Worlds of the World's Press." In G. Gerbner and M. Sieffert, eds., *World Communications: A Handbook*. New York: Longman.

Hermann, Charles, 1969. *Crises in Foreign Policy: A Simulation Analysis*. New York: The Bobbs Merrill Co., Inc.

Hollander, G. D. 1972. *Soviet Political Indoctrination: Development in Mass Media and Propaganda*. New York: Praeger.

Hutchings, R. L. 1983. *Soviet-East European Relations: Consolidation and Conflict 1968–1980*. Madison: University of Wisconsin Press.

Kaplan, F. L. 1977. *Winter Into Spring: The Czechoslovak Press and the Reform Movement 1963–1968*. Boulder: East Europe Quarterly.

Katz, P. P. 1978. "Detente and Pravda's View of the United States: A Quantitative Analysis." *Conflict*, 1:113–30.

LeDuc, D. R. 1981. "East-West News Flow: Imbalances." *Journal of Communications*. 33:135–41.

Nnaemka, Tony, and Jim Richstad. 1981. "Internal Controls and Foreign News Coverage." *Communications Research*, 8(1): 97–135.

Ostgaard, E. 1965. "Factors Influencing the Flow of News." *Journal of Peace Research*, 2(2): 37–68.

Pisarek, W. 1984. "Polish Actors in Socialist and Capitalist Press." In G. Gerbner and M. Sieffert, eds., *World Communications: A Handbook*. New York: Longman.

"Silence and Glee: Eastern Bloc Reacts to Poland." 1988. *New York Times*, 13 April, 6.

Simon, Jeffery. 1983. *Cohesion and Dissension in Eastern Europe: Six Crises*. New York: Praeger.

Vagvolgyi, Andras. 1989. "The Changes in The Media in Hungary." *East European Reporter*, 4(1): 34–36.

Wettig, G. 1977. *Broadcasting and Detente: Eastern Policies and Their Implication for East-West Relations*. New York: St. Martin's Press.

Presence of Immigrants and National Front Vote: The Case of Paris (1984–1990)

Nonna Mayer

Centre d'étude de la vie politique française

O ne of the main changes on the French electoral scene in recent years has been the rise of the National Front. Founded in 1972 by J. M. Le Pen, it amalgamates various components of the extreme Right. Since the Poujadist protest in the 1950s and the pro–"Algerie-Française" activism in the 1960s, the Right had lost most of its electoral support. In the parliamentary elections of 1981, it hardly drew 0.3 percent of the votes. In the previous presidential election, its leader couldn't even run as candidate.[1] The picture changed after the Left came to power. In 1983, in a number of by-elections, the National Front ran well, winning 16.7 percent of the valid votes in Dreux, 9.3 percent in Aulnay-sous-Bois, and 12.02 percent in Trinité-sur-Mer, the native town of its leader. The European elections of 1984 confirmed those local successes at the national level. Ever since, the National Front has been steadily attracting some 10 percent of the votes, and more than 14 percent of the electorate voted for J. M. Le Pen in the first round of the presidential election of 1988.

A Vote against the Immigrants?

Among the many explanations offered for this phenomenon, those most frequently put forward stress the problems aroused by the presence of a large population of immigrants. France today is home to approximately four million foreigners.[2] Since World War II, they have increased from 4 percent to 7 percent of the total population. The proportion was roughly the same in the 1930s, but the nationality of these immigrants has changed. In the 1950s, 80 percent were European, coming mainly from Italy, Poland, and Spain. Today Europeans account for less than half of the foreign

103

Graph 1. Integration index of the communities Living in France

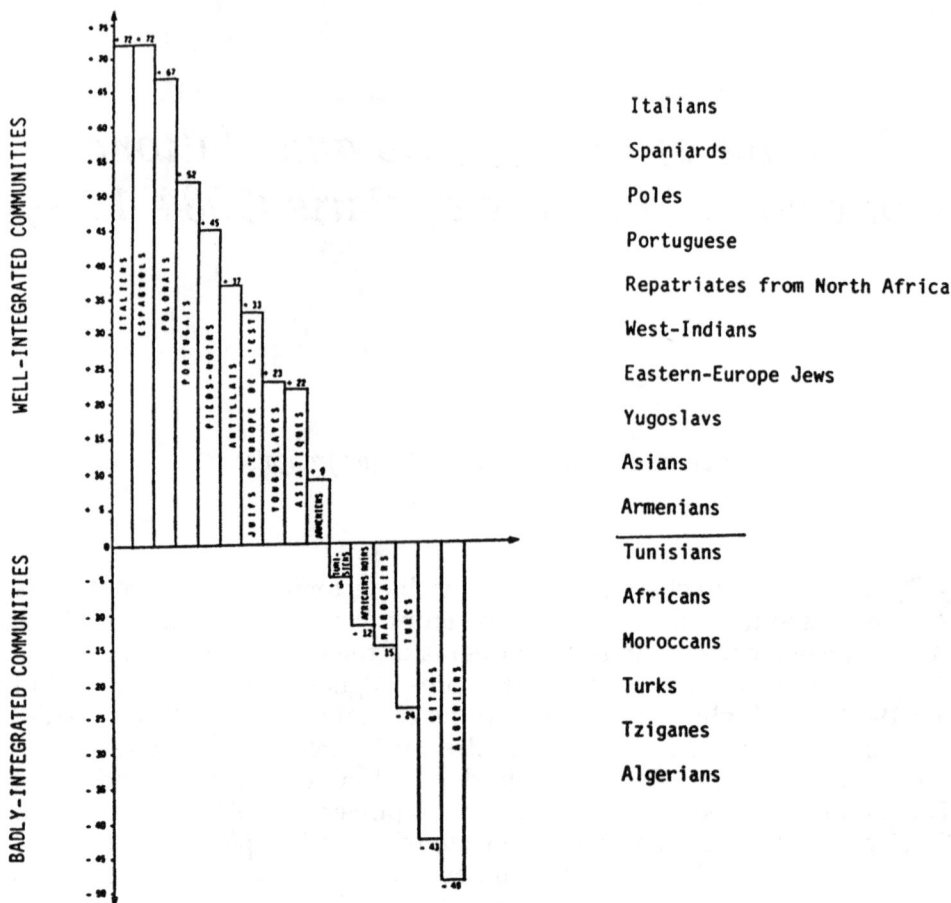

WELL-INTEGRATED COMMUNITIES

BADLY-INTEGRATED COMMUNITIES

Italians

Spaniards

Poles

Portuguese

Repatriates from North Africa

West-Indians

Eastern-Europe Jews

Yugoslavs

Asians

Armenians

Tunisians

Africans

Moroccans

Turks

Tziganes

Algerians

SOFRES survey for the MRAP (Movement against Racism and for Friendship between Nations), January-February 1984, *SOFRES-Opinion Publique 1985*, Paris, Gallimard, 1985, p. 80.

population resident in France. In the meantime, the proportion of Maghrebins (originating from Algeria, Tunisia, or Morocco) rose from 13 to almost 40 percent.[3] Because their ethnic, religious, and cultural differences are more striking, and because of the aftermath of decolonization, they seem to crystallize the anti-immigrant attitudes. A survey was conducted in February 1984, four months before the European elections, that questioned the perception of several ethnic communities. Each ethnic community was classified according to its score on an integration index, by subtracting the number of negative opinions it aroused ("badly integrated community") from the number of positive opinions ("well integrated"). All the Europeans had a positive score on the index, at its highest with Italians and Spaniards (+72). All the non-Europeans, with the exception of Asians (+22), had a negative score, at its lowest with the Algerians (−49).[4] Graph 1 shows the various ethnic groups' score on the index.

The speeches of J. M. Le Pen are aimed at these immigrants, who are blamed for unemployment, increasing crime rates, and more generally, France's troubles. Those who vote for the National Front, according to the surveys, cite the problem of immigration as the first motivation for their choice. It is actually where one finds more immigrants, in the urban and industrial departments of the eastern half of France, that the National Front gets more support. The parallelism between the maps of immigration and the maps of the extreme-Right electoral penetration is striking. (see, for example, Le Bras, 1986:200–20). Since 1984, there is a high positive correlation between the proportion of foreigners in the total population and the proportion of Le Pen voters at the level of the ninety-five metropolitan departments.[5]

Yet these findings are not corroborated by more detailed analyses done on smaller units, such as Perrineau's study of thirty-two communes in the suburbs of Grenoble (1985, 1986), or Rey's study of the forty communes of the Seine-Saint-Denis in the suburbs of Paris (Rey and Roy, 1986). These are both urbanized areas, with strong immigrant communities and a high level of votes for the National Front in 1984, as well as in 1985 and 1986. In neither case, however, does one find at the sub-departmental level a correlation between the proportion of Le Pen voters and the proportion of immigrants, or, more specifically, the proportion of Maghrebins.

There are several ways to interpret such a paradox. One is to see it as a typical case of "ecological fallacy," owing to the extensiveness and the heterogeneity of departmental-level analysis, and to consider that there is no *direct effect* of the presence of immigrants on the Le Pen vote. Another possibility is to look for a mediation between the departmental- and the subdepartmental-level of analysis. Based on a survey conducted in Grenoble, that showed that the feeling of insecurity is independent from objective, experienced insecurity, Perrineau hinted at a possible *indirect effect* of large ethnic communities: they may create what he calls a "halo effect" around them:

> The feeling of hostility against the immigrants, primary motivation of the extreme right vote, doesn't necessarily result from actual cohabitation with strong immigrant communities. Far from being immigration ghettos, the areas where the extreme Right makes its best scores often are centers on the periphery of which can be found large concentrations of immigrants. Thus the fears, rejections, worries that feed the vote for the National Front stem more from fantasy than from real, actually experienced troubles and dangers. (Perrineau, 1985:28)

From "Les Champs-Elysées" to "La Goutte D'Or"

The city counts more foreigners in its population (17 percent) than any other department, with the exception of the Seine-Saint-Denis. If the National Front vote was a function of the proportion of foreigners, it should reach its peak there.[6] Yet, if one orders the departments by decreasing National Front scores (percent of valid votes), Paris's National Front vote

Ethnic Politics and Civil Liberties

Table 1. Electoral Results of the National Front (1984–1989)

Elections	1984 (Euro.)	1986 (Parl.)	1988 (Pres.)	1988 (Parl.)	1989 (Euro.)
France					
Valid votes (%)	11.07	9.90	14.61	9.72	11.80
Registered voters (%)	6.11	7.44	11.75	6.30	5.70
Paris					
Valid votes (%)	15.24	10.99	13.38	9.87	14.07
Registered voters (%)	8.48	8.07	10.18	5.96	6.81

Source: CEVIPOF electoral file.

only ranked ninth in the European elections of 1984, fifteenth in the European elections of 1989, twentieth in the parliamentary elections of 1986, thirtieth in the parliamentary elections of 1988, and fifty-third in the previous presidential election. Table 1 shows the National Front's electoral results in European, parliamentary, and presidential elections between 1984 and 1989 in France and in Paris.

One should, however, take into account the uneven distribution of the foreign population in the city. For more than a century, Paris has been

Map 1: The Eighty Quartiers of Paris

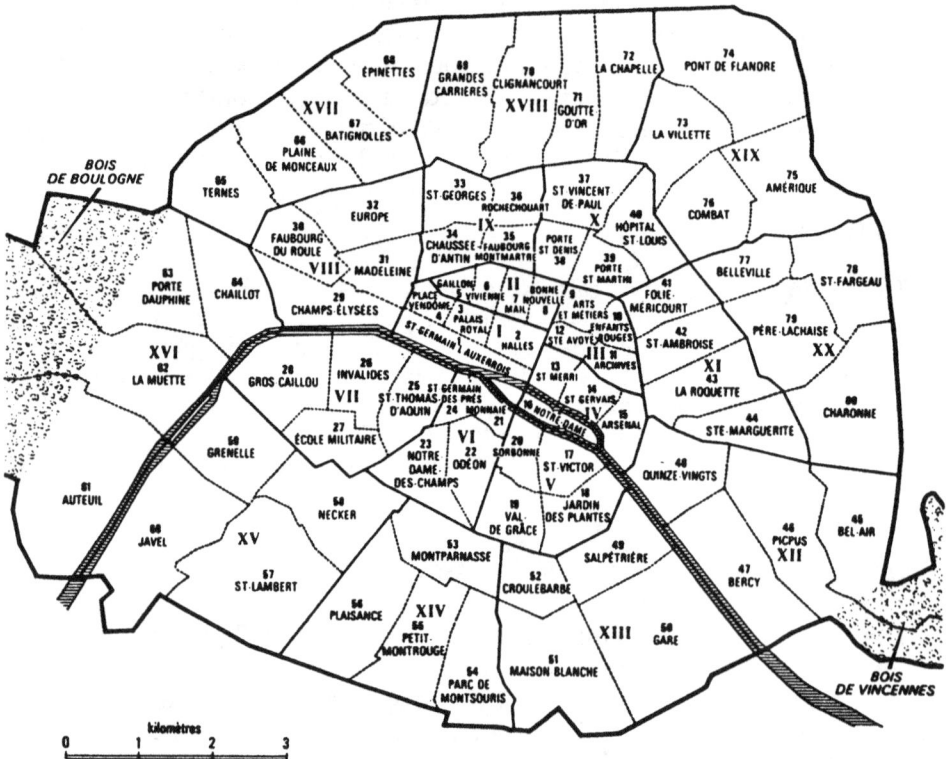

Table 2. The Foreign Population in Paris by Nationality (%)

Portuguese	14.5
Spanish	9.9
Yugoslav	6.0
Italian	3.2
Other Europeans	8.5
Algerian	14.2
Moroccan	8.7
Tunisian	6.5
Other African	9.8
Turkish	1.7
Other Asian	12.7
Other	4.3
Total Population	366,660

Source: 1982 census data.

administratively divided into eighty quartiers, four by arrondissement (Map 1), and as many villages, showing a great diversity in their social, ethnic, and political structures. The proportion of foreign residents in the population of these quartiers varies between 7 and 35 percent.

At the level of these eighty quartiers, one finds a constant correlation of about .50 (Pearson's R) between the proportion of foreigners in the total population and the proportion of valid votes for the National Front in the elections of 1984 (European), 1986 (parliamentary), 1988 (presidential and parliamentary) and 1989 (European).[7]

The explanation is less obvious if one considers the nationality of the foreigners living in Paris. Maghrebins come first (totaling about 29 percent), followed by Spaniards and Portuguese (25 percent) (Table 2). The relative importance of these groups is a good indicator of the ethnic balance in the quartier. Where Spaniards and Portuguese prevail, the foreign population is mainly European. Where North-Africans prevail, it is mainly non-European and therefore less integrated; according to the "direct effect" hypothesis, it is in these latter sections that the National Front vote should be the strongest.

Tables 3 and 4 show the correlation between National Front votes and ethnic and socioeconomic indicators. In 1984, the expected correlation is not evident. The National Front votes correlate more with the proportion of Spaniards and Portuguese in the population than with the proportion of North Africans (.48 versus .35, Table 3). If one measures them on the basis of the registered voters, instead of the valid votes, taking into account the important differences of voting turnout from one area to another, the correlation between the Le Pen vote and the presence of Spaniards and Portuguese climbs to + .57, and the correlation with the presence of North Africans disappears (Table 4).

The maps showing the proportion of foreigners in the quartiers in quintiles and the National Front votes in 1984 are clear enough. The Spanish and the Portuguese are concentrated in the west of Paris (Map 2), and the

Table 3. Correlation between the National Front Votes
and Ethnic and Socioeconomic Indicators (Registered Voters)

% Registered voters	Euro. 1984	Parl. 1986	Pres. 1988	Parl. 1988	Eur. 1989
Foreigners	.21	.41	.39	.37	.18
Maghrebins	−.05	.40	.61	.42	.01
Spanish, Portuguese	.57	.24	−.11	.10	.39
Working-class	−.07	.47	.72	.51	.01
Upper-class	.43	−.20	−.59	−.26	.26
Domestic services	.70	.28	−.12	.19	.49
Sup. Intell. Prof.	−.24	−.66	−.86	−.76	−.39

Table 4. Correlation between the National Front Votes
and Ethnic and Socioeconomic Indicators (Valid Votes)

% Valid voters	Euro. 1984	Parl. 1986	Pres. 1988	Parl. 1988	Eur. 1989
Foreigners	.48	.51	.47	.48	.47
Maghrebins	.35	.53	.67	.52	.39
Spanish, Portuguese	.48	.20	−.07	.13	.31
Working-class	.37	.60	.78	.61	.45
Upper-class	.00	−.34	−.64	−.35	−.16
Domestic services	.52	.22	−.10	.18	.36
Sup. Intell. Prof.	−.57	−.73	−.87	−.80	−.71

Note: Foreigners as proportion of the total population; occupations as proportion of the gainfully employed.

Maghrebins in the northeast (Map 3). Their proportion, which averages 5 percent of the total population of Paris, is double in La Chapelle (eighteenth), Saint-Louis (tenth), La Folie-Méricourt (eleventh); triple in Belleville (nineteenth); quadruple in La Goutte d'Or (eighteenth). Yet in the 1984 elections, it is the voters of the west and center of Paris, living in the quartiers of Europe, Champs-Elysées (eighth); Dauphine, Chaillot (sixteenth); Place Vendôme (first); or Plaine de Monceau (seventeenth) that gave more votes to J. M. Le Pen (Map 4).

This might be explained by the "halo effect": the people who don't live with the North Africans might be more receptive to the racist propaganda of the National Front, more prone to exaggerate the dangers and the nuisance of a neighborhood with a large North African community than those who actually live in such a neighborhood.

The elections of 1986 and 1988 invalidated this hypothesis. The support to the National Front candidates shifted to the northeastern quartiers. In 1986 and 1988 they drew most votes in La Chapelle, la Goutte d'Or, Saint Denis, and Belleville (Maps 5–7), and these votes were no longer correlated with the presence of the Spaniards and the Portuguese but with the presence of the Maghrebins (Tables 3 and 4).

These results fall in line with the direct-effect hypothesis, in terms of

Map 2: The Spanish and Portuguese in Paris (% of gainfully employed).

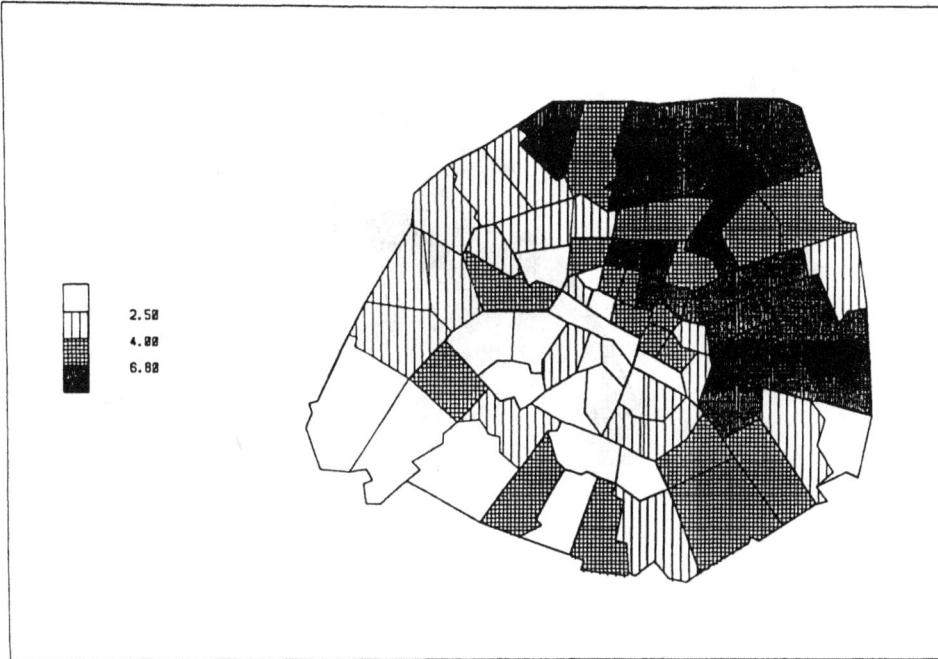

reactive xenophobia. Yet why would the voters in contact with the Maghrebins wait two years before turning to the National Front to express their hostility? And why would their hostility die off three years later? For in the European elections of 1989, the correlations shifted again. The Le Pen vote correlated better with the presence of the Spanish and Portuguese immigrants than with the presence of the Maghrebins (Tables 3 and 4).

It is equally difficult to analyze the National Front vote in 1984 and 1986 as an anti-Iberian vote. The Spanish and the Portuguese are among the best-integrated communities. And why would the voters react to their presence only at the time of the European elections? Our findings invalidate both the direct-effect and indirect-effect hypotheses. As soon as one breaks up the foreign population by ethnic groups, there is no systematic relation between their presence and the extreme-Right vote.

Their contrasted localization suggests another line of thought. Spanish and Portuguese are more often to be found in the west and center of the city, in the residential areas of the first, seventh, eight, sixteenth, or seventeenth arrondissements (Map 2). Their presence is correlated with indicators of "gentrification" of French families, such as the proportion of families owning more than one car, having upper-class and upper-middle-class occupations, and employing servants (Table 5). This can be explained by the exceptionally high proportion of Spanish and Portuguese who work in the "domestic services" sector, as caretakers, cooks, charwomen, watchmen, chauffeurs, etc. (38 percent on average, more than 50 percent in the seventh, eighth, and sixteenth arrondissements, compared to 5

Map 3: The Maghrebins in Paris (% of gainfully employed).

percent in the French population, see Table 6).[8] They have settled next to the well-off classes that can afford their services. In the French voting population alone, business owners, high-level executives, and professionals account for 36 percent of the gainfully employed in the seventeenth, 47 percent in the eighth, 49 percent in the seventh, and 52 percent in the fifteenth arrondissements. Here the National Front's good election results in the European elections reveal more the bourgeois character of its electorate in 1984 and 1989 than a surge of xenophobia against Spanish maids and Portuguese janitors. These results are positively correlated with all the indicators of gentrification. The best predictor of the 1984 Le Pen vote is the proportion of domestic-services employees (Tables 3 and 4).

The North-Africans, mostly blue-collar workers (see Table 6), are concentrated in the ill-favored neighborhoods of the northeast, which for centuries have attracted the poorer immigrants. Their presence correlates positively with the proportion of working-class people and the over-occupancy of housing units, and negatively with the indicators of gentrification (Table 5). In the French population alone, manual workers and menial clerks account for 50 percent of the gainfully employed in the eleventh arrondissement, 51 percent in the tenth, 54 percent in the twentieth, and more than 55 percent in the eighteenth and the nineteenth. There, the National Front's good election results reveal the working-class character of its electorate in 1986 and 1988, as much as its anti-immigrant attitudes. Its results are positively correlated with all the indicators of

Map 4: National Front Votes in Paris in the European Elections of 1984
(% of registered voters).

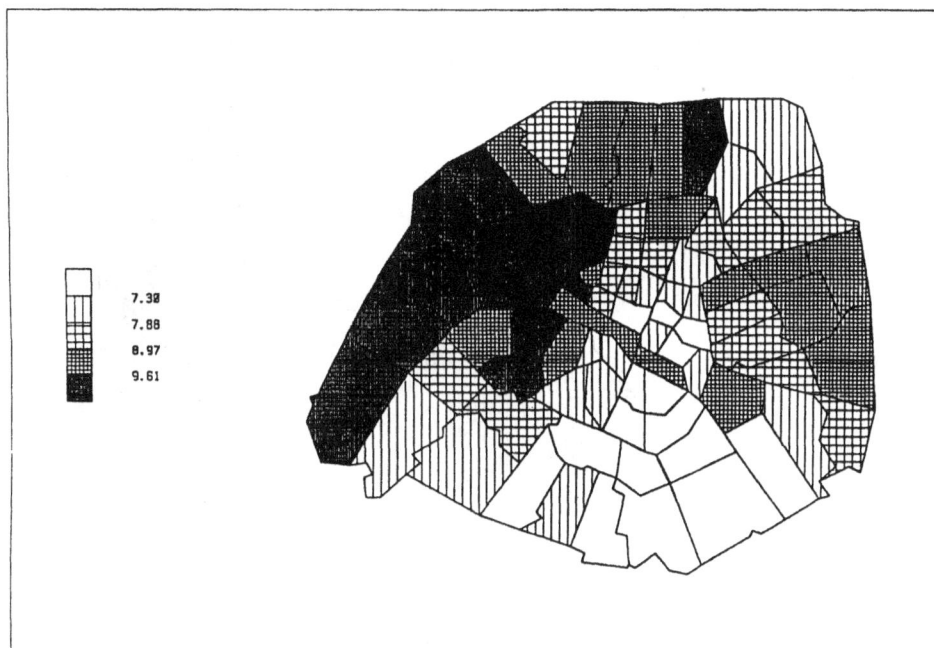

	7.30
	7.88
	8.97
	9.61

proletarianization, and the best predictor of the 1986 and 1988 National Front vote is the proportion of blue-collar workers among the gainfully employed.

This east-west opposition is not only social, but political. The north-eastern constituencies traditionally support the Left. For half-a-century they were the strongholds of the Communist party, and were gradually taken over by the Socialists.[9] The gentrified west is more conservative. At the time of the parliamentary elections of 1981, which gave the majority to the Socialists, the UDF-RPR coalition drew, in the first round, between 60 percent and 77 percent of the votes in the constituencies corresponding to the seventh, eighth, sixteenth, and part of the seventeenth arrondissements. In the constituencies corresponding to the eleventh, eighteenth, nineteenth, and twentieth arrondissements there was a second round, in which the Socialist won the seats.

This suggests that from one election to another, not only did the social bases of the Le Pen vote shift but its very meaning changed. In 1984 the exceptional mobilization of the bourgeois quartiers in his favor expressed the extreme opposition to the Socialist government by part of the right-wing electorate. The elections for the European parliament, of no domestic consequence, provided an outlet for an exasperation that the too-moderate ticket headed by Simone Veil couldn't convey. In the decisive parliamentary elections of 1986, the majority of these voters went back to the UDF or the RPR in order to defeat the Socialists. It is in these bourgeois

Map 5: National Front Votes in Paris in the Parliamentary Elections of 1986
(% of registered voters).

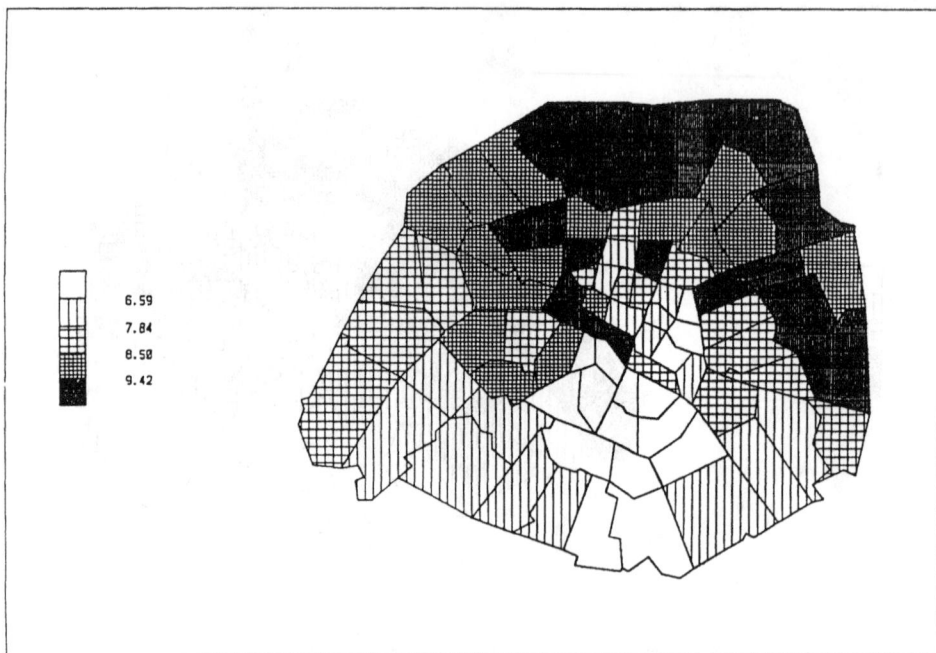

quartiers that the National Front's losses were the heaviest in 1986. Its marked progress in the northeast of Paris reflected the growing defection of the working classes disappointed by the Mitterrand experiment. The first round of the presidential election of 1988 provided the working classes with an even better opportunity to express their dissatisfaction, as the European elections had for the voters in the western parts of Paris in 1984, because the public opinion polls showed that Mitterrand was sure to be elected. Those who voted for Le Pen knew that their candidate had no chance; they could warn the Socialists, knowing that its right-wing opposition would not win.

Regentrification or Degentrification?

At first glance the 1989 elections do not fit into the same pattern as the previous ones. They look more like a remake of the 1984 European elections (Maps 4 and 8). Once again it is in the bourgeois quartiers that Le Pen draws more votes. Does that mean a "regentrification" of the National Front's electorate? Has its leader lost the support of the working classes he had won in 1986?

So far, the National Front scores by quartier have been measured in proportion of the registered voters. If we measure them in proportion to the votes cast, taking into account only the electors who actually went to the polls, the picture is slightly different, as Map 9 shows. On Map 4,

Map 6: National Front Votes in Paris in the Presidential Election of 1988
(% of registered voters).

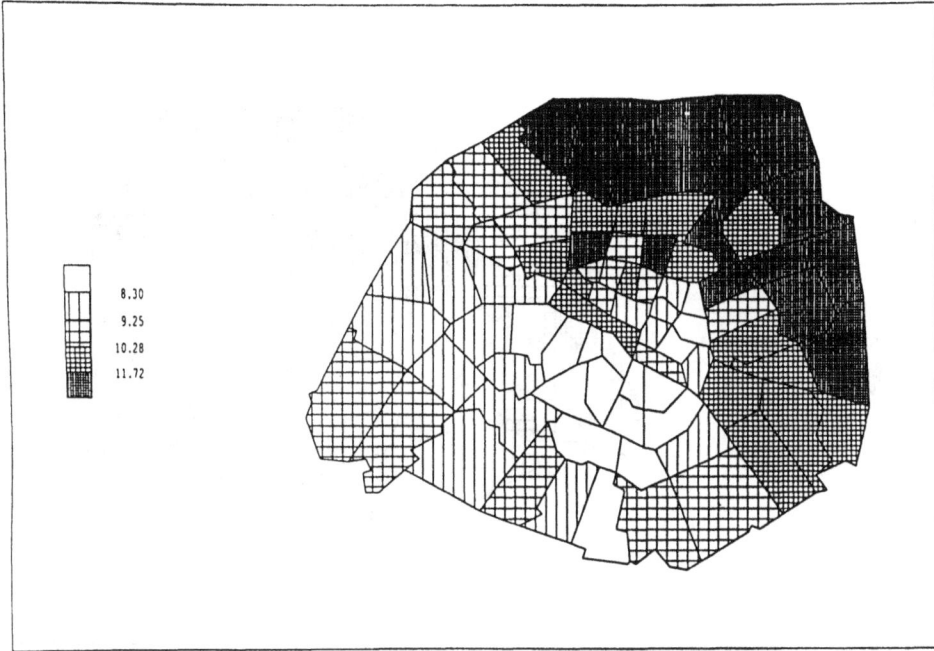

8.30
9.25
10.28
11.72

the 1984 National Front strongholds were strictly bourgeois. On Map 9
they are more mixed. If one ranks the quartiers by decreasing level of the
National Front vote, the working-class quartiers of the eighteenth and
twentieth arrondissements appear in the first quintile, just after the bourgeois
quartiers of the eighth and sixteenth arrondissements. Apparently the
double nature of the National Front vote has existed since the beginning.

Although the maps illustrating the National Front's votes in percentages
of valid votes cast for the 1986 parliamentary elections (Map 10), the 1986
presidential election (Map 11), and the 1988 parliamentary elections (Map
12) roughly correspond to the maps illustrating their votes in percentages
of registered voters in these elections, (Maps 5, 6, and 7, respectively), in
1989 discrepancies again appear, even more marked than those of 1984.
On Map 8 quartiers that most strongly voted for Le Pen appear in the
privileged west. On Map 13, which shows the National Front's votes, in
percentages of valid votes cast, in the European elections of 1989, it is the
opposite: they are clearly in the working-class districts of the northeast;
only five bourgeois quartiers remain in the first quintile. Thus depending
on which map one chooses to look at, the conclusion will be that there is
either a regentrification of the National Front electorate in 1989, or a continuation of the degentrification trend started in 1986.

The paradox stems from the exceptionally low rates of voter turnout
acknowledged in the northeastern quartiers in 1984 and 1989. Actually,

**Map 7: National Front Votes in Paris in the Parliamentary Elections of 1988
(% of registered voters).**

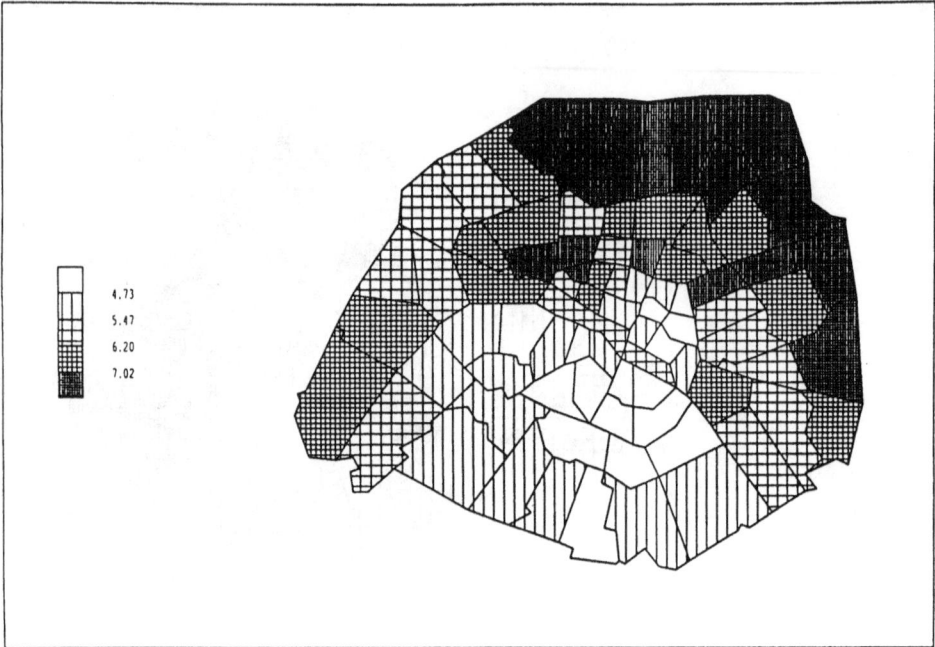

since 1986, even in 1989, when they do vote, the electors of the working-
class quartiers give more support to the National Front than do the electors of the bourgeois quartiers. But more often than in the gentrified West
they do not bother to go to the polls, especially in the case of European
elections with no direct political outcome.[10] This shows how important it
is to analyze electoral returns in terms of the proportions both of the
registered voters and of the valid votes cast.

The correlation analysis based on the National Front votes as a proportion of the valid votes cast tells the same story (Table 4). The Le Pen vote
in 1984 is clearly the most bourgeois: it is the most correlated with the
proportion of domestic services employees (.52). But it is already, to a
lesser degree, correlated with the proportion of blue-collar workers (.37).
After 1986, even in 1989, the latter correlation will increase and from then
on the Le Pen vote will be more correlated with the indicators of proletarianization than with the indicators of gentrification. On the whole, the
correlation between the National Front scores and the proportions of blue-
collar workers has increased between 1984 and 1989 (8 points), while the
correlation with the proportion of domestic services employees has decreased (16 points). The working-class support for Le Pen has not declined; on the contrary, it is stronger by the end of the period than at the
beginning.

Table 5. Correlation between the Ethnic and Socioeconomic Indicators

	%North Africans	% Spanish, Portuguese
Upper/upper-middle class	−.69	.65
Working class	.91	−.34
Employers	−.51	.81
Domestic services employees	−.20	.90
Number of people per room	.76	−.59
Families with 2 or more cars	−.55	.48

Note: Foreigners in proportion of the total population, occupations in proportion of the gainfully employed.

Table 6. The Population of Paris by Occupation and Nationality (%)

Nationality:	Spanish, Portuguese	Italian	Other EEC	North African	French	Total
Occupation						
Business, trade owner	1	11	8	7	8	7
Upper-management, professional	2	16	33	3	25	22
Middle-management	4	17	25	5	33	30
Clerk	10	15	19	14	27	25
Domestic services employee	38	11	6	12	5	8
Manual worker	46	30	8	58	12	18
(Number of People)	(54,156)	(6,584)	(10,448)	(56,060)	(906,876)	(1,095,448)

Source: 1982 census data.

Beyond the East-West Cleavage

The influence of the extreme Right throughout the period was not of course confined to the western and northeastern areas. As early as 1984, the National Front attracted voters in every constituency. In seventy-seven quartiers out of eighty its scores were better than the national average. Even at its lowest level, in the parliamentary elections of 1988, there was only one quartier, the Val de Grâce (fifth), where it drew less than 5 percent of the valid votes. Between elections, Le Pen's party gradually extended its grip from one side of the city to the other. Starting from the bourgeois quartiers in 1984 (seventh, eighth, sixteenth, and part of the seventeenth) it progressed, mostly in the working-class areas, between 1984 and 1986 (tenth, eleventh, eighteenth, nineteenth, and twentieth) and in the "petit-bourgeois" areas between 1986 and 1988 (eleventh to fifteenth).[11]

Only one group seems to have resisted steadily. Whatever the election, Saint Victor, Jardin des Plantes, Val de Grâce, Montparnasse, Montsouris

Map 8: National Front Votes in Paris in the European Elections of 1989
(% of registered voters).

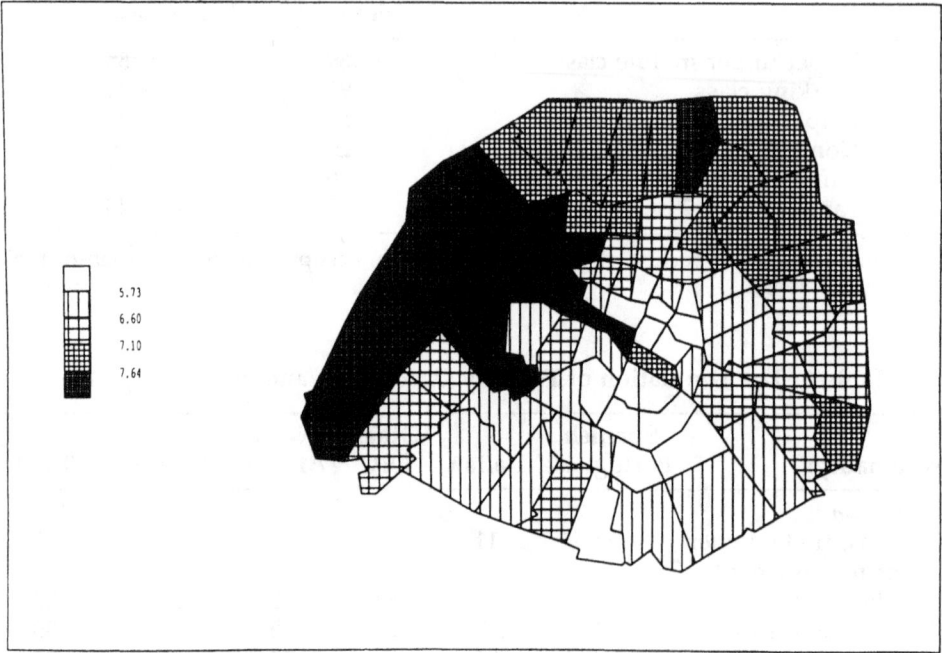

(fourteenth), Croulebarbe (thirteenth), Archives (third), and Saint Gervais (fourth) appear in the last quintile (in white on the maps), with the lowest percentage of National Front votes. Owing to the preponderance of the upper and middle classes among the gainfully employed, these quartiers can be labeled as bourgeois. Yet they differ from the western quartiers in the prominence of these professions that the French Occupational Code calls "superior intellectual professions": artists, journalists, lawyers, doctors, higher-level civil servants. They form a "new bourgeoisie," socially less conventional, politically less conservative, with a high level of education.[12] From 1984 to 1989 there is a high negative correlation between the percentage of these categories in the population of the quartiers and the scores of the National Front (Tables 3 and 4). But even there, the National Front vote is increasing. Between the parliamentary elections of 1988 and the European elections of 1989, the electoral gains of Le Pen's party were the highest in these very quartiers.

What the evolution indexes also stress is the instability of Le Pen's electoral base. His losses were the greatest in 1986 in his bourgeois strongholds of 1984. It was in the petit-bourgeois areas conquered in the presidential election of 1988 that he lost the most voices in the following parliamentary elections. These contrasting, ebb-and-flow voting patterns give the phenomenon an unexpected amplitude.

The case of Paris shows the complexity of the relation between the electoral rise of the extreme Right and the presence of the immigrants. The

Map 9: National Front Votes in Paris in the European Elections of 1984
(% of votes cast).

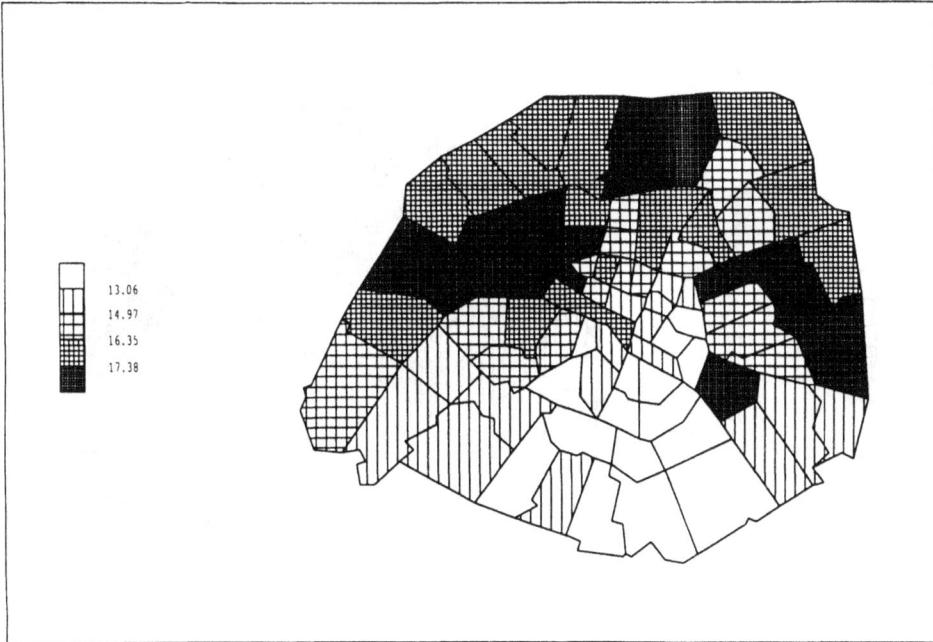

correlations we started with are deceptive. From one election to another, the correlations are no longer between the same immigrants, and the same voters. The very meaning of our ethnic indicators, in terms of the proximity and visibility of an ethnic group, neighborhood problems, the "halo" effect, and so on, is questioned by these findings. As much as ethnic indicators, they function as social and political markers of the city landscape, outlining the more-than-a-century-old opposition between the well-to-do and conservative west and the poor and radical east.[13] One could unmistakably list the eighty quartiers of Paris as upper class or working class, right-wing or left-wing, according to the respective proportions of North African or of Spanish and Portuguese immigrants in their population. Beyond the presence of these communities of immigrants, it is the social and political structures of the quartiers where they have settled that account for the Le Pen vote dynamics.

The Changing Le Pen Voters

To what extent can one generalize these findings? Our study reaches the limits of any ecological study. The fact that in 1984 Le Pen drew more votes in predominantly upper- and upper-middle-class quartiers doesn't necessarily mean that the upper- and upper-middle-class electors of these quartiers voted for him. The fact that in 1986 he drew more votes in predominantly working-class areas doesn't mean that the working-class electors voted for

Map 10: National Front Votes in Paris in the Parliamentary Elections of 1986 (% of votes cast).

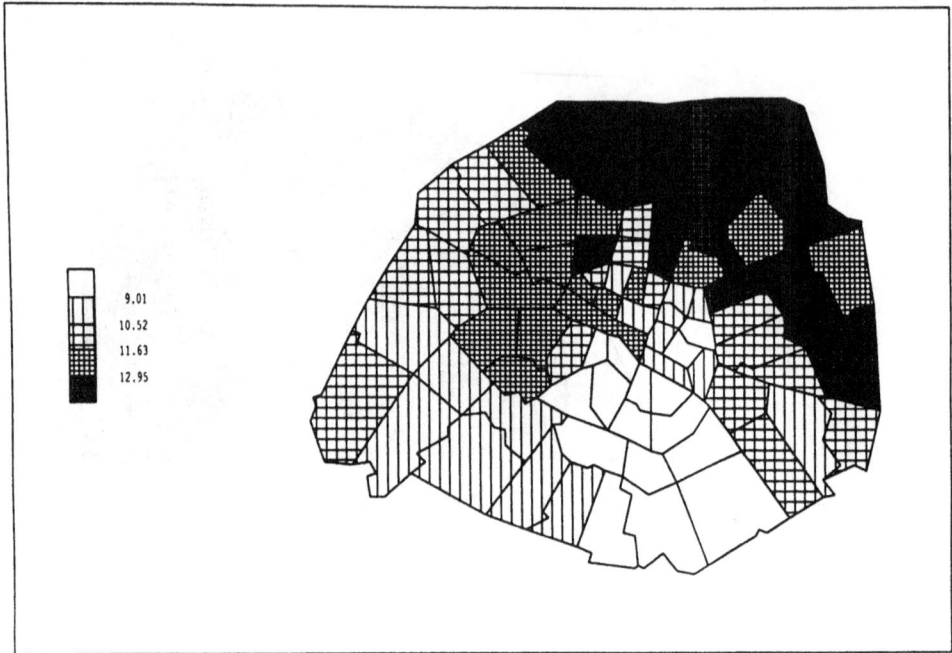

him. Furthermore, the political and social structures of the city are very specific. Therefore, the contextual analysis based on census data and constituency returns for Paris was augmented by the analysis of individual electoral behavior, on the basis of national exit polls and post-electoral surveys.[14]

The data confirm the sociological diversity of the National Front's support. Table 7 recapitulates the evolution of its support. Since 1984, Le Pen has attracted voters in every category of the population. It is among the entrepreneurs and the self-employed though, and particularly among shopkeepers and artisans, that he has always run best. In the first round of the 1988 presidential election they gave him almost one-third of their votes, more than to Mitterrand, Chirac, or Barre. In 1986, the leader of the National Front gained the support of the working classes. In four years their vote in his favor increased by 9 points. In 1988, le Pen drew as many voices as the Communist party candidate Lajoinie among the blue-collar workers (16 percent), and twice as many among the unemployed (19 percent). Contrary to what has often been suggested, there are practically no declared former Communists among the National Front voters, whatever the election (1981–1988) or whatever the political indicator used (party identification, voting intentions, past votes).[15] But if direct transfers from Communist to Lepenist vote are negligible, the "little people" who traditionally turned to the Communist party to defend them are increasingly

Map 11: National Front Votes in Paris in the Presidential Election of 1988 (% of votes cast).

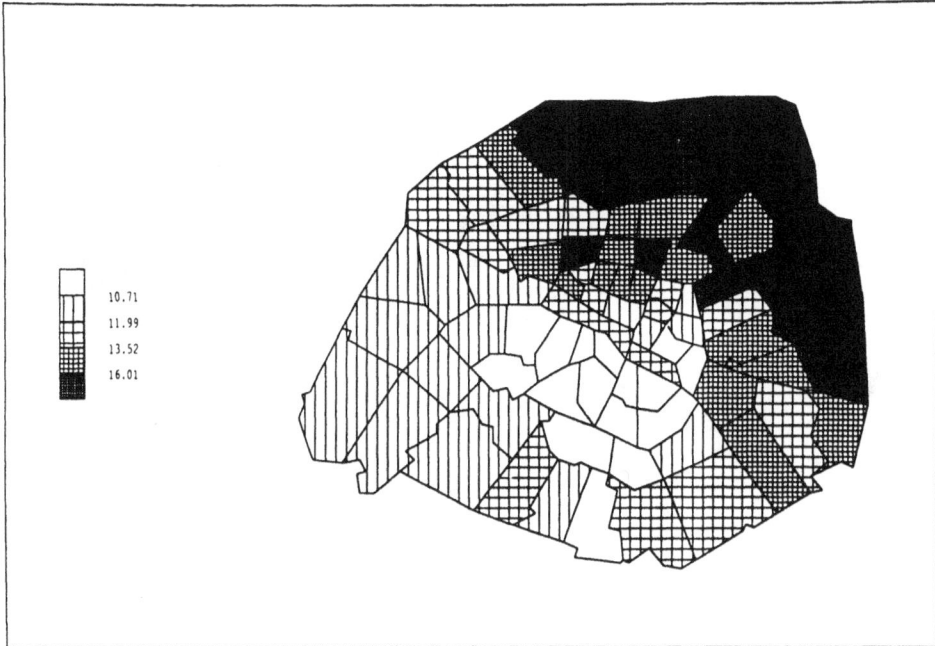

supporting the National Front. Although at the beginning of the period its clientele was markedly bourgeois and petit-bourgeois, by the end of the period it had acquired a more populist character.

Since 1989, there are signs of a conservative shift in the National Front's electorate. The proportion of women and older voters has increased since the last presidential election. The proportion of people with high incomes (15,000 F per month or more) has doubled, and the proportion of church-goers has gone up from 27 to 41 percent. These groups traditionally give more support to the right-wing parties. Indeed, the proportion of Lepenist voters who place themselves on the right side of the Left-Right scale (positions 5 to 7) increased between 1988 and 1989, from 66 to 78 percent (see Bourlanges, 1990). Yet one should not overstate this "regentrification" process. The basic structures of the National Front vote had not changed. It was still among small shopkeepers and manual workers that Le Pen drew the most votes (Table 8). His losses were more severe among upper-level managers and professionals (-8) and entrepreneurs (-9) than among the blue-collar workers (-4).

One should also take into account the specific nature of European elections. They always arouse less interest than presidential elections. In 1989, the rates of voter turnout went down to 49 percent, compared to 81 percent in the first round of the previous presidential election. But the voter turnout was much higher among the educated upper-middle class and

Map 12: National Front Votes in Paris in the Parliamentary Elections of 1988 (% of votes cast).

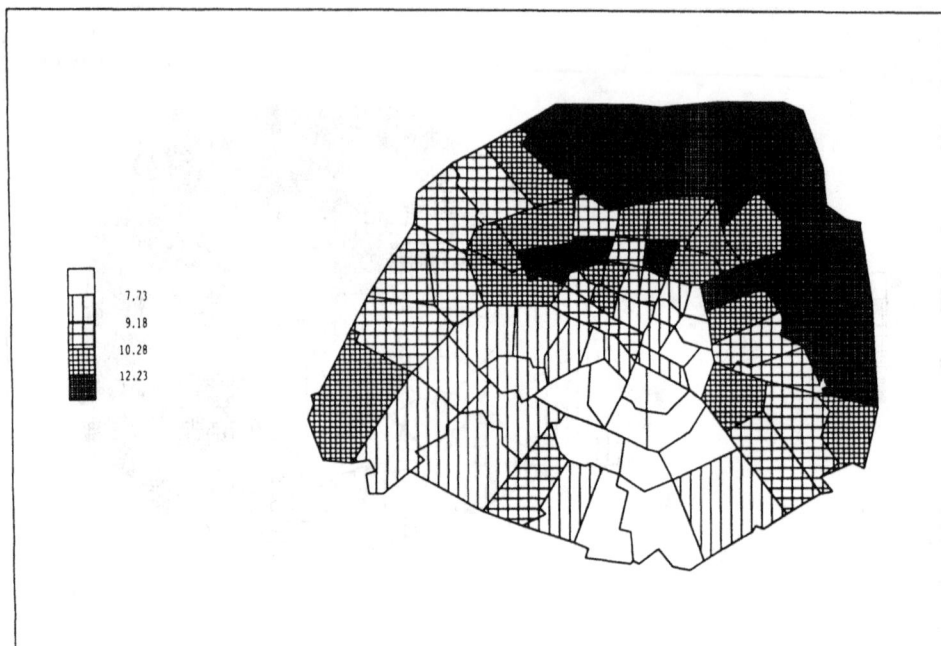

right-wing supporters, willing to express their opposition to the Socialist government.[16] This could partly explain the overrepresentation of these categories in the National Front's 1989 electorate.

The second point our survey data confirm is the political volatility of this electorate. In each election Le Pen loses some of his voters and gains new ones. Only one-third of his 1984 supporters who went to the polls in 1986 voted for his candidates, but 37 percent of the 1986 National Front electors were newcomers. In the presidential election of 1988, Le Pen only lost 10 percent of his 1986 voters, and two-thirds of his supporters were newcomers. They proved to be as mobile as their predecessors: in the next parliamentary elections, one-third of them did not vote for the National Front's candidate, and this time there were practically no newcomers.[17]

The third point surveys confirm is the protest function of the Le Pen vote, which accounts for its instability. There is a small group of voters that remain faithful to the National Front from one election to another, representing some 3 percent of the total French electorate. Every election enlarges this core of voters with discontented voters from every side of the political board. Each wave of newcomers has its distinctive ideological and social profile. The 1984 recruits were the most bourgeois and right-wing, the 1986 recruits were more left-wing and working-class, and the 1988 recruits were more petit-bourgeois.[18] They mostly return to wherever they came from once the election is over. For instance, 76 percent of the former left-wing voters who supported Le Pen in the first round of the 1988

**Map 13: National Front Votes in the European Elections of 1989
(% of votes cast).**

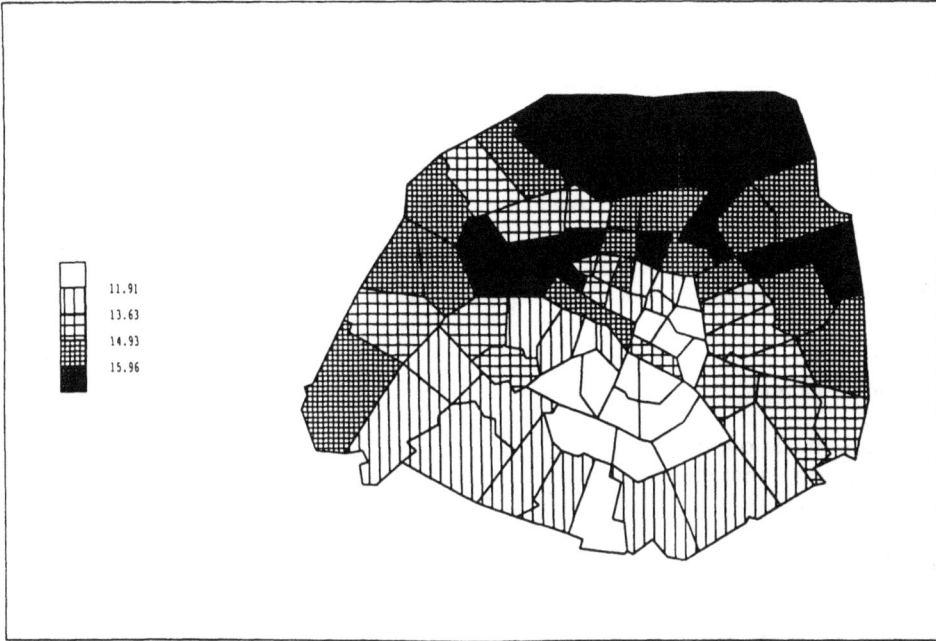

presidential election voted for Mitterrand in the second round, and 87 percent of the former right-wing voters voted for Chirac.[19]

In sharp contrast with the constant voters, the majority of the mobile voters do not identify themselves with the National Front; they do not consider themselves as part of the extreme right.[20] They do not vote *for* Le Pen, but *against* the other parties and the other candidates. In 1984, 79 percent of the Lepenist voters wished to "take advantage of this election to express their discontent" (compared to 53 percent of all the voters). In 1989, 82 percent of the Lepenist voters gave the same answer (compared to 40 percent). In 1986, 44 percent of the National Front voters (compared with 29 percent) wanted to express their "rejection of the other tickets" more than their "support to the ticket they chose."[21] A week before the first round of the 1988 presidential election, when asked which candidate they wished to see elected "at the bottom of their heart," only 28 percent of Le Pen's potential electors gave his name; 26 percent preferred Chirac, 17 percent Mitterrand, and 10 percent Barre. This surprising attitude, found in no other electorate, is typical of a protest vote (Jaffré, 1988).[22]

On the whole social, economic, and political factors seem more important than ethnic factors in accounting for the electoral rise of the National Front between 1984 and 1989. The lingering on of recession and unemployment and the inability of either the Right or the Left to cope with it have opened a space for the extreme Right. Only after the Socialist victory

Table 7. The National Front Voters in 1984–1988 (%)

	National Front voters in:		
	1984 (Euro)	1986 (Parl.)	1988 (Pres.)
Sex			
Male	13	12	17
Female	9	7	10
Age			
18–24 years	12	9	16
25–34	11	8	11
35–49	12	9	17
50–64	12	12	14
65 and over	9	9	12
Individual Occupation			
Farmer	13	11	18
Business, trade owner	21	14	31
Upper management, professional	12	9	17
Middle management	13	10	12
Clerk	12	7	14
Worker	7	13	16
No occupation	10	9	11
Sector of Activity			
Unemployed	13	14	19
Public sector employee	9	7	13
Private sector employee	13	12	14
Self-employed	17	13	24
Total	11	10	14

Source: BVA exit polls, 17 June 1984, 26 March 1986, 24 April 1988. National samples of 7,054, 4,564, and 2,837 voters.

of 1981, with the frustrations and disappointment it aroused, did the National Front become a credible alternative and immigration a prominent political issue.

The case of Paris suggests that, whatever the sensitivity of Le Pen's voters to the issue of immigration (more marked than in any other electorate)[23] their xenophobia doesn't need to be triggered by actual confrontation with immigrants and that their electoral choice is independent of immigrants' presence or absence. Proximity with large ethnic communities, and more specifically, with the North African communities, is neither a necessary nor a sufficient condition of the Le Pen vote. There are other types of contact with the immigrants than the residential ones: at school, in public transportation, at work, and so on. From the pioneering studies by G. Allport and R. M. Williams, one knows that residential, occupational contacts do not necessarily breed anti-immigrant attitudes. On the contrary, they may, in given circumstances, reduce them. Furthermore, there seems to be a phantasmagorical dimension in the relation between

Table 8. The National Front Voters in 1988–1989 (%).

| | National Front voters in: | | |
	1988 (Pres.)	1988 (Parl.)	1989 (Euro.)
Sex			
Male	18	12	14
Female	11	7	10
Age			
18–24 years	16	15	9
25–34	17	9	8
35–49	17	8	12
50–64	11	10	15
65 and over	12	10	12
Individual Occupation			
Farmer	13	3	3
Business, trade owner	27	6	18
Upper management, professional	19	10	11
Middle management	12	6	7
Clerk	13	8	11
Worker	19	19	15
No occupation	12	9	13
Total	14.5	12	10

Source: SOFRES post-electoral surveys. Conducted 19–25 May 1988, 14–23 June 1988, and 21 June–1 July 1989. National samples of 2,000 voters.

National Front voters and immigrants, which drives National Front voters against immigrants even though they have no contact at all (Perrineau and Lagrange, 1989).

To put it in the words of a journalist investigating Samoens, a small village of Haute-Savoie, where there were practically no foreign-born, but where the National Front had drawn 12.48 percent of the votes in the parliamentary elections of 1986, "one doesn't need to have the immigrants close to one's eyes, to have them far from one's heart." (Carton, 1987).

Notes

1. He failed to get the 500 signatures of elected representatives required.
2. According to the 1982 census of population, 3,680,100; 4,223,928 according to the statistics of the Ministry of the Interior in 1982, and 4,459,196 in 1987. According to the first results of the 1990 census, there has been no increase in the foreign population since.
3. According to 1982 census data. See INSEE/Ministère des Affaires Sociales et de la Solidarité Nationale, 1984:20.
4. This of course has not always been the case. The image of the Italians and of the Poles, for instance, was far less positive in the 1920s (see Schor, 1985:761; and Milza, 1986). The surveys conducted by the National Institute for Demo-

graphic Studies (INED) on the attitudes of the French towards foreign immigrants between 1947 and 1974 show a gradual amelioration of the image of Italians, Poles, Spanish, and Portuguese. But North Africans and black Africans have always been seen as less sympathetic and less capable of "adapting to French life." Only the Germans had a worse image, just after the war (see Girard, 1950, 1971, 1974).

5. Pearson's R of .79 in the European elections of 1984; .61 in the parliamentary elections of 1986 and 1988; and .67 in the presidential election of 1988 and in the European elections of 1989.

6. In his book *Les Trois France*, Le Bras records the following "Le Pen's equation": National Front votes (%) = 6 + (1.7 × Foreigners (%) + small residue (1986:216). According to this equation, in Paris the National Front should draw 6 + (1.7 × 16.8) = 34.56 percent of the valid votes!

7. Official electoral returns given by the city of Paris, and 1982 census data. On the origins of this research see Mayer, 1987. Source of all maps is Bernard Bouhet, Center for Computerization of Sociopolitical Data (CIDSP) of Grenoble.

8. See Taboada-Leonetti and Guillon, 1987:72. In 1975, the proportion of domestic employees among the Spanish women was up to 91 percent and among the Portuguese women to 87 percent.

9. Between 1973 and 1981 the Communist party's portion of the vote in Paris fell from 17.8 percent to 9.4 percent of the valid votes, while the score of the Socialist party went from 15.5 to 31.9 percent. After the parliamentary elections of 1981, the Communist party had no seats left and the Socialist party had thirteen (out of thirty-one). On the decline of the Communist party in Paris before 1981 see Platone, 1977.

10. In 1984, the proportion of abstainers varied between 48 and 52 percent in the working-class quartiers, between 33 and 40 percent in the gentrified ones. In 1989 the proportions varied between 55 and 60 percent, and between 45 and 50 percent, respectively.

11. That is, quartiers with an intermediate social structure, where the difference (positive or negative) between the proportion of the upper middle class (business owners, upper-level management, and professionals) and the manual workers among the gainfully employed is the smallest. These are the least working-class of the predominantly working-class quartiers, and the least bourgeois of the bourgeois ones.

12. For instance, they do not employ servants (the correlation between their percentage among the gainfully employed and the people employed in the "domestic services": .11), and more than average voted for Mitterrand in the first round of the presidential election of 1988.

13. On the permanence of the electoral structures of Paris, see Ranger, 1977.

14. There are some discrepancies between the exit polls and the ordinary survey data. If the former are very reliable to measure the voters' electoral behavior, they are sociologically more biased. Because the questionnaire is to be filled in by the respondent, the elderly voters and the less-educated voters (workers, unemployed, etc.) are underrepresented. So are the farmers, because the small rural polling stations are excluded from the sample. And the occupations of the respondents, because they are autodeclared, are generally less detailed than in the ordinary surveys.

15. At the most, 3 or 4 percent. See Platone and Rey, 1989.

16. Duhamel and Jaffré, 1990:179. The declared abstention was 47 percent in the total sample; it dropped to 38 percent among the voters with a higher edu-

cation and the upper- and upper-middle-class voters. 34 percent among those who had voted for Chirac in the first round of the 1988 presidential election, and 30 percent among those who had voted for Barre.

17. According to the CSA exit poll conducted on the day of the presidential election of 1988 on a national sample of 5.424 electors, only 56% of Le Pen's voters considered voting for the National Front candidates in case of anticipated Parliamentary elections. According to the SOFRES post-electoral survey, 66 percent actually did.

18. For a detailed comparison between the different waves of Le Pen voters, see Jaffré 1986; Charlot, 1988; and Mayer, 1989.

19. See Mayer and Perrineau, 1990. The study is based on a large CEVIPOF-SOFRES post-electoral survey (national representative sample of 4,032 French of voting age).

20. In 1988, 15 percent of Le Pen's presidential electorate classified itself at the extreme right end of the Left-Right scale; 33 percent declared a party proximity with the National Front. Mayer and Perrineau, 1990. In 1989, the proportion of the declared extreme Right Lepenist voters had increased, but it was not more than 22 percent (SOFRES post-electoral survey, June 1989).

21. See Duhamel and Jaffré, 1990: Chapter 12, p. 176, for a comparison between the SOFRES pre-electoral surveys in June 1984 and June 1989; and *SOFRES, L'Etat de l'opinion, Clés pour 1987*, Paris, Le Seuil, 1987, chapter 6, p. 112 (SOFRES exit poll, 16 March 1986).

22. SOFRES pre-electoral survey for a group of local newspapers, 1–2 April 1988.

23. Asked "Among these problems which are the two that counted the most in your vote of today" the 1989 Le Pen voters answered "The immigrants" (65 percent compared with 14 percent in the sample) and "Insecurity" (33 percent instead of 10 percent), while the average answer was first "the construction of Europe" and then "the protection of the environment" (IFOP-*Le Monde* exit poll, June 18, 1989, sample of 3,835 voters).

References

Bourlanges, Jean-Louis. 1990. "Le rendez-vous manqué de la rénovation." Pp. 37–41 in Duhamel and Jaffré, 1990.

Carton, Daniel. 1987. "Le vote Le Pen au ras des cantons." *Le Monde*, 5–6 July.

Charlot, Jean. 1988. "Le séisme du 18 mai et la nouvelle donne politique." Pp. 28–32 in Philippe Habert and Colette Ysmal, eds., *L'élection présidentielle 1988*. Paris: Le Figaro/Etudes politiques.

Duhamel, Olivier, and Jérôme Jaffré. 1990. *SOFRES, L'Etat de l'opinion 1990*. Paris: Le Seuil.

Girard, Alain. 1950. "Le problème démographique et l'évolution du sentiment public." *Population*, 2:333–52.

———. 1971. "Attitudes des Français à l'égard de l'immigration étrangère." *Population*, 5:827–76.

Girard, Alain, et al. 1974. "Attitude des Français à l'égard de l'immigration étrangère. Nouvelle enquête d'opinion." *Population*, 6:1,105–67.

INSEE/Ministère des Affaires Sociales et de la Solidarité Nationale. 1984. "Les Etrangers." *Migrations et Sociétés*, Paris: La Documentation francaise.

Jaffré, Jérôme. 1986. "Front National: la relève protestataire." Pp. 211–30 in Elisabeth Dupoirier and Gérard Grunberg, eds., *Mars 1986: La drôle de défaite de la gauche*. Paris: Presses Universitaires de France.

_____. 1988. "Le vote exutoire." *Le Monde*, 12 April.

Le Bras, Hervé. 1986. *Les Trois France*. Paris: Editions Odile Jacob.

Mayer, Nonna. 1987. "De Passy à Barbès, deux visage du vote Le Pen à Paris." *Revue française de science politique*, 36(6) (December): 891–906.

_____. 1989. "Le vote FN de Passy à Barbès." Chapter 12 In Mayer and Perrineau, 1989.

Mayer, Nonna, and Pascal Perrineau, eds. 1989. *Le Front National à Découvert*. Paris: Presses de la Fondation nationale des sciences politiques.

_____. 1990. "Why Do They Vote for the National Front?" Paper presented at the workshop on "The Extreme Right in Europe" at the ECPR joint sessions of workshops, 2–7 April, Bochum.

Milza, Pierre, ed. 1986. *Les Italiens en France de 1914 à 1930*. Rome: Ecole Française de Rome.

Perrineau, Pascal. 1985. "Le Front National, un électorat autoritaire." *Revue Politique et Parlementaire*, July–August: 24–31.

_____. 1986. "Quel avenir pour le Front National?" *Intervention*, 15 (January–March): 33–42.

Perrineau, Pascal, and Hugues Lagrange. 1989. "Le syndrome lepéniste." Pp. 228–46 in Mayer and Perrineau, 1989.

Platone, François. 1977. "Les structures du vote de gauche à Paris." *Revue française de science politique*, 27, no. 6 (December): 820–47.

Platone, François, and Henri Rey. 1989. "Le FN en terre communiste." Chapter 13 in Mayer and Perrineau, 1989.

Ranger, Jean. 1977. "Droite et gauche dans les élections à Paris: le partage d'un territoire." *Revue français de science politique*, 27 no. 6 (December): 789–819.

Rey, Henri, and Jacques Roy. 1986. "Quelques réflexions sur l'évolution électorale d'un département de la banlieue parisienne." *Hérodote*, 43 (October–December): 6–38.

Schor, Ralph. 1985. *L'opinion française et les étrangers (1919–1930)*. Paris: Publications de la Sorbonne.

Taboada-Leonetti, Isabelle, with Michèle Guillon. 1987. *Les immigrés des beaux quartiers*. Paris: CIEMI-L'Harmattan.

Symposium I: Latino Politics in the 1990s

Introduction

F. Chris Garcia

University of New Mexico

The decade of the 1980s was heralded as being "the Decade of the Hispanics." However, as the 1980s drew to a close, it was evident that, although some minor gains had been made, Latinos by and large were disappointed in the changes that had occurred over the past ten years. The most notable gains seem to have been made in Latino political representation. At the end of the decade there were more elected and appointed public officials of Hispanic origin than there had been at any time in U.S. history. However, socioeconomic data pointed to only minimal gains, and even some regression, in areas such as employment, income, education, housing, and health. In addition to these objective indicators of well-being, there was also a widespread feeling among Latinos that the achievement of Latino political empowerment and equal status was still a long way off. This was particularly frustrating since relatively large advances, initiated in the late 1960s and early 1970s, had led to great expectations for the 1980s; yet progress toward equal opportunity and parity had leveled off. This was all the more disturbing in light of demographic projections that indicated that there had been and would continue to be a tremendous increase in the proportion of Latinos in the U.S. society—a phenomenon that was projected to continue through at least the next two or three decades.

Consequently, as Latinos entered the 1990s, most assessments of the 1980s were tinged with disappointment. Some of the hopefulness expressed for the 1990s revealed an optimism that did not seem to be based on any particular new information about the system, nor did it seem to be based on possibly more successful strategies or innovative conceptual approaches. No careful analyses provided a solid foundation for sanguine expectations. There was only a hope that things would be better, perhaps simply and somehow inevitably because there would be more Latinos in society, and eventually the dominant society would have to deal with a large proportion of its population in a more benevolent and egalitarian manner. Social and political observers agreed that more, and more effective, organization and mobilization were necessary, since these are general elements in political success, but why this had not occurred sooner and why the 1990s would be particularly supportive or promotive of these was not clearly spelled out.

It is true that during the 1980s successful legal challenges to many local at-large electoral systems (with the courts declaring them null and void) have resulted in some additional Latino representation from Latino areas. In some areas, electoral participation rates improved. However, there was also some evidence indicating that Latino participation in some cases had declined. Latinos were still significantly underrepresented, holding less than 1 percent of the nation's elective offices though comprising 9 percent of the population.

A few advances were made due to the successful lobbying in Washington by national Latino advocacy organizations, such as the National Council de la Raza and the National Association of Latino Elected Officials. Yet, organizations such as the Mexican American Legal Defense and Education Fund (MALDEF) and the League of United Latin American Citizens (LULAC) also experienced several internal problems that may diminish their effectiveness.

The main thrust of Latino politics in the 1980s had been electoral and litigational, but it is not clear how much more can be done in these areas to increase the well-being of the Latino communities. Certainly, higher electoral participation among Latinos would mean that the group would have more influence, and litigation could continue to redress personal and organizational injustices. However, both of these strategies may be approaching a point of diminishing returns without the addition of some new conceptualizations, strategies, and approaches for Latino politics in the 1990s.

It is to add some expert perspectives to this dialogue over Latino politics in the 1990s that the participants in the Latino politics symposium direct their analyses and musings. It is always risky business for anyone to go on public record with projections for the future, and social scientists have not been particularly adept at making accurate long-term projections. However, these symposium papers present some perceptive analyses of and challenging ideas about past and current approaches to Latino politics, along with some likely scenarios for their future.

There are common threads found running through most of these papers. There must be some new synthesis, or at least a restructured dialectic, that will produce something very different and more successful than Latino politics have produced in the past. More of the same probably will not suffice to make any significant difference. Perhaps as a precondition, Latinos need to look inward and resolve some internal contradictions and inconsistencies. Perhaps a new collective consciousness under the label of Hispanic or Latino is needed in order to transcend, at least partially, the great heterogeneity of the Latino population. Some new associations and coalitions must be formed, some at the attitudinal level, others taking organizational forms. Some of these will be within the Latino communities themselves, perhaps emphasizing some common Hispanic cultural ties as symbolic rallying points. The danger of such an approach, of course, is that attachments that tie Latino communities together along cultural lines may further estrange those groups that otherwise might be allies but that do not share these cultural manifestations. So perhaps a variety of strategies and approaches must be employed, depending not only upon the political players, but also upon the stage, (that is, the area and circumstances) and the particular issue at hand. Rudy de la Garza examines some of these "endogenous" factors that will affect future Latino political success, especially the naturalization of the burgeoning Latino immigrant population.

It may very well be, as Luis Fraga posits, that as Latinos strive for greater equality, the distinctiveness of the Latino culture must necessarily be diminished. Conversely, as cultural ties weaken, an important political resource may be lost. In any case, new coalitions and associations must be formed. Certainly ad hoc coalitions on certain kinds of issues, particularly in urban areas, may include other racial minorities, particularly African Americans. James Jennings details how distinctive ethnic and racial minorities must work together to advance common interests and must work hard to diminish sources of conflict. Otherwise, it is likely that the position of a great proportion of disadvantaged minorities will deteriorate further.

Latinos must not be prejudicially opposed to any alliance that will advance common interests; principled pragmatism must be the guiding precept. Luis Fraga sees Latinos working together with certain elements of the core cultural majority. In that interplay between minorities and majorities, which will involve compromise and negotiation toward finding a common ground for action, the perception of the public interest can be broadened to include both Latino and Anglo special interests.

Issues around which interests may coalesce may include pressing domestic concerns such as education; economic well-being, including health care and housing; the reduction of crime; and control of the drug problem. These are issues that will be high on the nation's agenda and will not be distinctive to any one ethnic group. If the U.S. economy continues to deteriorate or even show signs of weakness, then nonminority as well as minority citizens will increasingly be seeking new ways to maintain or improve their situation. In the past, hard times have often meant that the more secure majority has been even more resistant to sharing benefits with minorities. However, due to the increasing economic inequities and the deterioration of the middle class, the changing demographic composition of our society, and the attainment of some positions of security and influence by Latinos, such exclusion or repression can no longer occur so easily. A new, constructive, positive approach to shared interests and shared approaches to new common problems must be the result, or all segments of society will suffer.

Some domestic issues will call for particular approaches; others will call for different strategies. In order to be most effective, Latinos will have to engage in a great deal of internal assessment and evaluation. Perhaps some issues that Latinos have tried to push onto the public agenda will have to become more a responsibility of the Latino communities themselves. For example, bilingual education in the nation's public schools may have to assume the form of a transitional pedagogy if it is to be publicly supported; its function as language maintenance may have to be supported by the Latino community through the establishment of its own language and cultural educational institutions. As Ron Schmidt observes, education may be at the top of the agenda for the nation and for Latinos. The nation's public school systems are approaching a crisis stage. It is very possible that a major reformulation of their structure, support, and operation will occur in the 1990s. Latinos will find many allies among other minority groups, as well as among the majority, who will be anxious to participate in an improved reformulation of education.

Joining education as a priority issue will be our economic condition. The last part of the 1980s and the first part of the 1990s provided strong evidence that the economic situation of many Americans was worsening. The gap between rich and poor was growing. Middle- and lower-income Americans of all races and ethnic groups found themselves in increasingly dire straits and were more and more critical of traditional political institutions and processes. Faith and trust in government was diminishing rapidly. Indeed, low-income, core-culture Americans seemed to be less enthusiastic about the efficacy of themselves and their political institutions, as well as less optimistic about their future economic and political status, than are Latinos. Many Latinos are actually more enthusiastic about the possibilities of becoming a part of the system and reaping its benefits in the future (that is, being upwardly mobile) than are non-Latinos.

In this stage of internal reassessment and introspection, Latinos must give considerable attention not only to which issues to approach in what manner and to various possibilities for coalitions and alliances, but also to their own organizational situation, including the problem of leadership. Considerable thought, time, and effort must be spent on organizing resources, such as money, motivation, knowledge, and population, in the most effective manner possible. Considerable resources must also be directed to the building of a leadership cadre and to the support of these key persons in a renewed and revitalized organizational base. Latinos can neither afford the luxury of being internally divisive or nonsupportive of their leaders, nor can they be relatively unskilled in organizational activities.

In the international arena, as Cold War tensions and concern with Eastern Europe and the Soviet Union decrease, perhaps more and more of our foreign policy will be focused on the Third World areas of Asia, Africa, and Latin America. At the same time, demographic projections are that many of the new citizens of the United States will come from these latter areas. There are opportunities as never before for the United States to play a new role in a new world order characterized by peace and international understanding. As the United States becomes more and more a microcosm representative of the global population, Latinos can play a unique and significant role in relations with Latin America. However, Latinos in the United States must be major players in the politics of the United States before an international role will be appropriate.

Apparently, the 1990s will be a period of increased internationalization and globalization of politics, with the confrontation between communist and noncommunist ideologies being less significant. Democratic ideology and practice, which involves considerations of equality and the incorporation of all significant populations, will be the focus of both national and international politics in the 1990s.

Maria Torres sees democratization and incorporation coming in both the United States and Latin America and hopes that the United States will adopt a less threatening international posture. This will allow a normalization and reform of politics in Latino communities here and in Latin America.

The new Latino politics of coalitions and alliances, the strengthening of organizational bases, more internal mutual support and self-responsibility, the reexamination of the strategic and long-range importance of cultural politics, the critically differentiated approaches toward various issues, and a new and enlightened internationalism—all will have not only practical implications, but also major significance for the scholarly investigations of Latino politics. In fact, as Rodney Hero points out, Latino scholars now should incorporate newer theoretical approaches and/or use new analytical techniques that can contribute to our understanding of Latino politics in the future and can also help Latino political practitioners be more clear about their own purposes and objectives.

New approaches by scholars of Latino politics and new strategies developed by Latino political practitioners must go hand in hand as never before; that is, they must be in a symbiotic relationship in order to proceed intelligently and effectively into and through the 1990s. Smart and wise Latino politics, in its reformulated manifestations, will advance not only the well-being and happiness of Latinos, but should also have salutary effects on all Americans and indeed on all democracies, increasingly a larger and larger portion of the global community.

Self-Determination, Cultural Pluralism, and Politics

Luis Fraga

University of Notre Dame

Historically, Latino politics have been distinct from much mainstream politics in three fundamental respects. First, they have been anti–status quo. In this regard they have been a politics that have promoted change in policies, procedures of election, and overall access to governmental decision making. At times this focus on change has been antisystem, although most often the type of change advocated has been one that attempted to push American political practice to live up to reasonable interpretations of America's own political promise (Acuña, 1972; Garcia and de la Garza, 1978; Shockley, 1974). Second, they have been egalitarian. That is, the central focus of the calls for change has been to include Latino interests equal to those of middle- and upper-class Anglos, and at times African Americans, in politics (Browning, Marshall, and Tabb, 1984). This has been demonstrated most clearly in the calls for policy parity by Latino political leaders in areas such as voting, education, housing, employment, and criminal justice. Third, Latino politics have very often focused on maintaining a distinct "cultural community." The elements of this community include the Spanish language and pride in distinct origins, family relationships, celebrations, food, and, to an extent, religion. This cultural distinctiveness of Latino communities has been used to enhance popular mobilization, establish candidate credibility, and, most notably, to limit assimilation as an unquestioned goal and strategy in politics (Rendon, 1971; Acuña, 1972).

The continued presence of Latino communities in the United States with distinct political interests has been due largely to their lack of opportunity to advance within society. The barriers to advancement are well known and include discrimination, segregation, and violence. One of the primary promoters of these barriers has been an exclusionary political-

132

economic system that has allowed, if not promoted, separation from the mainstream. The lack of self-determination which Latino communities have been allowed to exercise, has enhanced the presence of cultural pluralism in the United States.

A Latino politics of the 1990s will be very distinct from its predecessors, in that the three dimensions described above will no longer be as compatible with each other. In fact, the very success, especially since the 1970s, of Latino politics in realizing both system modification and greater equality today threatens the maintenance of a cultural community with clearly distinct political interests. And it has been this sense of a distinct culture that has been the inspiration for many of the efforts directed at change and equality. Greater opportunities for the free exercise of self-determination threaten cultural pluralism for Latinos more than exclusion and exploitation ever could.

However, this disjunction between cultural maintenance and change-oriented egalitarianism can be reconciled. It will require, however, a recognition of the limits of interest-group politics and its focus on policy parity, and a much broader understanding of community that explicitly includes the public interest. It will require the attainment of what I shall term the *informed public interest*. The attainment of that reconciliation is the fundamental challenge to Latino politics in the 1990s.

To develop these concerns, I shall focus on two major criticisms that have been levied upon contemporary Latino politics and that should become even more severe in the 1990s. Each of these criticisms flows from an understanding of the major change that has occurred in the recent past in American political development. That change is the enhancement of access by African Americans and certain language minorities, including Latinos, to the system of governance through greater formal representation resulting from alterations in the systems of election and representation through the Voting Rights Act. For the six states of Arizona, California, Florida, New Mexico, New York, and Texas, the number of Latino elected officials has increased from a total of 1,185 in 1973, to as estimated 3,321 in 1989 (NALEO, 1990). This is an increase of just over 280 percent. Although the 1989 figure is still substantially below population parity, it is a dramatic increase.

An impassioned argument is made by Thernstrom (1987) and other critics of the development of the Voting Rights Act that the imposed inclusion of minority communities in formal representation leads to several undesirable consequences for the polity. The major consequence worthy of consideration is that imposed representation of racial and ethnic communities institutionalizes, and thus makes permanent, ethnic and racial conflict within the regime. Minority and nonminority representatives, the argument continues, participate within a system of representation where an incentive system has been designed to reward ethnically and racially exclusive rather than inclusive, constituency service. Cooperation and compromise, to the extent that they occur, represent aberrations in the structured legislative process. As a result, ethnicity and race continue to be dimensions through which both legislators and the public evaluate public policy. The elimination of ethnocentrism and racism in American society becomes even less likely.

This argument, which laments the structural changes that have led to greater representational equity for Latinos, is misguided in several respects. The transformation of the representational regime, which has given Latinos more of an opportunity to select their first-choice candidates to office, simply reflects identified cleavages within the polity. It neither initiates nor causes these divisions. Nonetheless, it can perpetuate their presence. To the extent that such perpetuation is achieved, it merely reflects underlying divisions within the society that have existed for many decades. It is irrational to think that a constituency will continue to identify its political interests as distinctive from a majority solely because of its representation. The constituency will identify its interests consistent with its understanding of reality. That reality is one where ethnicity and race are relevant in assessing the costs and benefits of public policy. Denying racial and ethnic cleavages does not eliminate them.

Moreover, the proponents of this argument are misguided in their implicit understanding of the representation of Latino interests as largely primordial, or, at least, inconsistent with a properly evolving polity (see the critical discussion in Rothschild, 1981). Although ethnic divisions can result in considerable violence, as has been demonstrated recently in countries as varied as Sri Lanka, the Soviet Union, Hungary, and Yugoslavia, this is unlikely to be the case for Latinos in the United States today. Contemporary ethnic representation in a polity as developed as the United States is more likely to be as sophisticated and appropriately strategic as the representation of any other interest, such as those organized by industry, labor, or region. To conclude otherwise requires that one assume that the Latino representative does not have the capacity to distinguish between advocacy and policy success in a majoritarian legislature. If the representative of a Latino constituency is to provide for his or her community, he or she must be more than an instigator of conflict. The representative must be able to convince representatives of other constituencies that his or her plan also serves their constituencies' interests in an effort to secure the necessary number of legislative votes to achieve initial enactment. Latino ethnic representation, when that representation is a minority of the interests represented in a legislature, must and can adapt to the requisites of legislative success in the modern polity. Coalition building, compromise, and the force of legislative argument and legislative politicking are the means to such success. Majoritarian legislative decision making provides no guarantees to any minority; Latino ethnic interests are no exception.

Notice the implication of the argument thus far. Because of the system modification that has provided greater representational equity to Latinos, and in order to serve the needs of Latino communities, the representative of these communities must begin a process of redefining his or her community's interests in terms that are convincing to representatives of other constituencies. What is suggested is that the representative must begin a process of politically redefining the Latino community.

Herein lies the disjunction between greater opportunity for self-determination and the maintenance of traditional cultural communities. A strong argument is made by some critics of the representatives of minority communities that this enhanced ethnic and racial formal representation has been largely symbolic and very minimally beneficial to the larger mass of the most materially disadvantaged and opportunity-disadvantaged African Americans and Latinos (see Reed, 1988). At least three major disadvantages result. First, ethnic and racial communities develop a false sense of hope that these representatives will be able to provide them with beneficial public policies. At best the representatives can provide some public policies that largely benefits middle-class elements in minority communities, such as greater municipal employment, appointments to boards and commissions, more favorable minority-firm contracting, or the pursuit of capital-directed economic growth with a faith in the benefits of "trickle down." Second, the larger Anglo community develops a false sense that real progress has been made. As a result, they either become complacent, and assume that no further access to governance need be gained by ethnic and racial communities, or accept no responsibility for developing constructive solutions to the social and economic conditions confronted by many minority communities. Third, these ethnic and racial representatives are inhibited from developing the necessary class focus in their policy analysis and advocacy, which is necessary if any real systemic change is to occur that will benefit most African Americans and Latinos. Geographically based ethnic and racial representation inhibits this interethnic class focus.

The response to these critics provides the reconciliation of the disjunction between greater self-determination and the maintenance of a distinct cultural community. The above critical analysis makes two errors. One, it incompletely understands benefits to ethnic and racial communities in terms of material parity. Material parity, of course, should be an ultimate standard with which to measure the status of segments of the population. However, there exists a prior stage in the conceptualization of material progress for minority communities. That stage is one where the public interest is broadened to include the interests of minority communities. An exclusive focus on material parity suggests a zero-sum understanding of benefit. The public interest described here understands benefit to be mutually satisfactory to minority and nonminority communities. This *informed public interest* understands viability. Minority and nonminority communities must be allowed to appreciate that not all problems for which changes may be sought are within the purview of government. This informed public interest is beyond interest group politics. Parity is an insufficient justification for the receipt of favorable policy. The informed public interest begins to make progress toward a more inclusive discourse of politics that requires all demand making to be stated and justified in terms that are acceptable to the broader, longer-term interests of the regime.

The analysis also misunderstands the nature of the community within ethnic and racial groups. How can a Latino politics that expects main-stream politics to change (that is, to adapt, evolve, and accommodate) to incorporate Latino interests not have the same expectations of change (that is, again adaptation, evolution, and accommodation) of itself? A Latino political community, like Latino culture, is not static. The 1990s will be the time when a reconsideration of the dimensions of that community will be possible. And as suggested, the major dimension to be reconsidered is the one that addresses the *sense of purpose* of the group. As a way of constructively surviving the threatening actions of mainstream society, Latinos have appropriately placed a high priority on maintaining their cultural distinctiveness. However, what has always been absent in this strategy of maintenance was a clear goal that justified the maintenance beyond maintenance. The attainment of an informed public interest can provide that purpose by requiring both representatives of Latino communities and scholars and intellectuals of Latino politics to ground their calls for policy benefit in terms consistent with the needs of the larger community.

In the end, the 1990s will be the time when Latino communities, largely through their elected representatives, will begin to outline, through self-determination, the dimensions of that public interest. It is expected that this informed public interest is likely to take Latino representatives and their constituencies away from understandings of the traditional virtues of their ethnic communities. If Latinos do not do this through self-determination, it is likely that it will be done to them by others. A change in the nature of Latino communities is inevitable. Through an understanding of purpose that contributes directly to an enlightened general polity, the preservation of a worthy Latino community is inevitable as well.

References

Acuña, Rodolfo. 1972. *Occupied America*. San Francisco: Canfield Press.

Browning, Rufus P., Dale Rogers Marshall, and David H. Tabb. 1984. *Protest Is Not Enough*. Berkeley: University of California Press.

Garcia. F. Chris, and Rodolfo O. de la Garza. 1978. *The Chicano Political Experience*. North Scituate, MA: Duxbury Press.

National Association of Latino Elected Officials (NALEO). 1990. *1989 Roster of Hispanic Elected Officials*. Washington, DC: NALEO Educational Fund.

Reed, Adolph, Jr. 1988. "The Black Urban Regime: Structural Origins and Constraints." *Comparative Urban and Community Research*, 1:138–89.

Rendon, Armando B. 1971. *Chicano Manifesto*. New York: Macmillan Publishing Co.

Rothschild, Joseph. 1981. *Ethnopolitics*. New York: Columbia University Press.

Shockley, John Staples. 1974. *Chicano Revolt in a Texas Town*. Notre Dane, IN: University of Notre Dame Press.

Thernstrom, Abigail M. 1987. *Whose Votes Count?* Cambridge, MA: Harvard University Press.

Latino Politics: A Futuristic View

Rodolfo O. de la Garza

University of Texas at Austin

D emographers predict that, given current reproductive and immigration trends, Latinos will be the nation's largest minority group by the year 2010. Understandably, Latino leaders often use these projections to assert that Latinos will be a formidable political force in the future. Making such claims is much easier than realizing them, however, and if they unrealistically raise expectations, such assertions may have negative consequences.

Rather than rely exclusively on demographic projections to estimate future Latino political influence, it is useful to consider the effects of additional factors that, given our current understanding of Latinos and American society, will affect the political future of Latinos. These additional factors may be broken down into endogenous and exogenous categories; that is, those factors that Latinos are in a position to influence substantially and those that are largely beyond their influence. The major exogenous factors are immigration, national and state-level conditions, party competition, legal decisions, and national shifts in public opinion. The principal endogenous factors include Latino organizations, naturalization and the political incorporation of immigrants, development of a pan-national origin identity, relations with blacks, and patterns of electoral participation.

It should be obvious that the line between these categories is not fixed, and that today's exogenous factors could become endogenous in the future. Moreover, endogenous variables are not necessarily more significant than are the exogenous to future Latino political influence. For example, continued large-scale illegal immigration and prolonged economic recession could give rise to substantial increases in anti-Latino sentiments among the general public, which could become manifest in public policy and party platforms. Court decisions, particularly regarding affirmative action, reapportionment, and redistricting, could dramatically increase or

137

decrease Latino political clout. Changes in levels of party competitiveness could similarly alter Latino political influence. If, for example, Anglo identification with the Democratic party continues to diminish, resulting in expanding Republican hegemony, Latinos, who in sizeable majorities identify themselves as Democrats, may find themselves increasingly influential within a party whose influence continuously declines.

As has been noted, however, such developments are essentially beyond Latino control. Therefore, the remainder of this paper will examine those factors that will affect future Latino political power and that they can directly influence.

Latino Organizations

Although several Latino organizations have long histories, their presence as national organizations and as participants in national policymaking is a recent phenomenon. The beginnings of their effective presence in Washington can be traced to the Carter years of 1976–1980 (de la Garza, 1984). Ironically, it was also during those years that their combined presence and influence reached its apogee. The Reagan administration ushered in a less-hospitable political environment and sharply reduced the programs with which many of these organizations were involved. Since then, Latino organizational presence in Washington has declined in terms of both the number of organizations still active and the size of their staffs. Today, players include the National Council de la Raza (NCLR), the National Association of Latino Elected Officials (NALEO), Aspira, the National Puerto Rican Coalition, the Mexican American Legal Defense and Education Fund (MALDEF), the Congressional Hispanic Caucus, the League of United Latin American Citizens (LULAC), and the National Coalition of Hispanic Health and Human Services Organizations (COSSMO). While some of these may have an important impact on specific issues (NCLR and, to a lesser extent, NALEO seem to have influence on a wide range of issues), overall it is difficult to discern their collective influence on policy. For example, Senator Moynihan's 1988 welfare reform reflects attention to the conditions of the black community but not to the situation of Latinos, suggesting that these organizations were unable to affect the shaping of this key legislation. Similarly, although Latino organizations did influence key aspects of the Immigration Reform and Control Act (IRCA) of 1986, IRCA was enacted despite vigorous protestations by NCLR and others that it would result in anti-Latino discrimination (de la Garza, 1991).

All of these organizations have limited autonomy because of virtual dependency on funding sources, such as the corporate world, foundations, and federal contracts, that are beyond their control. Corporate donations are of diminishing utility since these are disproportionately from the alcohol and tobacco industry, both of which are under increasing attack for targeting minority populations now that Anglo America is becoming abstemious (Maxwell and Jacobson, 1989). Foundations are neither reliable nor permanent sources of funds, and their support diminishes as their priorities shift or as political conditions change (Oppenneimer-Nicolau and Santiestevan, 1990). The once-vibrant National Association of Chicanos in Higher Education became moribund when it lost foundation funds. The Southwest Voter Registration Project has suffered substantial declines in funding despite undeniably significant achievements and continued patterns of electoral participation. As noted previously, changes in federal priorities between the Carter and Reagan administrations affected service organizations similarly. To the extent that these shortcomings are overcome, that is, as Latino organizations increase the support they receive from their own constituents, their individual and collective influence will increase. This is a principal reason why the Cuban American National Foundation, a newcomer to the Latino world of organizations but one that receives its funds primarily from its members, is so effective (Moreno, 1990). Cubans, it must be recognized, are more affluent than other Latino groups. Nonetheless, there is no doubt that the expanded Mexican American and Puerto Rican middle and upper-middle class has resources with which to increase substantially the support it provides Latino organizations. The continued absence of such support points either to a major weakness in the collective commitment to Latino issues from the Latino community or to an indictment of Latino organizations for their inability to tap that commitment.

It would also seem especially important for Latino organizations to develop an effective unified umbrella organization, so that Latino views would be continuously and effectively voiced on a wide range of issues. This would be possible so long as the organization focused on domestic issues toward which Latinos of various national origins share a general consensus (Pachon and DeSipio, 1990). Such an organization could function without threatening the individual identities of its membership. At present, while there is increased cooperation among the several key groups, the possibility of formal institutionalized collaboration is uncertain.

Another institutional void that Latinos need to fill is in the area of research organizations. There is currently nothing for Latinos like the Joint Center for Political Studies, which speaks out regularly and authoritatively from an intellectual perspective on black political and economic issues. The Tomas Rivera Center and the National Council de la Raza have fledgling efforts in this regard, but both suffer from the suspicion that their product reflects their role as advocacy groups. The Inter-University Program for Latino Research is also a fledgling organization that may evolve to play the kind of role described here. However it comes into being, such an organization is essential if Latinos are to be in a position to influence policy.

Relatedly, there is no mechanism for an ongoing dialogue between the Latino intelligentsia and Latino political leaders. The recent appearance of popular publications that appeal to mass Latino audiences notwithstanding, there is no magazine such as *The New Republic* or the *Nation* where issues are raised and debated. There are few newspapers with editorial pages that systematically include columns on Latino issues and Latino perspectives of national and international issues. There are also no national radio or television programs that voice these views. Without such outlets, it will remain difficult for Latinos to develop, clarify, and communicate their arguments to themselves and to the nation at large.

Naturalization and the Political Incorporation of Immigrants

For decades, Latino citizens did nothing to stimulate naturalization among Latino immigrants. Now, led by NALEO, organizations are recognizing that this is the most untapped segment of the potential Latino electorate, and they have initiated naturalization and political incorporation campaigns. As recently as 1980, Mexicans did not rank among the top ten immigrant groups in terms of naturalization rates. Since 1985, they have ranked among the top three (Immigration and Naturalization Service, 1988:92).

As naturalization and incorporation efforts continue, the number of Latino voters will increase dramatically. In 1988, there were Latinos ineligible to vote because of noncitizenship than there were Latino voters (NALEO, 1989a:v). However, Latino immigrants cite the desire to vote in U.S. elections as a principal reason for naturalizing. More significantly, 81 percent of Latino naturalized citizens register to vote, compared to 70 percent of the nation at large (NALEO, 1989b). This, initiatives focusing on mobilizing naturalized immigrants into electoral politics are likely to enjoy substantial success.

It should be noted that naturalization efforts will affect the several Latino groups of different origin differently. As native-born citizens, Puerto Ricans find them irrelevant. Cubans will be decreasingly affected since immigration from Cuba has slowed dramatically, and it is likely that those who came and wanted to naturalize probably have already done so. The population of Mexican origin, especially in the Southwest where it is concentrated, will be most affected since it makes up approximately 65 percent of the total Latino population nationally. In the Southwest it constitutes over 90 percent. Central Americans are another group that could be specifically targeted for significant results. These differential impacts could increase the role that Mexican Americans play in national Latino initiatives.

Development of a National Identity

Preliminary results from the Latino National Political Survey (LNPS) indicate that traditional labels of national origin such as "Mexican American," "Puerto Rican"' and "Cuban" are overwhelmingly preferred to inclusive terms such as "Hispanic" or "Latino." Furthermore, more LNPS respondents prefer to identify as "American" than as "Latino," and only slightly more prefer "Hispanic" to "American." Relatedly, when asked if all Hispanics/Latinos are very similar or not very similar culturally, significantly more selected the latter. Even more noteworthy is the fact that respondents overwhelmingly agree that the political interests of Cubans, Mexican Americans, and Puerto Ricans are not very similar (de la Garza et al., 1990).

Rhetoric aside, much is yet to be done if the several national-origin groups are to develop a shared identity that may be accommodated under one label such as "Hispanic" or "Latino" (Garcia and Garza, 1990; Ortiz and Brownstein-Santiago, 1990). Many factors, such as geographical dispersion, history, and policy preferences impede the creation of such an identity. There is also considerable resistance in some quarters to its growth. Noteworthy leaders of the several national-origin groups, for example, have protested against such an identity. It should not be assumed, therefore, that such an identity will evolve automatically. Without such an identity, it will be difficult for Latino leaders to maximize their potential political clout as they need it. For such an identity to become real, therefore, leaders may have to develop specific strategies to win over their respective constituencies.

Relations with Blacks

The quality of Latino-black relations will have an important impact on the political status of Latinos in the future. While it is often claimed that Latinos and blacks are part of a rainbow coalition that will lead to a majority-minority dominant coalition, there is also evidence that major issues may divide the two (Perspectives, 1980; Chaves, 1990). These include

1. Resentment among many blacks over Latino access to affirmative action programs that blacks believe were designed for them (Changing Relations Project Reports,[1] 1990).
2. Tensions because of the perception that immigration results in job displacement and the reallocation of public resources to Latinos rather than to blacks.
3. Tensions resulting from Latino population growth that produces Latino majorities in schools that previously had black majorities, administrators and staff. Latino demands for curricular reform and staffing changes thus become Latino-black competitions. Similar results occur because of the Latinoization of police forces and the all-too-frequent charges of police brutality against Latino cops by blacks. Miami and Houston in particular are experiencing these situations.
4. Battles over reapportionment and redistricting. Population is the foundation for allocating legislative seats. The number of state legislative seats is fixed, while the number of congressional seats allocated to each state may vary slightly as a result of the census. Given that, in cities with substantial Latino and black populations, these groups

often live in juxtaposition and that Latino population growth greatly exceeds black population growth, any increase in legislative seats designed to accommodate the growth of the Latino population could come at the expense of blacks (see O'Hare, 1989).

Mutually satisfactory responses to these issues would obviously benefit both groups. Such outcomes will not be easily achieved, and Latino and black leaders will therefore need to be diligent to avoid the divisiveness that could result from exacerbating these differences.

Patterns of Electoral Participation

Latino political futures will greatly differ depending on whether the following patterns change or are maintained:

1. Latino, especially Mexican American and Puerto Rican, voters turnout at rates far lower than rates for whites or blacks. In 1988, 62, 54, and 46 percent of eligible Anglo, black, and Latino adults voted, respectively. Latino influence will remain minimal so long as this trend continues.
2. Mexican Americans and Puerto Ricans vote solidly Democratic. This will increase their influence within the Democratic party but may decrease their overall influence if the Democratic party continues to decline in influence. In other words, Mexican Americans and Puerto Ricans may play key roles in selecting the Democratic nominees for statewide and national office, but that is of little benefit when those candidates lose the general election.
3. Younger, more affluent Mexican American voters switch to the Republican party or become independents (Garcia, 1987:13), as evidenced by the increase in high-level appointments by former President Reagan and President bush and by Republican governors in key states such as Texas and California. Ironically, however, in Florida, Cuban support for the Republican party may liberalize the party on domestic policy; that is, Cuban support may move it toward increased support for social spending and opposition to nativist language policies (Moreno, 1990). If this trend also develops among Mexican American Republicans, it could push both parties to respond more positively to Latino domestic policy concerns.

Conclusion

These factors suggest that the opportunity exists for Latinos to significantly improve their political status, but they also point out obstacles that could limit such gains. At present, the factor most likely to increase Latino political clout is naturalization. Ironically, a second positive trend is in the increased bipartisanship of Latinos. The most serious problems have to do with Latino electoral turnout and black-Latino relations. The former is a

long-standing problem that has not significantly improved despite elimi-
nating the barriers, such as English-only ballots, strict registration requirements, and at-large election systems, that have been used to explain low
rates of electoral participation.

In conclusion, Latinos are in a position to increase their political clout in
the 1990s. The extent to which they do so will depend on factors beyond
population growth. Latino leaders would therefore do well to focus on
those factors and forego population-based predictions that, if taken seriously, could have negative effects. After all, Latinos are unlikely to mobilize if they believe that numbers alone will make them politically powerful.

Notes

1. The Changing Relations Projects was a two-year ethnographic study of relations between established residents and immigrants in six cities. Rodolfo O. de
   la Garza is a member of the project Board. Contact him for further information
   regarding the project.

References

Changing Relations Project Reports. 1990. See note 1.
Chavez, Linda. 1990. "Rainbow Collision." *The New Republic*, 19 November, pp.
14–16.
de la Garza, Rodolfo O. 1984. "And Then There Were Some: The Role of Chicanos
as National Political Actors, 1967–1980." *Aztlan*, 15, no. 1 (Spring): 1–24.
_____. 1991. "Immigration Reform as a Civil Rights Issue: A Mexican American
Perspective." In Gillian Peele and Bruce Cain, eds., *Developments in American
Politics*. London: Macmillan Education Limited.
de la Garza, Rodolfo O., Angelo Falcon, F. Chris Garcia, and John Garcia. 1990.
Unpublished results from the Latino National Political Survey.
Garcia, F. Chris. 1987. "Comments on Papers Presented on the Panel on Latinos
and the 1984 Election." In R. O. de la Garza, ed., *Ignored Voices: Public Opinion
Polls and the Latino Community*. Austin, TX: Center for Mexican American Stud-
ies, University of Texas.
Garcia, John, and Mlita Garza. 1990. "Common Experiences Meld Diverse His-
panic Groups." *Hispanic Link*, 24 September, p. 3.
Immigration and Naturalization Service Statistical Yearbook, 1988. Washington, DC:
Immigration and Naturalization Service.
Maxwell, Bruce, and Michael Jacobson. 1989. *Marketing Disease to Hispanics*. Wash-
ington, DC: Center for Science in the Public Interest.
Moreno, Dario, 1990. "The Political Empowerment of Cuban-Americans." Paper
presented at Inter-University Program for Latino Research Conference, San
Luis Obispo, May 25-26.
Moreno, Dario, and Nicol Rae. Forthcoming. "The Conservative Enclave: Cubans
in Florida." In R. O. de la Garza and Louis DeSipio, eds., *Latinos and the 1988
Election*. Austin, TX: Center for Mexican American Studies, University of Texas.
National Association of Latino Elected and Appointed Officials (NALGO). 1989a.
National Roster of Hispanic elected Officials. Washington, DC.
_____. 1989b. 7 September. Press Release.

O'Hare, William P. 1989. *Redistricting in the 1990s: A Guide for Minority Groups.* Washington, DC: Population Reference Bureau.

Oppenneimer-Nicolau, Siobhan, and Henry Santiestevan. 1990. *From the Eye of the Storm.* Washington, DC: Hispanic Policy Development Program.

Ortiz, Vilma, and Cheryl Brownstein-Santiago. 1990. "Unifying Label Vital for Latino Empowerment." *Hispanic Link*, 17 September, p. 3.

Pachon, Harry, and Louis DeSipio. 1990. "Latino Legislators and Latino Caucuses." *New Directions for Latino Public Policy Research*, Working Paper no. 11. IUP/SSRC Committee for Public Policy Research on Contemporary Hispanic Issues, The Center for Mexican American Studies, University of Texas at Austin.

Perspectives, pp. 12–18. 1980. Washington, DC: U.S. Commission on Civil Rights.

Latino Politics in the 1990s:
A View from California

Ronald J. Schmidt

California State University, Long Beach

T he aim of this essay is to identify and articulate some of the key challenges facing Latino politics in the United States for the next decade. For several decades a central preoccupation of those political scientists who had a special interest in the Latino populations of the United States has been the problem of "empowerment": Why do Latinos not have a power position in the United States political economy commensurate with their numbers? How do they get their "fair share"? This essay stands within that tradition of enquiry, and it argues that the 1990s will be a crucial decade for Latinos because of the inexorable working out of demographic and economic changes that have been in motion for at least twenty-five years. The essay will focus primarily on California—partly because this state has by far the largest number of Latinos (34 percent of Latinos in the United States, according to the Census Bureau in 1988), and partly because the forces highlighted herein are most advanced in California and may, therefore, be harbingers for the future of Latino politics generally.

The *demographic* story underlying this analysis has been often repeated: it is a story of the unprecedented and explosive growth of the Latino population. There is not space to repeat the story here. Suffice it to say that Latinos are experiencing the greatest numerical increase of any ethnic group in the nation (a 34 percent growth rate in the 1980s, according to the Census Bureau, compared to 7 percent growth rate for the population as a whole), and demographers expect that early in the next century it will be the largest minority group in our population (Houston, 1988; Valdivieso and Davis, 1988).

In California, as elsewhere in the Southwest, Latinos have been the largest minority ethnic group for some time, and demographers expect that the 1990 census will show that 25 percent of the state's population is Latino. A recent report, moreover, predicts that the population in California will be 30 percent Latino by 2000, that Anglos will lose their majority status by the end of the century, and that Anglos and Latinos will constitute roughly equal portions of the state's population about twenty years later (Roderick, 1990).

In addition to the sheer numbers, it is politically important to note that the growth stems almost equally from two sources: massive immigration, and relatively high birth rates in the Latino population. These sources of growth are important politically because, in addition to ensuring that a significant portion of the Latino population will be ineligible to vote (as noncitizens), both together ensure that this population will be relatively young. Thus in 1988 the median age in the United States was 32.2 years, compared to only 25.5 years for Latinos (Valdivieso and Davis, 1988:3).

It is a truism in political science that young people have a significantly lower rate of participation in politics than do their elders, and several recent surveys of American youth indicate that this is an even more pronounced pattern with the present generation of young adults (Oreskes, 1990). This may help to account for the fact that voters in recent California elections have had a median age over 50, and it is estimated that it will reach 60 by the end of the century (Walters, 1990:17). These demographic realities may also help to account for the fact that in the 1986 statewide elections in California, Anglos made up 57 percent of the population but 85 percent of the electorate, while Latinos composed almost 25 percent of the population and only 6 percent of the voters (Walters, 1989). The point to be emphasized, in any case, is that one of the principal challenges for Latino empowerment in the 1990s will continue to be the huge task of political incorporation—not only the incorporation of Latino immigrants but of a whole generation of the young as well.

The second change to be highlighted here in relation to Latino empowerment is economic. Both conservative (Phillips, 1990) and liberal (Zeitlin, 1990) political analysts have recently emphasized that one of the most important changes in the U.S. political economy in the last decade was significant growth of economic inequality and a decline of the middle class as a proportion of the U.S. population. Latinos, along with the African-American population, have been particularly affected by these economic changes. A 1989 report issued by the National Council of La Raza found a significant drop in Latino family income in the 1980s, and a concomitant increase in the proportion of Latinos living below the poverty line. Most discouraging was the finding that poverty increased among married-couple Latino families, from 13.1 percent to 16 percent (Davis, 1989).

And once again this phenomenon seems to be particularly pronounced in California, where publicists and analysts routinely refer to the state's developing "two-tier" economy or to the emergence within the state of a "Third-World" economy of enlarging rich and poor classes and a declining middle class (Leigh, 1990; Tietz and Shapira, 1989; Ong et al., 1989). This phenomenon has been particularly significant in its impact on Latinos in California. Recent studies on Southern California's economy, where the concentration of Latinos is highest, have found substantial increases in below-poverty-level wages for full-time workers. Not surprisingly, there-fore, Latinos made up 64 percent of Los Angeles county's low-wage, full-time workers in 1987, but 34 percent of the county's population (Ong et al., 1989:36). Similarly, in 1986–1987 Chicano males in Los Angeles, County had average earnings equal to only 61.4 percent of Anglo male earnings, lower than those of any other racial or ethnic group (Ong et al., 1989:90).

In summary, the economic changes of the past decade have not been kind to the Latino community in California or nationally. As was true of the United States population as a whole, the 1980s brought upper-scale Latinos increased prosperity, but the growing number of Latinos at the bottom of the economic scale found themselves with a decreasing propor-tion of the nation's wealth. By 1988, in fact, the Tomas Rivera Center had convened a conference to analyze the question of whether William J. Wilson's analysis of the "underclass" could be used accurately to under-stand the large and growing impoverished segment of the Latino popu-lation.

The point to be emphasized here is that the intersection of the two changes highlighted above—the demographic and the economic—has im-mense political importance for Latinos, and increasingly, for the nation as a whole. Taken by themselves, as noted above, the demographic changes in the community represent an enormous challenge of political incorpo-ration. Yet those changes cannot be taken alone, for the deterioration of the Latino community's economic position poses equally serious political challenges. That is, just as youthfulness and noncitizenship affect the power position of the Latino community, so too does its economic base. For it is also a truism in political science that low-income groups—particularly those not organized into unions or other such associations—play a lesser role in politics and wield far less power than do the more affluent (Wolfinger and Rosenstone, 1980). Without the intervention of other political factors, then, the intersection of the demographic and eco-nomic changes described above may be expected to reduce the power position of Latinos in the United States over the next decade, despite their increasing numerical importance in the general population.

Latino political elites (and indeed all who are concerned about the well-being of the nation), then, face some serious questions of strategy and policy. Challenges to minority vote dilution such as gerrymandering or citywide elections, will continue to be important, as will support for var-ious forms of ethnic-preference policy (for example, affirmative action hiring, minority set-aside programs for contractors, or broadcasting li-censes). The data presented above, however, lead me to argue that these efforts—by themselves—will be insufficient to change the power position of the Latino community in the decade ahead. The maturation of a huge generation of Latino youths—many of whom are poor, many of whom are not citizens of the United States, most of whom can be expected to have little impulse toward political participation—represents a demographic and economic wave likely to overwhelm the effects of even successful law suits to counter vote dilution and to sustain ethnic-preference policies.

What are the implications of these data, then, for a strategy of empowerment for Latinos? First, the generation of Latino youths represents an enormous pool of human resources and political potential that cannot be allowed to go waste (see Hayes-Bautista, Schink, and Chapa, 1988 for a related analysis). This means that public education must remain at the top of the Latino policy agenda and must be moved to the top of the national agenda generally. The evidence is overwhelming that educational attainment is the single most important variable in determining rates of political participation (Wolfinger and Rosenstone, 1980:23–30) and in determining the occupational tier of a given worker in our increasingly two-tier economy (Leigh, 1990). Yet during the 1980s Latinos continued to fall farther behind the population as a whole in levels of educational attainment (Houston, 1988).

Again, however, even successful educational reform is not sufficient to rectify the problem of Latino empowerment in the United States political economy. For there are structural changes in both the political and economic sectors that need to be addressed as well. After all, the transformation of California's economy toward a Third-World pattern is not simply a function of low educational attainment among the recent immigrant population. Rather, structural changes in global economic relationships, abetted by the policies of the past two Republican administrations, have been instrumental in the decline of the middle class and in the impoverishment of low-wage workers. Growth sectors in the past several decades have been in low-wage and high-wage service occupations, while the manufacturing sector, which provided a toehold into the middle class for many Latinos in the previous generation, has suffered a decline. A serious effort at coming to grips with the subject of Latino empowerment, then, will require a political strategy that addresses questions of economic class and inequality (see Torres, 1988 for an elaborated analysis of this point).

Structural changes in the nation's political system, finally, must also be addressed on the Latino agenda for the 1990s. A century ago, the last great wave of immigrants to this country was incorporated into the polity through political party machines with a strong motive to encourage immigrants to become citizens and to vote (Buenker, 1978). Today, however, the process of becoming a citizen is no longer under the control of the party machines nor, indeed, are there party machines in the same sense. In "reformed" states like California, political parties can scarcely be said to exist at all, outside the legislature or the minds of potential voters when they register for primary elections. Without effective party organizations, politicians bent on winning election are far more fixated on raising the enormous sums necessary to pay for their advertising campaigns than they are in recruiting young people, immigrants, or the poor into the political system.

Still, numbers count in electoral political regimes. Given the political motivation and organizational base, the vast number of Latinos *can* be converted into large numbers of votes, which *can* be converted into political power and a transformed policy agenda. The point is that the same demographic data—large numbers of youth and recent migrants to the United States—presently resulting in lower political participation rates could be converted into the Latino community's greatest political asset. The task is to build the organizational and programmatic bases from which these incorporation and conversion processes can be mounted. Ultimately, this is the primary challenge for Latino politics in the 1990s.

References

Buenker, John D. 1978. *Urban Liberalism and Progressive Reform*. New York: W. W. Norton & Co., Inc.

Davis, Kevin. 1989. "Latino Poverty Grew over Decade, Study Finds." *Los Angeles Times*, 16, December A28.

Hayes-Bautista, David E., Werner O. Schink, and Jorge Chapa. 1988. *The Burden of Support: Young Latinos in an Aging Society*. Palo Alto: Stanford University Press.

Houston, Paul. 1988. "Census Bureau Says More Latinos Finish Education." *Los Angeles Times*, 7, September, I14.

Leigh, Nancey Green. 1990. "What Happened to the American Dream? Changing Earning Opportunities and Prospects of Middle-Class Californians, 1967–1987." *California History* 68, no. 4 (Winter 1989/90): 240–47.

Ong, Paul, et al. 1989. *The Widening Divide: Income Inequality and Poverty in Los Angeles*. Los Angeles: UCLA School of Architecture and Urban Planning.

Oreskes, Michael. 1990. "Profiles of Today's Youths: Many Just Don't Seem to Care." *New York Times*, 28, June pp. A1, 11.

Phillips, Kevin. 1990. "Reagan's America: A Capital Offense." *New York Times Magazine*, 17, June 26–28, 40, 64.

Roderick, Kevin, 1990. "Californians: 30 Million and Counting." *Los Angeles Times*, 16, May pp. A1, 16.

Teitz, Michael B., and Philip Shapira. 1989. "Growth and Turbulence in the California Economy." In Rodwin and Sazanami, eds., *Deindustrialization and Regional Economic Transformation: the Experience of the United States*. Winchester, MA: Unwin and Hyman.

Torres, Rodolfo D. 1988. *Latinos in the U.S. Economy: A Critique and Reformulation of Theories of Income Inequality and Policy Alternatives*. New York: Centro de Estudios Puertorriquenos, Hunter College, City University of New York.

Valdivieso, Rafael, and Cary Davis. 1988. "U.S. Hispanics: Challenging Issues for the 1990s." *Population Trends and Public Policy*, no. (December): 1–16.

Walters, Dan. 1989. "The 'New' California." A keynote speech presented to the Conference on "Envisioning California," Sacramento, February.

_____. 1990. "California: A State of Change." Pp. 1–18 in Walters, ed., *California Political Almanac, 1989-90 Edition*. Santa Barbara: Pacific Data Resources.

Wolfinger, Raymond E., and Steven J. Rosenstone. 1980. *Who Votes?* New Haven: Yale University Press.

Zeitlin, Maurice. 1990. "U.S. Misery in Inequality: Ignoring the Grim Truths." *Los Angeles Times*, 20, May pp. M4, 8.

Will Cuba Be Next? What about Miami?

Maria Torres

DePaul University

A decade ago, as thousands of people jammed the Peruvian Embassy in Havana trying to leave Cuba, Cuban-American newspapers and radio stations heralded the downfall of Fidel Castro.

Today, again, Cuba watchers are debating whether Castro will last beyond this year. Some are arguing that this time tougher U.S. measures against Cuba will guarantee his downfall.

U.S.-Cuban relations frame the contours of Cuban-American politics. For Cuban Americans, their future is intimately tied to the successful resolution of thirty years of conflict.

Aging Cuban-American organizations have set up military training camps, as they have for the last thirty years every time it looked like the Revolution was faltering. Added to the exiles' arsenal are government committees studying ways of quickening Cuba's government's demise and bracing for the imminent impact that such changes will bring to south Florida. Miami's Police Department has contingency plans for the night of festivities once Castro falls. Self-anointed presidential hopefuls, such as Jorge Mas Canosa, have hired experts, including Milton Friedman, to concoct economic and political plans for their future governments.

There is no doubt that Cuba's government is at a crossroads. A critical part of its international economic and political frame of reference is in flux. All over the world, state-controlled planned economies are decentralizing and privatizing. One-party political structures are giving way to multiparty representation. The ideological and practical aspects of these changes are beginning to have a profound impact on Cuban society.

Nevertheless, at least two important facts differentiate the Cuban situation. First, Cuba's government came to power through a popular revolution, a factor not present at least in the case of the nations of Eastern Europe. Second, since the first U.S. incursion into Cuban politics in 1898,

150

Cubans have perceived the United States as an intruder—much like Poles viewed the Soviets—and viewed Castro, like Walesa, as the person who unshackled his people from their oppressor.

These two facts in and of themselves do not guarantee the survival of the present government. They do, however, continue to frame the political debate in Cuba. This is especially true after the U. S. invasion of Panama, which served as an unsettling reminder to Cubans of the available political alternatives in Latin America.

The changes in Eastern Europe are an important impetus for debate in Cuba, but beyond the backdrop of the East/West view is a more critical challenge to the system from inside: that posed by Cuba's younger generations. Most people in Cuba today were born after the Revolution. Their educational, social, and, in most cases, economic standing are a result of the successes of the Revolution. While the majority of Cubans may have had harder lives without the Revolution, they have no life experience with which to internalize this distinction. Thus, they have become a catalyst for change.

Most of these young people have a stake in the present-day system, so they seek not to overthrow or substantively change the regime, but merely to participate in its future in a more democratic fashion. They do not rule out the possibilities of direct elections of the members of the National Assembly or of the president, and they are enthusiastic about Gorbachev's reforms.

Generational pressure is also a growing reality in the Cuban-American community in the United States, as its younger members are increasingly disinclined to support attempts to take over the island. Most believe that change will occur in Cuba through internal processes. They are curious about their parents' homeland, but more concerned with their lives in the United States. Increasingly they advocate for a more democratic culture in their own community.

Both in Cuba and in the Cuban-American community, debate about the future of Cuba or U.S.-Cuban relations is extremely difficult.

In Cuba, while broad discussions are taking place within the confines of the party, in public people are rallied into a unified position allowing little room for debate or dissent. Human rights activists are accused of being agents of the United States government and are jailed under laws that prohibit the right of assembly and criticism.

Last year the FBI named Miami the capital of U. S. terrorism, after eighteen bombs went off in the homes and businesses of Cuban-Americans working to better relations with Cuba. Hard-line organizations, such as the Cuban-American National Foundation, accuse those who support better relations with Cuba of being agents of the Castro government. They throw their repressive weight around in Washington and in Cuban-American communities throughout the United States. Recent examples of this occurred when Foundation members successfully lobbied State Department officials to deny visas to the world-famous Cuban Orquesta Aragon, who was to perform in a city-sponsored event in Chicago. They were also involved in urging Treasury Department agents to break into the home of Ramon Cernuda, director of a Miami-based Museum of Cuban Art, in the middle of the night to confiscate his paintings, because some had been painted by artists living in Cuba. The courts found that Cernuda's constitutional rights had been violated, and many were deeply troubled about the antidemocratic nature of the political culture propagated by conservative exiles.

It is interesting to note that there is a debate about a more democratic culture between generations of Cubans on both sides of the Florida Straits. Aggressive U. S. policies toward Cuba have had the effect of furthering the position of the antidemocrats on the island and in the United States.

Meaningful political and economic openings in relations with Cuba occurred during the Carter administration, when policies were aimed at negotiating with the Cuban government rather than at attacking the regime. Political prisoners were released, elections were held, and free peasant and craft markets flourished.

It seems clear that the United States needs a more productive alternative to the thirty-year-old, unsuccessful, policy of harsh posturing and an economic embargo aimed at strangling the island government—TV Marti being the latest example. Simply opening up relations and encouraging exchanges would be a more engaging and constructive approach. Removing Cuba's most notorious external threat would inevitably contribute to opening the political space on the island. It would also allow the Cuban-American community to rid itself of its obsession with overthrowing the current Cuban government. And this would help Cuban-Americans to normalize their politics.

The only ones who would object to such an approach are those who are not really concerned with economic and political progress in Cuba or in the Cuban-American community, but who, rather, are interested in holding on to their own power—whether in Havana or Miami.

Questions and Approaches in Understanding Latino Politics: The Need for Clarification and Bridging

Rodney E. Hero

University of Colorado, Boulder

Understanding "Latino Politics in the 1990s" is an important task both in terms of actual, practical politics, and in terms of how those politics are studied. There are a number of significant issues that have, to this point, affected the *study of* Latino politics and that are likely to continue to do so into the 1990s. Several issues that seem particularly significant regarding research approaches and questions about Latino politics will be noted and addressed in this discussion. The comments offered below also seek to underscore the need for conceptual clarification and theoretical bridging. That is, it appears that names or labels, concepts, and the like have been used ambiguously or too casually in the study of Latino politics. Also, the literature on mainstream politics and cognate research on Latino politics have not been brought together adequately.

Major questions that require more careful attention in the study of Latino politics include definitions of the phenomena and of descriptions of the theoretical approaches, assumptions, and questions that underlie scholarly (and popular) efforts to understand and comprehend Latino politics. It can be noted at the outset that the very notion of Latino politics implies separate and distinctive social and political phenomena that are neither simple nor easily understood. But, to a considerable degree, these matters have not been well understood or have not been adequately accounted for in much, perhaps most, research and discussion. This, then, is one area where the study of Latino politics raises important theoretical and empirical questions that are closely interrelated.

Individual self-identification is a major issue, which has ostensible implications for group behavior as well as for group political and social

153

cohesiveness (Lampe, 1982). Ethnic identification is often taken for granted in much social science research, and political science research has probably taken this issue for granted to a greater degree than other social science disciplines (cf., however, Garcia, 1981). The subtlety and complexity of identification issues and processes have been recognized and debated extensively (Munoz, 1989; Acuña, 1988; Garcia, 1981). It has been increasingly perceived that identity is itself an issue or "problematic" worthy of attention; that it may, indeed should, be seen as a dependent variable and not solely as an independent variable. The creation and use of particular labels (such as "Mexican American," "Chicano," "Latino," or "Hispanic" is not just a simple act of naming. Rather, it situates or constitutes individuals and groups. There is, in short, a political and/or social construction of ethnicity that must be understood as part of the study of Latino politics. But that has not influenced how issues of Latino politics are studied. The simple, easy acceptance and use of official group designations, particularly the Census Bureau's term "Hispanics," needs to be understood as itself political. Inattentiveness to this may also introduce theoretical and methodological imprecision into research.

Studies of Latino politics also raise questions concerning appropriate theories or explanations, theories that have broader implications for the understanding of American politics. Despite considerable questioning and criticism, much if not most of the research on Latino politics has implicitly followed a pluralist or behavioralist approach (cf. Garcia and de la Garza, 1977). By and large, the assumption has been that Latinos are like most other ethnic groups, and are but one of a number of groups that compete with other groups for political influence on a relatively equal basis. Therefore, the focus has been on traditional, conventional questions of "normal" politics, even though, the notion of a Latino politics implies significant differences. There are reasons to question the adequacy of such an interpretation for Latino politics, even in pluralism's modified forms (see, for example, Manley, 1983 on "neopluralism" and "pluralism I and II").

There have been few analyses that consciously incorporate alternative perspectives on Latino politics such as "coalitional bias" or "systemic power" interpretations (Stone, 1986, 1980; cf. Flores, 1989). Coalitional bias suggests that in day-to-day governance all groups are not looked upon as equally desirable coalition partners, and that ethnic or racial and social-class status are often intertwined, serving as cues to what groups are more or less desirable, more or less socially and politically important. Systemic power arguments alert scholars to the significant ways in which power is exercised through the "logic of situations" and indirectly, not just in readily apparent and direct ways. Better understanding of contemporary minority politics requires attention to these possibilities.

Similarly, much of the research has focused on a number of political research issues that gained prominence in the 1960s; primary among these is the impact of governmental structure—particularly district versus at-large elections— on the election of Latinos to city council positions (Bullock and MacManus, 1989; Hero and Beatty, 1989). These are not unimportant questions (Meier, Stewart, and England, 1989). But the substantive sig-

nificance of the election of "ethnics" to city councils and to mayoral positions—where Latino election has occurred most frequently—may have
been overstated historically (Wolfinger, 1974; Erie, 1985). And those elections seem increasingly less significant in light of broader social developments, and related theorizing, in the 1980s.

There have been a number of scholars—from rather different ideological
perspectives—who have pointed to major alterations and changes in the
status of urban governments. Peterson (1981) has argued that cities should
avoid redistributive policies, presumably those policies most germane to
Latinos and other disadvantaged groups, and stress developmental policies; allocational policies are a third type. Building on Peterson's arguments, Sharp (1990) has contended that urban politics are bifurcated between
allocational policies—which include such matters as police patrol alloca-
tions, snow removal, trash collection—and developmental politics. Allocational policies tend to have high levels of visibility and controversy, and,
to a considerable degree, allocational policies may reflect an overall plu-
ralistic pattern of power. Developmental policies, which are presumably
at the heart of urban governmental concerns, most often have low visibility and conflict and exhibit an elitist pattern of power, dominated by
banking, corporate, and development interests. Redistributive policies,
Sharp implies, are, at most, peripheral. Others who question the role of
contemporary cities are Gottdiener (1987), who has written of the "decline
of urban politics," and Kantor (1988), who writes of the "dependent city"
(also see Elkin, 1987).

To be sure, these interpretations have been challenged; nonetheless,
they cannot be ignored, and they have had a major impact on thinking and
analysis of urban politics. Yet much of the mainstream research, particularly what might be called the "empirical/behavioral" work, has either not
acknowledged or has not adequately accounted for this. There have been
a number of studies that have examined the impact of various elements of
local governments' electoral structure on the election of Latinos, but with
little or no attention to the theorizing about urban government during the
1980s. Thus, the important question of what urban elections, and, indeed,
urban politics more generally, mean as an avenue for the political and
social mobility of Latinos in the coming decade has yet to be squarely
faced, theoretically or practically.

At another level, issues of Latino politics need to be considered in light
of broader themes of American democratic politics. Hochschild (1988, 1984),
for instance, has suggested that the African-American situation in the
United States is not simply an exception or anomaly but may in some ways
be necessary or symbiotic to the workings of the American political system. Are Latino politics also symbiotic, or are they an exception? Hochschild's questions are important, and her work has pursued these issue
from the standpoint of school desegregation policies (1984). Later work
has addressed less visible but equally significant aspects of these issues:
issues of "second generation discrimination" in the educational arena,
that is, the discrimination that may occur after formal desegregation and
that manifests itself in such institutional practices as ability grouping,

disciplinary policies, and educational outcomes. Analyses of institutions and their potential biases need to be given greater attention. Institutions and policies that appear to facilitate and enable group advancement may, in the course of "normal" practices, also constrain and impede individual and group development. These are themselves political issues and have larger political implications.

There are a number of relatively specific issues that require attention and need to be linked to other literature as well. It has long been suggested, for instance, that Latino interest groups function differently than do mainstream interest groups; they tend to be multifunctional and have several other unique characteristics (Vigil, 1987). At the same time, scholars have argued that interest group activities in the United States have been supplemented or supplanted by "issue networks" (Heclo, 1978). Research in state politics has indicated that minority groups may now have a presence in state politics, but that that presence is not necessarily to be equated with power (Thomas and Hrebenar, 1990). What do, or might, these arguments mean for Latino interest groups and Latino politics? And, in the many analyses of political culture in the American states (spawned Elazar's work [1984]), the significance of Latinos to political culture has hardly been considered. Bridges need to be built here.

It is often implied in much of the research on Latinos (and other minority groups) that their only interests or goals are for redistributive policies (see, for example, Browning, Marshall, and Tabb, 1984). The possibility that groups such as Latinos may have political values and perspectives that can broaden or modify social and political discourse and debate is thus precluded, virtually by definition. At the same time, this heavy emphasis on redistributive issues draws attention away from the ways in which Latinos are affected by other, nonredistributive policies. This social-psychological and policy segmentation obscures, rather than clarifies and links, Latino politics with larger political and policy processes.

If there is to be advancement in the study of Latino politics in the 1990s the approaches, and their associated assumptions, need to be questioned, understood, and addressed. Following that, the linkage of Latino politics research with and to research in other issues in American politics is necessary. In the absence of attention to these concerns, our understanding of Latino politics and of the broader American political system will be incomplete or inadequate.

References

Acuña, Rodolfo. 1988. *Occupied America*. New York: Harper and Row.
Browning, Rufus P., Dale Rogers Marshall, and David H. Tabb. 1984. *Protest Is Not Enough*. Berkeley, CA: University of California Press.
Bullock, Charles S., III, and Susan A. MacManus. 1989. "Structural Features of Municipalitites and the Incidence of Hispanic Councilmembers." Paper presented at the annual meeting of the Southwestern Political Science Association.
Elazar, Daniel J. 1984. *American Federalism: A View from the States*. New York: Harper and Row.

Elkin, Stephen. 1987. *City and Regime in the American Republic*. Chicago: University of Chicago Press.

Erie, Steven. 1985. "Rainbow's End: From the Old to the New Urban Ethnic Politics." Pp. 249–75 in Lionel Maldonado and Joan Moore, eds., *Urban Ethnicity in the United States: New Immigrants and Old Minorities*. Beverly Hills, CA: Sage.

Flores, Henry, 1989. "The Selectivity of the Capitalist State: Chicanos and Economic Development." *Western Politicl Quarterly*, 42 (June): 377–96.

Garcia, F. Chris, and Rodolfo O. de la Garza. 1977. *The Chicano Political Experience: Three Perspectives*. Duxbury.

Garcia, John. 1981. "Yo Soy Mexicano. . .: Self-Identity and Sociodemographic Correlates." *Social Science Quarterly*, 62 (March): 88–98.

Gottdiener, M. 1987. *The Decline of Urban Politics*. Newbury Park, CA: Sage.

Heclo, Hugh. 1987. "Issue Networks and the Executive Establishment." In Anthony King, ed, *The New Political System*. Washington, DC: American Enterprise Institute.

Hero, Rodney E., and Kathleen M. Beatty. 1989. "The Elections of Federico Pena as Mayor of Denver: Analysis and Implications," *Social Science Quarterly*, 70 (June): 300–10.

Hochschild, Jennifer. 1988. "The Double-Edged Sword of Equal Opportunity." In Ian Shapiro and Grant Reeher, eds., *Power, Inequality, and Democracy*. Boulder, CO: Westview.

_____. 1984. *The New American Dilemma: Liberal Democracy and School Desegregation*. New Haven: Yale University Press.

Kantor, Paul, with Stephen David. 1988. *The Dependent City: The Changing Political Economy of Urban America*. Boston: Scott, Foresman.

Lampe, Philip. 1982. "Ethnic Labels: Naming or Name Calling?" *Ethnic and Racial Studies*, 5 (October): 542–48.

Manley, John. 1983. "Neopluralism: A Class Analysis of Pluralism I and Pluralism II." *American Political Science Review*, 77 (June): 368–83.

Meier, Kenneth, Joseph Stewart, Jr., and Robert England. 1989. *Race, Class, and Education: The Politics of Second Generation Discrimination*. Madison, WI: University of Wisconsin Press.

Munoz, Carlos, Jr. 1989. *Youth, Identity, Power: The Chicano Movement*. New York: Verso.

Peterson, Paul. 1981. *City Limits*. Chicago: University of Chicago Press.

Sharp, Elaine B. 1990. *Urban Politics and Administration: From Service Delivery to Economic Development*. New York: Longman.

Stone, Clarence. 1980. "Systemic Power in Community Decision Making." *American Political Science Review*, 78 (December): 978–90.

_____. 1986. "Race, Power, and Political Change." Pp. 200–222 in Janet K. Boles, ed., *The Egalitarian City*. New York: Praeger.

Thomas, Clive S., and Ronald J. Hrebenar. 1990. "Interest Groups in the States." Pp. 123–58 in V. Gray, H. Jacob, and R. Albritton. eds., *Politics in the American States*. 5th ed. Glenview, IL: Scott, Foresman.

Vigil, Maurilio. 1987. *Hispanics in American Politics*. Lanham, MD: University Press of America.

Wolfinger, Raymond. 1974. *The Politics of Progress*. Englewood Cliffs, NJ: Prentice-Hall.

Blacks and Latinos in the American City in the 1900s: Toward Political Alliances or Social Conflict?

James Jennings

University of Massachusetts, Boston

T he social and political relationships between blacks and Latinos in the
big cities of America will be one of the most pressing issues for urban
politics in the 1990s. This development represents a new and major challenge to mayoral leadership. The demography that characterizes the American city, the social and economic similarities between blacks and Latinos,
and national and international political trends underlie the importance of
evolving social relationships between blacks and Latinos in urban settings. As political economist Kenneth M. Dolbeare asks,

> What will it mean, for example, to have predominantly black and Hispanic
> populations in almost all the major cities, with nearly all-white surrounding
> suburbs? . . . Is it reasonable to expect working coalitions between Hispanics
> and blacks? We know that there is a high potential for new minority political
> power, but not much about its prospects for realization. (Dolbeare, 1986:14).

As further suggested by political scientist Rufus P. Browning and his
colleagues, raising this question is justified by focusing on blacks and
Latinos in particular because "Blacks and Latinos are the two largest minority groups in the United States, composing 18.1 percent of the national
population in 1980 and much larger proportions in many states and cities"
(Browning et al., 1990:6).

It is clear that the bigger American cities and key electoral states are
becoming increasingly populated by blacks *and* Latinos, and also in some
cities, by people of Asian descent. In 1980, for example, there were twenty-
six cities across the United States that had 100,000 or more inhabitants and

158

Table 1. Rate of Increase in Population Growth by Race and Ethnicity,
1980–1990

	% Increase
White	6.2
Black	12.7
American Indian, Eskimo, and Aleut	18.9
Latino	34.0
Asian or Pacific Islander	70.3

Source: Rafael Valdivieso and Cary Davis "U.S. Hispanics: Challenging Issues for the 1990s" Population Reference Bureau, Inc., Washington D.C., December 1988

where blacks and Latinos *each* comprised at least 10 percent to the total population (U.S. Department of Commerce, 1989: Table 39). The number of cities where a combined black and Latino proportion has reached or exceeded 20 percent increased between 1980 and 1990. Furthermore, the population of communities of color are growing much more rapidly than is the white population. Table 1 shows the rate of increase in population growth for major groups between 1980 and 1990.

The growth illustrated in Table 1 for Latinos is taking place in urban areas. In 1985 there were at least forty-four Metropolitan Statistical Areas with at least 100,000 Latinos residing in them; it is important to note that these geographical areas are also those where the black population is rapidly increasing in numbers (Word, 1989).

These figures suggest that the growth of the Latino population has created vast political potential for this group. A large proportion of the Latino population is concentrated in nine states that contain 40 percent of the congressional seats in the United States, as well as three-quarters of all the electoral votes needed to elect a president. While Latinos only comprised 7.3 percent of the total U.S. population in 1985, they comprised 15 percent or more of the population in the following states: California, Texas, Arizona, and New Mexico. In the following states Latinos comprised between 7.5 and 15 percent of the total statewide population: Colorado, New York, Florida, and New Jersey. The total electoral votes in all of these states is 169, more than half of what is needed to elect a president (270) (Bureau of the Census, 1988). And the electoral votes will increase for these states, precisely due to the growth of the Latino, Asian, and black populations, after legislative reapportionment based on the 1990 Census.

Table 2 illustrates the growth of the Latino voting-age population between 1970 and 1980, in the major growth states for Latinos.

In some of the bigger states in this list, however, the black percent of the total voting-age population is also high and continuing to increase. In 1980, in California, for example, blacks made up 7.5 percent of the voting-age population, in Florida it was 10.8 percent, in Illinois it was 13.6 percent, in New Jersey it was 11.7 percent, in New York it was 13.1 percent, and in Texas it was 11.0 percent. In all of these big states the black proportion of the total voting-age population has increased since 1980 (see Joint Center for Political Studies, 1985). Both blacks and Latinos are part of

Table 2. Growth of Latino Voting-Age Population: 1970–1980

State	Number of Hispanics (1980)	% Growth
Arizona	265,688	+88
California	2,775,170	+11
Colorado	204,301	+70
Florida	629,292	+130
Illinois	379,208	+73
New Jersey	307,321	+85
New Mexico	292,714	+82
New York	1,061,852	+35
Texas	1,756,971	+82

Source: Hispanic Policy Development Project, *The Hispanic Almanic* (New York: 1984)

a broad demographic and, possibly therefore, political and social trans-formation of the United States. The nature of this transformation will be partially dependent on the political relationships between these two groups.

The query posed by Dolbeare implies that blacks and Latinos can be approached monolithically; this is not true. There are major social and economic differences within the overall Latino community that should not be overlooked in investigating relationships between blacks and Latinos. As the Latino population continues to grow, social and economic differences within and between various Latino groups may become more prominent and salient as political issues (see for example, Nelson, 1919; Garcia, 1989; for some discussion regarding the possibility of political differentiation within a Latino community, see Jennings, 1989). While the median age for Mexican Americans, or Chicanos, was 23.6 years in 1989, for Cubans it was 41.4 years! The labor force participation for Puerto Ricans in this year was 54.2 percent, but for Chicanos it was 67.8 percent, and for Cubans it was 62.3 percent. There are also significant deferences between Puerto Ricans, Chicanos, Cubans, and persons from countries in Central and South America regarding unemployment rates, poverty, percent of female-headed households, median income levels, and occupational characteristics (U.S. Department of Commerce, 1990, also McKay, 1985). Some of these differences may explain how relationships between blacks and Latinos evolve in different urban settings.

The growth of both black and Latino populations in cities is generally associated with increasing levels of poverty compared to whites in the United States. Blacks and certain sectors of the Latino population are experiencing increasing social and economic problems that seem to show the need for greater amounts of economic assistance and resources, as well as greater attention on the part of urban mayoral leadership. But despite significant social and economic similarities between blacks and some groups of Latinos, it is quite possible that a cleavage will emerge between these two communities of color. The kind of cleavage suggested here is different than discussed in earlier works focusing on urban political or mayoral leadership. Political scientist Clarence N. Stone describes one focus of some of these earlier works:

Banfield, in particular in his work with James Q. Wilson, talked about urban conflict primarily in terms of a cleavage between a provincial and tradition-minded ethos linked to machine politics and a cosmopolitan and modern-minded ethos linked to good government reform. This cleavage, rather than class or racial conflict, was the focus of Banfield and Wilson's understanding of city politics (Stone, 1988:138).

In 1968, the Kerner Commission identified major political and social cleavages in urban America along racial and class lines; this report focused on the economic chasm between the haves and the have-nots (National Advisory Commission on Civil Disorders, 1968). The continuing prominence of this kind of economic cleavage was again recognized in a twenty-year review of the Kerner Commission's findings (Harris and Wilkins, 1988). But the cleavage between haves and have nots, while continuing to characterize urban politics, will now become even more complex as it is impacted by the particular political and social relationships between blacks and Latinos—generally, two "have-not" groups.

Many social and political issues that urban mayors have to try to resolve are now colored by the political relationships between blacks and Latinos. For example, in places like Miami and Houston conflict between police and community reflects, in part, ethnic division and hostility between blacks and Latinos. In both these cities, instances of police brutality have involved Latino officers abusing black residents. In the area of education, there are instances both of political conflict and of cooperation between blacks and Latinos in cities like Chicago and New York. Electoral redistricting struggles in places like Los Angeles and Boston have, to a certain degree, reflected black and Latino political solidarity. Police and community relations, education, and redistricting are but a few issues that have always confronted the mayor's office; today, these same issues become even more complex and pressing as a result of the growth and political maturing of two communities of color, neither of which has been accepted or integrated fully into the higher echelon of private and corporate wealth in urban America.

Due to the lower social and economic status of blacks and Latinos and their particular political needs, at least two scenarios are possible in projecting an answer to Dolbeare's query. One scenario is characterized by political conflict between blacks and Latinos, as may have been the case at various times in cities like Miami, New York City, and Detroit. But the other scenario is one of blacks and Latinos joining to push a common political agenda, as was witnessed in the Harold Washington mayoral campaigns in Chicago, the Mel King mayoral campaign in Boston in 1983, and the David Dinkins mayoral victory in New York City. Both scenarios can have a major impact on the political direction of the American city. One writer suggests further, and in stronger terms, that acting together politically these two groups actually have the power to significantly influence the direction of the American economy at a national level. (Gallegos, 1986). But even though the coalitions among communities of color can have a significant impact in these areas, as political scientist Rodney E. Hero stated, "Those coalitions . . . probably are not as simply created, or maintained, as it sometimes appears" (Hero, 1989:349).

The mayor of a big city can assist in building a common political front between blacks and Latinos, or the mayor can seek short-term political advantages by encouraging one group to act as an electoral counterweight to the other group. There was some evidence of the latter response at the national level when Ronald Reagan and the Republican party attempted to mold the Latino electorate as a political counterweight to loyal black Democrats. There are also local instances of mayors attempting to utilize one group of black or Latino citizens to counter the political influence of the other group. Former mayors Kevin White in Boston, and Edward Koch in New York City were accused of attempting such strategies at various times during their administrations.

The implications for each of these scenarios are significant for the overall politics and economic direction of the American city. If conflict between blacks and Latinos becomes the political norm, then we should not expect much progress toward a public policy that responds to the economic and social needs of the poverty-level and working-class strata in each of the communities. The major reason for this claim is that the political influence of one group seeking social changes may be countered or dampened by that of the other group. If blacks, Latinos—and people of Asian descent—do support common political agendas and coalitions, however, then it may mean that have-not interests could develop stronger platforms by which to challenge actors representing and benefiting from the economic and wealth status quo in urban America.

Further Research

Several questions and issues should be explored in order to investigate further some of the possibilities suggested in this brief essay. First, what is the history of black and Latino political relationships in different cities and regarding various policy issues? What conditions or factors lead either to political cooperation or competition between blacks and Latino activists? Under what conditions have multiracial coalitions led to the election of black, Latino, or Asian candidates? What characteristics are found in those places where black and Latino political cooperation has been evident? What political or social tools or processes contribute to cooperation or competition, and what is the role of the mayor in the American city as far as this question is concerned? And what kinds of demands upon government will emerge as a result of political collaboration between blacks and Latinos? Will these demands be different than the traditional benefits sought from local government? These questions will become more significant and important as both blacks and Latinos continue to numerically dominate an increasing number of American cities.

References

Browning, Rufus P., et al. 1990. *Racial Politics in American Cities*. New York: Long-man Publishers.

Dolbeare, Kenneth M. 1986. *Democracy at Risk: The Politics of Economic Renewal*. New Jersey: Chatham House Publishers.

Gallegos, William. 1986. "The Sunbelt Strategy and Chicano Liberation." *Forward*. 5 (Spring): 1–32.

Garcia, F. Chris, ed. 1989. *Latinos in the U.S. Political System*. Notre Dame, IN: University of Notre Dame Press.

Harris, Fred R., and Roger W. Wilkins. 1988. *The Quiet Riots: Twenty Years after the Kerner Report*. New York: Pantheon Books.

Hero, Rodney E. 1989. "Multiracial Coalitions in City Elections Involving Minority Candidates: Some Evidence from Denver." *Urban Affairs Quarterly*, 25, no. 2 (December): 342–351.

Jennings, James. 1989. "Future Directions for Puerto Rican Politics." In Garcia, 1989.

Joint Center for Political Studies. 1986. *Black Elected Officials: A National Roster, 1985*. Washington, DC.

Mckay, Emily G. 1985. "A Demographic Summary of Hispanic Americans." Washington DC: National Council of La Raza.

National Advisory Commission on Civil Disorders. 1968. *Report*. Washington, DC: Government Printing Office.

Nelson, Dale C. 1979. "Ethnicity and Socioeconomic Status as Sources of Participation: The Case of Ethnic Political Culture." *American Political Science Review*, 73 (December): 1024–38.

Stone, Clarence N. 1989. "Paradigms, Power, and Urban Leadership." In Bryan D. Jones, *Leadership and Politics*. Lawrence, KS: University Press of Kansas.

U.S. Department of Commerce. Bureau of the Census. 1988. "The Hispanic Population in the United States: March 1988 (Advance Report)." Current Population Reports, P-20, no. 431. Washington, DC: Government Printing Office.

_____. 1989. *Statistical Abstract of the U.S., 1989*. Table 39. Washington, DC: Government Printing Office.

_____. 1990. "The Hispanic Population in the United States: March 1989." Current Population Reports, P-20, no. 444. Washington, DC: Government Printing Office.

Word, David L. 1989. "Population Estimates by Race and Hispanic Origin for States, Metropolitan Areas, and Selected Counties: 1980 to 1985." U.S. Department of Commerce, Bureau of the Census, Current Population Reports P-25, no. 1040-Rd-1. Washington, DC: Government Printing Office.

Symposium II:
African-American Politics in the 1990s

Introduction

Byran O. Jackson

California State University, Los Angeles

P olitics within African-American communities across the United States is undergoing change. In large part this change stems from a number of factors, including first and foremost the rise of a new generation of black politicians resulting from the retirement or replacement of older black political leaders. We find associated with this particular change a reorientation in the style and character of political strategies used by black politicians. Unlike the 1960s when African Americans used racial solidarity and protest as their major vehicles toward political empowerment, today's black politicians are opting for strategies with less racially polarizing overtones.

Furthermore, even the sociodemographic makeup of African-American communities has changed. More often than not, inner-city blacks are finding themselves sharing their neighborhoods with Asians and Latinos immigrating from all parts of the Far East and Latin America. The common ground for most inhabitants of these areas is poverty linked to social decay and violence. Those African Americans who can afford it move, leaving the poorest of the poor behind.

During the late 1960s and early 1970s, African-American mayors were elected for the first time in many of our nation's largest cities. These elections brought hope for political empowerment that would be translated into economic advancement for the African-American community. Nevertheless, while New York City and Los Angeles, our nation's two largest cities, have African-American mayors, the quality of life for African Americans in both cities is rapidly declining.

In 1984 Jesse Jackson brought still another theme to the political history of African Americans. His bid for the U.S. presidency renewed the struggle for socioeconomic and political advancement not only for African Americans but for all people of color falling under his rainbow coalition. Jackson's bid for the presidency represented a shift in the focus of the struggle for African-American political empowerment, from the local level to the national level of government.

The changes in the social and political environment of African-American communities pose new questions and areas of debate for scholars studying African-American politics. Can the appeal to broader audiences by African-American politicians be pursued without diluting or undermining the articulation of the pressing needs of the African-American community for the sake of developing "winning coalitions"? Can African Americans form political alliances with their new immigrant neighbors? Can political power be translated into economic power for African-American citizens?

The presentations found in this symposium take a sobering examination of the many changes taking place on the African-American political landscape. In doing so, they begin to address the themes suggested by these questions. Aldon Morris opens the symposium with a pointed essay titled "The Future of Black Politics: Substance versus Process and Formality." The author evaluates black political empowerment in light of the lack of improvements in the socioeconomic conditions of African Americans. Whether it is "the politics of deracialization" or "black solidarity," the author cautions that the true test of an appropriate political strategy for African Americans is its ability to produce black economic empowerment. The debate on the future of black politics must be centered on this major concern.

Charles V. Hamilton follows with a critical examination of the deracialization trend in African-American politics. The author points to the necessity for maintaining black solidarity in America's pluralist society while eschewing the notion that deracialized campaigns represent a progressive element in African-American politics.

The selection by James Jennings included in the first symposium on Latino politics should also be considered here. Jennings observes the ethnic change occurring in central-city neighborhoods with large concentrations of African Americans. And the central question guiding his paper is whether blacks and Latinos can join in meaningful coalitions.

Despite the large increase in African-American elected officials at the state and local levels, there remain serious deficiencies in policy development and implementation in a number of important areas. Elsie Scott takes a retrospective view on the changes in law enforcement and law enforcement policy as it relates to the African-American community. The optimism brought by law enforcement reforms during the late 1960s and early 1970s dissipates in light of 1990s statistics showing declining opportunities for blacks in the law enforcement arena, as well as an increase in black incarcerations, to a level that exceeds that in South Africa.

What is the impact of Jackson's rainbow coalition on African-American politics? Katherine Tate examines the ends of the rainbow and its impact on party politics in the United States. She empirically examines the impact of the Jackson campaign on reshaping black attitudes and behavior and lays to rest some speculations found in this area.

Finally Ronald Walters offers an assessment of recent elections in which African-American politicians conducted deracialized campaigns. Walters, who views black politics in pragmatic terms, asserts that the study of black politics should not be reoriented to accommodate racial crossovers by black politicians. Instead, in his view these represent two separate political traditions requiring distinct assessments of their costs and benefits.

The Future of Black Politics: Substance versus Process and Formality

Aldon Morris

Northwestern University

A a the decade of the 1990s opens, the material conditions of the black masses have deteriorated drastically. Yet, at the same time the number of black elected officials have skyrocketed to an all-time high. This is a paradox that was not supposed to happen. During the heyday of the civil rights and black power movements, it was widely believed that attaining the ballot, and the political power it would generate, were the keys that would unlock the doors of black empowerment. Black leaders, activists, and ordinary people marched, went to jail, and endured physical violence to obtain the ballot. Some even paid the supreme price by sacrificing their life so that African Americans could achieve the ballot. But twenty-five years later a bitter revelation stares the scholar and lay person in the face: the election of black politicians does not automatically empower the African-American community, and it is even possible for that community to become less empowered as the number of black elected officials increases.

This paradox is real. In the latter half of the twentieth century poverty has increased, especially in inner cities throughout the nation, where blacks are heavily concentrated (Wilson, 1987). Indeed, one-third of black families live below the poverty line and thousands more live near that line (Jayne and Williams, 1989). About half of all black children live in families below the poverty line. Black per capita annual earnings are 56 percent that of whites, which means that, relatively, blacks are now worse off than they were during the late 1960s, when black protest was commonplace. Umemployment is rampant in the black community, especially among young black males: the odds of young white men having jobs are about 2.5 times those for young black men (Jayne and Williams, 1989). The situation is acute for black women because, even though they are discriminated against on the basis of race and sex, they still must support half of all black families by themselves with astonishingly few resources.

Human suffering and pain lie beneath these statistics. Children are going to school and bed with stomachs pulsating with pain becuse of a lack of food. Some don't make it: 18.2 black babies out of 1,000 die before their first birthday. Poverty is the root of much evil. It generates hostility; a thriving, dangerous drug trade; lack of both educational opportunities and hope for the future; and murder. The black homicde rate is astronomical: each year blacks kill over 8,000 other blacks. Half the prisons' inmates in the nation are black, which means that there are fewer marriages and fewer economically productive black males. The African-American community is in deep trouble, and the prospects for its future become bleaker with each passing hour.

The civil rights movement was successful in its effort to seize the franchise for millions of southern blacks and create favorable political conditions for the exercise of the franchise by blacks outside the South. Indeed, "the number of black elected officials has risen from a few dozens in 1940 to over 6,800 in 1988" (Jayne and Williams, 1989:15). As Bobo and Gilliam (1990:379) point out, black elected officials are to be found in state legislatures, city councils, and school boards, and as mayors of major cities. Currently there is a black governor of Virginia, and Andrew Young conducted an impressive but unsuccessful campaign to become the first black governor of Georgia. Reflecting this trend of black political progress, a black man—Ron Brown—is the current National Chairman of the Democratic party, and Jesse Jackson waged significant campaigns to become president of the United States in 1984 and 1988. In short, the civil rights movement ushered in a small-scale revolution in electoral politics, making it possible for significant numbers of blacks to hold office for the first time since Reconstruction.

Nevertheless, office holding and real empowerment can be two different realities altogether, as the data already cited suggest with respect to the black community. Moreover, in many cases black mayors, for example, have had sufficient time to empower the black community, for in "major cities such as Atlanta, Detroit, Gary, Los Angeles, and others, black mayors have controlled city hall for more than a decade" (Bobo and Gilliam, 1990:379). In my view, it is time to seriously consider the argument that black elected officials, no matter how well intended, cannot empower the black community. If true, this is a harsh conclusion, given the heroic struggles in the past by African Americans to obtain the franchise, and the current obsession with electoral politics by black leaders. But these are precisely the reasons why this strategy of political office seeking must be questioned, for such a myopic quest could push the black community even lower than its present subordinate position.

The ability to exercise power is the essence of politics. Empowerment means having the leverage to allocate to one's constituency valuable resources that are unequally distributed within a society. In America valuable resources—money, wealth, good jobs, access to medical and legal services, ability to engage in consequential decision making, and the like—

are unequally distributed along class, race, and gender lines. Thus, the black community is in a subordinate position because historically and currently it has been the victim of an interlocking system of class, race, and gender oppression. This oppression has left the black community relatively powerless, because it lacks the leverage to allocate valuable resources to its members. From this vantage point, black empowerment refers to a state in which political and economic representatives of the black community have real power to allocate valuable resources—especially economic resources—to their community, enabling it to effectively compete and bargain with other communities from a position of strength, rather than of dependency.

The analytical value of this political-economy approach to black empowerment seems obvious. Yet black empowerment is often defined as mere representation and influence, rather than as the actual exercise of power (Bobo and Gilliam, 1990). Employing these narrow criteria of empowerment, analysts often conclude that significant black empowerment has already occurred. This restricted view of empowerment probably stems from the tremendous political struggles African Americans had to wage to break into electoral politics on a significant level. It is important to remember, however, that black people had to generate real power outside conventional channels in order to gain widespread access to the electoral arena. It was protest politics in the context of a grass-roots social movement that made electoral politics accessible to the black community.

Weber (1947) defined power as the ability to realize one's own will even in the face of resistance. The white power structure of the South, coupled with the large white urban political machines of the North, vehemently resisted the efforts of blacks to gain meaningful access to the electoral arena. Nevertheless, widespread black protest in the streets during the 1950s and 1960s produced an acute crisis in America by causing the social order to unravel throughout the South and in many locales outside the South. Organized protest by masses of black people was the foundation of power from which African Americans seized the franchise and won political offices even in the face of stiff white resistance.

A major reason why politicians and political apparatus emerge within a group is to solidify, manage, and protect group interest, especially economic interests. In this respect the paramount responsibility of the American state and its associated political parties is to protect and promote the economic interests of America's white upper classes. In the black community this process has worked in the reverse. Black politicians and black political machinery are proliferating, while the black community remains economically oppressed and locked out of the economic mainstream of the larger society. In many cases blacks are seeking and winning political offices already permeated with an institutional logic that protects and promotes white interest. In any case, black politicians usually find themselves seeking and presiding over political structures only marginally attached to their own group's interests. The essence of such politics is to substitute procedures and formality for substantive group interest. Under such conditions black politics have become the art of warring over empty shells, while the masses bear the cross of hunger and pain.

In fact, contemporary black politics have rejected their heritage and historical mission. The civil rights movement generated modern black politics, but by the late 1960s the key leaders of that movement made it clear that economic empowerment was the next step in the battle for black liberation. Thus, before he was assassinated, Martin Luther King and the Southern Christian Leadership Conference (SCLC) concluded:

> We can now see ourselves as the powerless poor trapped within an economically orientated power structure. . . .
>
> Our insight into the structure of American society teaches us that the right to vote or to eat in any restaurant, while important, does not penetrate the "power plant" and therefore does not actually affect conditions of living. We have learned that fruitful existence in America requires money, for the society offers no degree of mobility, creativity, or power to those without it. (Southern Christian Leadership Conference, 1968:2)

The analysis here is that real black empowerment flows from economic resources rather than from the mere acquisition of political office. Yet contemporary black politicians proceed as if their election to office is tantamount to black empowerment. The black masses are urged to register, vote, and mobilize the community for the purpose of electing blacks. What becomes paramount is winning city hall, seats in Congress, the governor's mansion, an aldermanic post, and the White House. In this logic the silent promise of the politician is "vote for me and I will set you free." The masses are convinced on a subtle level that once elected, black politicians will provide them with good jobs, economic parity, and social justice.

The question of whether black politicians have the wherewithal to empower the black community is sidestepped. Yet it is the real question that must be addressed head on by black politicians, leaders, and community activists if black politics are to be pursued intelligently. If this fails to happen, the black community may very well be rushing toward a political train disguised as a black liberator, but whose real destination is deeper black subordination. From all indications, office seeking appears to be the black politics of the future. The major strategy discussions in the community and leadership circles center around how to run the best campaign, how to appeal to white voters, how to select the best candidate, and how to appeal to a fragile black electorate riddled with class differences.

It is curious that debates addressing black economic empowerment and the development of strategies to accomplish such empowerment are virtually nonexistent among black political leaders. Yet it was precisely this agenda that emerged logically from the political struggles of the 1950s and 1960s. This quest for black economic empowerment led to the assassinations of black protest leaders and the heavy repression of the civil rights and black power movements. Indeed, white economic and political elites realized that money and other valuable resources would have to be distributed more equally in order for blacks and the poor to become economically empowered.

There are good reasons why black political leaders avoid generating or sharpening a debate focusing on black economic empowerment. Such a debate would reveal their lack of capacity to actually implement fundamental economic change within the black community. The masses would come to see that the winning of political offices is not synonymous with empowerment, and that such political behavior is susceptible to becoming largely a ritual of process and formal office holding. Therefore black political leaders engage in the far-easier task of debating formal political procedures and how to win office. Electoral politics are probably the black politics of the future because black political leaders have developed a vested interest in steering the community down this barren route.

Nonetheless, an ongoing national debate on black economic empowerment would be fruitful for black political leaders and for the larger African-American community. To be useful, this debate would have to be pursued vigorously and honestly and include serious input from black political leaders, activists, scholars, business leaders, and clergy, as well as members of the African-American community. Such a debate should be deeply rooted in hard economic and political data, as well as in philosophy, and speculative thinking. It should be conducted within the institutions of the African-American community, and it should be democratic so as to prevent any particular segment of the community form directing it into narrow channels.

I believe that from this debate would emerge a number of important conclusions that could be utilized in building a politics of substance for the future. First, a dynamic relationship between black political leaders and the black masses must develop and be promoted if black politics are to become empowering and politically significant. Such a relationship is essential, because the inherent dynamics of electoral politics separate politicians from the masses and encourage only those superficial ties geared toward mobilizing the vote for the next election. This separation is catastrophic for the African-American community, because, unlike the white politician, whose role is to manage and protect an already-empowered constituency, the black politician must work for empowerment itself, which can only be accomplished in concert with the masses. In the absence of a dynamic relationship that unites leaders and masses, black politics will remain trapped in procedures and formalities and be characterized by internecine warfare among politicians, similar to that that erupted in Chicago following the death of Harold Washington.

Second, black electoral politics must embrace black protest politics; otherwise the former will remain impotent in terms of black empowerment. It is now commonplace for politicians and the black masses to view protest politics as weapons of the 1960s that have become obsolete for the modern period, where "real politics" are conducted in legislative halls and the offices of politicians. However, for a potent black politics to emerge capable of generating real empowerment, black politicians themselves must become empowered. Mass black protest is a critical ingredient capable of empowering black politicians. With the election of black politicians, the black masses have tended to become politically quiescent, believing either that their elected officials would realize their interests, or that protest would embarrass black office holders or be perceived by hostile white forces as public attacks against black office holders. This is unfortunate, because black protest could create the social conditions under which black politicians could more effectively wrestle economic and social goods from a recalcitrant society and could utilize those resources in an overall effort to empower the African-American community. In short, a mobilized, protesting constituency is one that cannot be ignored and that in fact, becomes an important factor in the equation of power politics.

Black protest would also serve to counter the conservative tendencies inherent in electoral politics. Black politicians, like all politicians, must be kept honest and focused on the goal of black empowerment, and it is black protest that can keep them in check. Moreover, black protest is a central force that pulls the black community into the political process making them knowledgeable and politically efficacious. Without mass involvement and protest, it is unlikely that large economic corporations, the government, and other powerful white interests will share societal resources more equitably with the African-American community. Thus, the election of black officials ought to generate black protest rather than repel it, and black leaders, especially activists, must function as the vanguard in the generation and management of black protest. Black protest politics and electoral politics are the twin cornerstones necessary in the empowerment of the African-American community.

Third, black electoral politics are not likely to be dynamic and creative if they continue to be dominated by black males. What the African-American political community needs now are new, fresh, ideas concerning the strategies that should be explored and implemented in the search for black empowerment. Black women have unique insights rooted in their experience of class, race, and gender oppression and their familiarity with black family dynamics. These insights need to be incorporated into the political dialogue by the African-American community. For example, knowledge of how women support families on few resources is important, because it would help inform us about how to economically empower black families. Black women political leaders could also help empower the black community by revealing how sexism operates in this context. Sexism is a real liability in the black community, because it works against the mobilization and productivity of women and men.

In conclusion, I have argued that the current obsession with black electoral process, at the expense of actually empowering the African-American community, is a disturbing development. The current brand of black electoral politics stresses political procedures and office holding rather than actual activities and ideas capable of producing black empowerment. It was also stressed that economic empowerment is the crucial step that must be undertaken if black politics are to remain meaningful and useful.

If black politicians fail to grapple with real economic empowerment, they will have rejected the historic mission hammered out by the heroic struggles of the civil rights and black power movements. Finally, we need a critical political science and sociology that will be able to conceptualize exactly what constitutes black empowerment and the tools that can measure the degree to which black empowerment has occurred as well as the degree to which the goal continues to elude us. It is time to open debate on how to achieve complete black liberation.

References

Bobo, Lawrence, and Franklin D. Gilliam, Jr. 1990. "Race, Sociopolitical Participation and Black Empowerment." *The American Political Science Review*, 84:377–93.

Jayne, Gerald, and Robin Williams, Jr. 1989. *Common Destiny: Black and American Society*. Washington DC: National Academy Press.

Southern Christian Leadership Conference Program Office. 1968. "Statement of Purpose: Poor People's Campaign." Washington, DC.

Weber, Max. 1947. *The Theory of Social and Economic Organizations*. Talcott Parsons ed. New York: Free Press.

Wilson, William J. 1987. *The Truly Disadvantaged*. Chicago: University of Chicago Press.

The Politics of Deracialization in the 1990s

Charles V. Hamilton

Columbia University

E ach decade in the last half of the twentieth century has presented a peculiar, dynamic brand of politics by African Americans. And it is not at all certain that the precise shape of the phenomenon could have been predicted at the beginning of each period. What is certain, however, is that black politics are a result of the continuing interaction of forces in the larger society grappling over the vexing, perplexing issue of race, and the role of public policy in relation to that issue. How the larger society responds to demands for racial equity will continue to be the stimulant for action and analysis. As much as some would prefer to act as if race per se were no longer an important intervening variable in public policy, the likelihood of this being true of American political life is slim in the final decade of this century. The precise issues on the policy agenda will alter, of course, but to suggest that race and racism will *not* be manifest remains more an understandable predilection than reasonable prediction. If we view politics as the struggle over authoritative allocation of scarce resources, it follows that many criteria—including race—will affect those decisions. The social and economic ramifications of a multiracial multiethnic society are too deeply embedded in the American system to conclude otherwise.

At the turn of the 1990 decade, it is difficult to escape the conclusion that the state of national and international economies will greatly determine the nature and results of political demands. So much of what African Americans need and demand will depend on scarce resources that agendas, and outcomes will be debated and analyzed in terms of a zero-sum game. What one group gains, another loses. If the focus is on civil rights, more than a few people will want to question exactly what citizens *by right* ought to have. This will be as much a political struggle as a constitutional or legal one. We will continue to fuss over important questions of historical causes and subsequent appropriate remedies. We will continue to argue that current conditions are more properly understood as results *not* of blatant past racial segregation and discrimination, but of relatively recent structural inequities of society—mainly economic. We will continue to debate whether the wisest political strategy will be to couch demands in more overt racial terms, or to blunt such strategies (the term "deracialization" will be heard increasingly) in favor of approaches that seek to form broader-based coalitions.

At all times, we will be focusing on the most efficacious way to pursue a politics of resources—namely, how best to extract from a shrunken pie the goods and services so badly needed by those who, for various reasons, have the least. What will make this a particularly difficult problem will be the many different interpretations of "for various reasons"; and how *that* is decided will in large measure determine how the policy issues are dealt with.

At national, state, and local levels, demands will be made to take into account the "special" needs of those least able to help themselves. But should this account be predicated on racial designation, or on other less ascriptive determinants? If the former, will this aggravate racial polarization, creating even deeper divisions in the body politic? If the latter, will this simply be a continuing refusal to recognize the pernicious persistence of racism as a factor in public life? This battle will be fought in virtually every arena of official decision making. But it is very likely the case that we will see much more dispersion of strategies than was previously the case.

Though for so long national executive and judicial branches (especially the U.S. Supreme Court) were the initial arenas of race-equity advocates, the 1990s will probably see much more effort expended in the national legislative arena and the state and local arenas. This switch began, surely, in the 1970s, accelerated under the Reagan administration in the 1980s, and, for the 1990s, will probably characterize the transformed politics of African Americans. Neither is this an insignificant matter, because different pressure points in the fragmented American system call for different strategies and tools of action. Elections and lobbying, perhaps more than lawsuits, will be the initial (but by no means the only) vehicles for policy change. At the same time, no one should be sanguine that such strategies will necessarily have quick payoffs. Whatever else is true about the American political system, it is certainly the case that such legislative politics are usually slow and painfully incremental.

In the ensuing decade, African Americans will turn increasingly to the process of electing people to office who are perceived as more responsive to the concerns of the race as a group. On its face, such goals are not unexpected. There is no identifiable group in American society that does not calculate its status in such self-interested terms. But should political demands be made in race-specific terms? Or are they more appropriately pursued in conjunction with the needs of other groups perceived as similarly situated (again, the "deracialization" approach)?

Contrary to considerable conventional wisdom, blacks have always attempted to reconcile their socioeconomic demands with those of others. The history of black attempts to form viable coalitions with others is a long one. The problem, however, has been that for the most part they have had few important takers, especially when the agenda concerned economic issues. Certainly this is the case with the New Deal, as the history of much of the social legislation of that period will attest—the initial coverage of Social Security (1935) being one glaring example. Likewise, few students of black political history should be ignorant of the fate of A. Philip Randolph's Freedom Budget in the 1960s or the failure to pass a meaningful Humphrey-Hawkins Full Employment Bill in the 1970s. It is not that African Americans have lacked the vision and willingness to pursue "deracialized" politics. They simply have not had sufficient white allies to make the strategy viable. Whatever one thinks of Jesse Jackson personally, his program in the 1980s ought to have appealed to many more whites than they did. With all the poor and economically marginal whites in the country, it is curious—but sadly revealing—that there were no white candidates with the stature or courage to challenge Jackson for leadership of the truly liberal-progressive wing of his party. For the most part they collapsed to the center, and blacks are aware enough to know that therein lies little prospect for serious resolution of the problems for the poor and most vulnerable. Therefore, the failure to build viable coalitions on the Left has not been the result of black unwillingness, but of white unavailability. The 1990s will, and ought to, see continued efforts in this direction, but given the picture of looming protracted economic austerity, no one should be naive about the difficulty of this strategy. But it should be clear what a "politics of deracialization" is: a means of testing whether the country is prepared to join with blacks in moving toward truly progressive policies. It should not be seen as a means of co-opting black demands.

As before, there will be suggestions that African Americans should not be too dependent on one major political party, namely, the Democratic party. Perhaps they should, the thinking goes, consider a balancing strategy—either supporting the Republican party more often and/or forming an independent force.

Supporting the Republican party would make sense only if there were policy incentives for doing so. Blacks vote overwhelmingly Democratic because that party, on the whole, normally is stronger on the issues of concern to the group. The Republicans are aware of what they have to do to reverse that practice. The fact is that in presidential elections the Republicans have made other decisions, focused on other groups, and done quite nicely in the bargain. For blacks to switch under such circumstances, without a corresponding switch in Republican party policy performance, would hardly satisfy the real socioeconomic needs of the masses—whatever it might do for the fortunes of a few black elites. Contrary to some popular commentary, the black electorate is not led blindly into the Democratic party fold by self-seeking leaders. There *have* been occasional desertions to more attractive Republican candidates. If there is to be a switch in the 1990s to the Republican party, it will be on the basis of the perceived advantage of *indivisible* benefits for the many, not *divisible* benefits for the few.

However, others have suggested the option of not aligning with either major party. For the mass of voters, this would mean opting out of many critical primary elections, and that has questionable value. But in certain circumstances, especially at local levels where the arithmetic might be favorable and manageable, the creation of an independent third political forces could be viable. This is even more promising if the current mood to limit state and local legislative terms bears fruit. Likewise, we should be aware that, with the steady decline of the party- in-the-electorate, we have been witnessing over the years more emphasis on individualized candidate strategies. This has been demonstrated with the increasingly individualized nature of election campaigns—candidates forming their own organizations and contesting elections. Such developments can signal increased opportunities for candidates thinking about organizing in black communities.

In the final analysis, politics have to be seen as the continuing struggle to maximize benefits for the largest number of constituents. Precisely because African Americans remain disproportionately economically deprived, it should not be difficult to determine what benefits are needed. Results are not difficult to measure. Strategies to achieve desired results can and ought to be diverse and flexible. In the American system, politics, for those most successful over time, are an instrumental process. A *progressive* black politics in the 1990s will provide important opportunities to test and fine-tune that craft.

The Politics of the Police in the 1990s: Race-Related Issues

Elsie L. Scott

Deputy Commissioner of Training, Police Academy, City of New York

political issues of the U.S. police system in the 1990s closely parallel issues of the 1960s. In the late 1960s, many of the nation's cities exploded in racial uprisings. Black people took to the streets to express displeasure about substandard housing, lack of jobs, and racism in general. The underlying causes were deeply rooted in social and economic factors, but the precipitating factor in all of the major outbursts was police action (National Advisory Commission, 1968).

President Lyndon Johnson appointed the National Advisory Commission on Civil Disorders (the Kerner Commission) to study the causes of the uprisings and to make recommendations for preventing future occurrences. The Commission concluded that "to many Negroes police have come to symbolize white power, white racism and white repression. And the fact is that many police do reflect and express these white attitudes." (p. 11).

The Kerner Commission made a number of recommendations for reducing tensions and hostility between the police and the black community. Two of the major recommendations were;

- adoption and strict enforcement of policies that prohibit misconduct such as harassment, brutality, or discourtesy, and
- intensive recruitment of black police officers and adoption of fair promotional procedures to ensure the rapid increase of blacks in supervisory positions.

There is evidence that some attempts have been made to implement these recommendations. In 1981 the Commission on Accreditation for Law Enforcement Agencies was formed to develop standards for proper

Table 1. Employment of Black Police Officers in Large U.S. Cities

City	Percentage of Black Officers	
	1967[a]	1988[b]
New York, NY	5	11
Chicago, IL	17	22
Philadelphia, PA	20	20
Detroit, MI	5	57
Baltimore, MD	7	23
San Francisco, CA	6	9
Boston, MA	2	17
Washington, DC	21	41
Memphis, TN	5	29
New Orleans, LA	4	33
St. Louis, MO	11	23
Atlanta, GA	10	56
Pittsburgh, PA	7	22
Oakland, CA	4	25
Newark, NJ	10	28

Sources: [a]Kerner Report, 1968: 321; [b]Walker 1968: 4.

law enforcement administration, training, and operation. In chapter 1 of their *Standards for Law Enforcement Agencies* (1983), the issues of ethics, limits of authority, and the use of force are addressed. The use-of-force standard states that "an officer may use deadly force only when the officer reasonably believes that the action is in defense of human life" (Commission on Accreditation for Law Enforcement Agencies, 1983: 1–2).

Most urban police departments now have written policies and disciplinary procedures for persons who violate policies. Research has shown that these policies have had an impact in some cities. A study by Larry Sherman (1986) showed that between 1970 and 1984, the number of civilians killed by police in major U.S. cities dropped by 50 percent.

Policies and departmental disciplinary procedures have sometimes worked when the criminal justice system has failed to indict a police officer in a misconduct case. For example, a white policeman was not indicted by a Dallas grand jury for the shooting death of a 70-year-old black woman who had called the police to report a burglary in progress at a neighbor's home. The Dallas Police Department, nevertheless, fired the officer after it was found that he had failed to use options other than deadly force.

Black police were vigorously recruited after a number of discrimination lawsuits were filed. A comparison of statistics on the employment of black officers in some of the fifty largest cities at the time of the Kerner Report and statistics for 1988 reveals significant improvement. For example, Detroit's police force went from 5 percent black officers in 1967 to 57 percent in 1988 (see Table 1). There was an increase in the percentage of blacks in command-level positions within the largest cities, from 4.4 percent in 1975 to 8.0 percent in 1985 (Lewis; 1987).

Despite the bright picture portrayed by policies and statistics, in 1990 the police system is still a political issue in the black community. After a decade-and-a-half of lessening tensions and fewer complaints from the black community, there is a concern by many that the increased frustrations on both sides concerning the drug crisis will lead to weakening relationships.

Fears about police safety have led some law enforcement officials to call for a change in the almost universally accepted deadly force policy, which states that deadly force should be used by police only in situations where there is a threat to life. The recommendation to change the policy to allow the shooting of fleeing felons and to allow warning shots has been made despite the U.S. Supreme Court decision in *Garner v. Tennessee* that seemed to outlaw police shooting of fleeing felons, and despite the adoption of the defense-of-life policy by all the major law enforcement associations and the Commission on Accreditation for Law Enforcement Agencies.

The adoption of policies that restrict the use of force by police officers has reduced police shootings, but it has not eliminated "questionable" shootings of blacks by the police and perceived injustice by the court system. For example, in 1984 Eleanor Bumpurs, a 66-year-old black woman, was killed in New York City by a white policeman when she lunged at him with a knife during an eviction dispute. The officer was acquitted of manslaughter and the outraged black community mounted a strong protest. In 1987, statements by the Hillsborough County, Florida, state's attorney alleging justifiable force in each of four black deaths during the previous five months led to a lawsuit filed by the NAACP and protests by black citizens. The city of Miami exploded several times in reaction to a shooting of a black person by a white or Hispanic officer.

Black males continue to be overrepresented in the police-shootings statistics. A number of studies have documented the racial disparities in police shootings (see Takagi, 1974; Milton et al., 1977; Fyfe, 1981). A more recent study of the discharge of weapons by the Dallas police during a two-and-one-half-year period beginning in 1985 revealed that 50 percent of the firearms discharges by Anglo and black officers involved black subjects, and 75 percent of the shots fired by Hispanic officers involved black subjects (Alpert Group, 1987).

Criminal justice researchers, with few exceptions, have attempted to explain that the racial disparities in police shootings do not mean that there is racism in the system. Fyfe, for example, argues that racism cannot be confirmed when one examines evidence about weapon usage by black victims of police shootings.

It is interesting to note that the black community does not protest against every shooting of a black person by the police, and that almost 100 percent of the protests have involved a white or Hispanic officer, not a black officer. Whites have seldom protested against the shooting of a white person by police, and not one instance could be found in which whites protested against the killing of a white citizen by a black officer. It is logical to assume that, if a black officer were to kill a white person in circumstances similar to some of the circumstances about which blacks have protested, a public outcry would be heard from the white community.

Whites and blacks seem to define justifiable force in different ways. Whites seem to use the legal definition and, therefore, can justify the taking of a black life because a police officer feared that a 70-year-old woman might have had a knife. Blacks seem to have a broader definition of the circumstances under which an officer is justified in taking a life. New York City Police Commissioner Lee Brown probably best explains the difference. He states that he feels that officers should not use the legal criteria of justifiable force, but should decide if the force is *necessary*— could some other methods or means be used to effect the desired result? If the force was necessary, then it is justified.

The statistics on the hiring of black police officers may also be somewhat misleading. Affirmative action consent decrees have been the most important factor in bringing about an increase in the number of black police officers (Lewis, 1987). The fact that most of these consent decrees have been court mandated rather than voluntary does not leave much room for optimism about the future of black employment in police departments. Some of these consent decrees have been challenged by white police officers, who have charged reverse discrimination. Recent Supreme Court decisions have limited the federal protection against employment discrimination based on race (*Martin v. Wilkes; Patterson v. McLean; Wards Cove*). In *Martin v. Wilkes*, for example, the Supreme Court sided with white fire fighters in Birmingham, Alabama who had challenged the provisions of a consent decree.

Even with the court-mandated consent decrees, most cities have not reached racial parity—the percentage of blacks on the police force does not equal the percentage of blacks in the labor force. In Lewis's study, he found that in every city that had reached racial parity, the labor force was less than 20 percent black.

The future of blacks in policing is made even dimmer when one observes the large number of black police officers who are eligible to retire. Many blacks who are presently on police forces were recruited after the racial uprisings of the late 1960s. With a twenty-year retirement system in many cities, these blacks have now reached or will soon reach their retirement eligibility year. Many of these blacks are in executive or command positions, and the number and percentage of blacks presently occupying middle-level management positions are not very large (Jones, 1990). The retirement of blacks from executive positions with no blacks in line to replace them may lead to a crisis in black police leadership. Lewis's study found that black political leadership (mayors and police chiefs) was important in achieving affirmative action gains in police departments. Black chiefs of police and police officers have also been credited with improvements in relations between the police and black citizens, by respecting citizens and reducing incivilities practiced by white police officers.

Increasing racial tensions and acts of racial violence and harassment in society at large have led to speculations about the possibility of riots like the 1960s riots. Many of the same factors that caused the 1960s uprisings, such as "frustrated hopes" and "black ghettos," are still present in society, and one shooting of a black by a police officer that is perceived to be unjust can trigger a violent reaction from blacks. A twentieth-anniversary assessment of the conditions since the Kerner Report concluded that, instead of the violent riots that were observable by all, "quiet riots" are occurring that are destroying as much human life as the 1960s riots (Harris and Wilkins, 1988). Whether the "riots" are quiet or loud, there is an urgent need for the country to address its racial problems. The police are probably better prepared to handle race riots, but the police are not responsible for addressing the underlying causes of riots or racial tensions in this country. Instead of rolling back the civil rights protections developed during the 1960s and 1970s, there is a need to ensure enforcement of the laws in a just way and for an assurance to black youth that their lives are valuable.

Reference

Alpert Group. 1987. "Review of Deadly Force Training and Policies of the Dallas Police Department." Unpublished report.

Commission of Accreditation for Law Enforcement Agencies. 1983. *Standards for Law Enforcement Agencies: The Standards Manual of the Law Enforcement Agency Accreditation Program*. Fairfax, VA: Commission on Accreditation for Law Enforcement Agencies, Inc.

Fyfe, James J. 1981. "Race and Extreme Police-Citizen Violence." In R.L. McNeely and Carl E. Pope, eds., *Race, Crime and Criminal Justice*. Beverly Hills: Sage.

Harris, Fred, and Roger Wilkins. 1988. *Quiet Riots: Race and Poverty in the United States*. New York: Pantheon Books.

Jones, Lt. Seymour. 1990. Interview conducted 30, June Washington, DC.

Kerner Report. 1968. See National Advisory Commission on Civil Disorders, 1968.

Lewis, William G. 1987. "Toward Representative Bureaucracy: An Assessment of Black Representation in Police Bureaucracies." Paper presented at the second annual Black Law Enforcement Chief Executives Symposium, Oakland, California.

Milton, Catherine H., Jeanne W. Halleck, James Lardner, and Gary L. Abrecht. 1977. *Police Use of Deadly Force*. Washington, DC: Police Foundation.

National Advisory Commission on Civil Disorders. 1968. *Report*. Washington, DC: U.S. Government Printing Office.

Sherman, L.W. 1986. "Citizens Killed by Big City Police, 1970–84". Washington, DC: Crime Control Institute, Crime Control Corporation, N.Y., NY.

Takagi, Paul. 1974. "A Garrison State in a 'Democratic' Society." *Crime and Social Justice*, Spring-Summer: 27–33.

Walker, Samuel. 1989. "Employment of Black and Hispanic Police Officers, 1983–1988: A Follow-Up Study." Occasional paper, Center for Applied Urban Research, University of Nebraska at Omaha.

The Impact of Jesse Jackson's Presidential Bids on Blacks' Relationship with the Democratic Party

Katherine Tate

Harvard University

In a 1983 paper on black Democrats, "Black Voting, Bloc Voting, and the Democrats," I. A. Lewis and William Schneider reported that, while 44 percent of blacks in a *Los Angeles Times* survey felt that most Democrats are sincerely committed to helping blacks get ahead, a nearly equal percentage of blacks (40 percent) thought that most Democrats " don't really care much about Black people." The perception that the Democratic party takes the black vote for granted was widely shared by blacks throughout the 1980s and contributed to Jesse Jackson's 1984 bid for the Democratic party's presidential nomination. Indeed, if Jackson had chosen to run as an independent candidate in the 1984 presidential election, many blacks would have voted for him rather than for Walter Mondale or Ronald Reagan. In the 1983 *Los Angeles Times* poll, 35 percent said that they would vote for Jackson if he ran as an independent. In a 1984 national telephone survey of black Americans, over half (53 percent) claimed that they would vote for Jackson as an independent.[1] Lewis and Schneider conclude that, although blacks constitute the base of the party, they are, nevertheless, a "restive element"—quite willing in light of their ideological intensity and critical stance toward Democratic leadership to abandon their party in favor of Jackson or an alternative, pro-black, third-party candidate.

The Jackson candidacy seriously tested the Democratic party's long-standing relationship with blacks. On the one hand, leaders and representatives of the Democratic party struggled with the dilemma of maintaining their biracial coalition of liberal blacks and conservative white Southerners while dealing effectively with Jackson. The party had to find a way of accommodating Jackson without appearing either to have slighted him or to have caved in to his demands. On the other hand, black Democrats struggled with their clear preference for Jackson against the pragmatic decision to fully support the party's nominee in the interest of party unity. Jackson received higher evaluations among blacks than did Mondale in 1984. He earned an average of 74 on a "feeling thermometer" scale of 0 to 100, compared to 63 for Mondale. Furthermore, 57 percent of those polled said that they voted for or would have voted for Jackson in the 1984 primary, while only 27 percent voted for or would have voted for Mondale. Even though blacks voted overwhelmingly Democratic in the 1984 and 1988 presidential elections, both the party and blacks have charged each other with failing the test that Jackson's candidacies have imposed. Today, the party still does not know if it can count on the black vote in presidential elections, especially now that there is a 1992 Jackson candidacy on the horizon. Similarly, quite a few black Democrats continue to maintain that the party does not take them or their representatives seriously enough. A minority of blacks felt that Jackson had been mistreated by the party in 1984. Slightly more than one-fifth (21 percent) of the 1984 survey respondents felt that the Democratic party treated Jackson worse than it treated the other candidates in the race for the nomination.

In 1988, Jackson managed to strengthen his base of support among white liberals and blacks. At that point, additional numbers of blacks were more willing to support an independent Jackson bid for the presidency. In the 1988 reinterview of black voters, 60 percent said that if Jackson ran as an independent, they would vote for him rather than for Michael Dukakis or George Bush. In the aftermath of these two elections, and with a 1992 Jackson candidacy quite possible, it is important to assess the overall impact of Jackson's candidacies on blacks' relationship with the Democratic party. In this essay, I first outline the history of blacks' relationship with the Democratic party from the New Deal era to the emergence of Jesse Jackson as a presidential contender in 1984. Then, utilizing data from he 1984–1988 National Black Election Study,[2] I assess the impact of Jackson's candidacies on black loyalty to the Democratic party and–on black turnout in the 1984 and 1988 presidential elections. Finally, I discuss the implications of a third Jackson bid for the Democratic party's nomination and the extent of blacks' support for the party in 1992 and beyond.

Blacks and the Democratic Party: Roosevelt to Kennedy

When black Republicans began voting Democratic in national elections during the 1930s and 1940s, their alliance with the party was not considered permanent, since blacks generally voted Democratic during the period out of economic necessity (Weiss, 1983). Few could forget that the party was largely controlled by the South, which depended on lynching, supremacist violence, and legal devices to disenfranchise blacks. Most blacks were, in fact, Roosevelt Republicans. Furthermore, not only did blacks not play a critical role in the New Deal coalition forged by Roosevelt, but they also got little in exchange for their votes. Although he champi-

Figure 1. Black Party Identification, 1952–1988

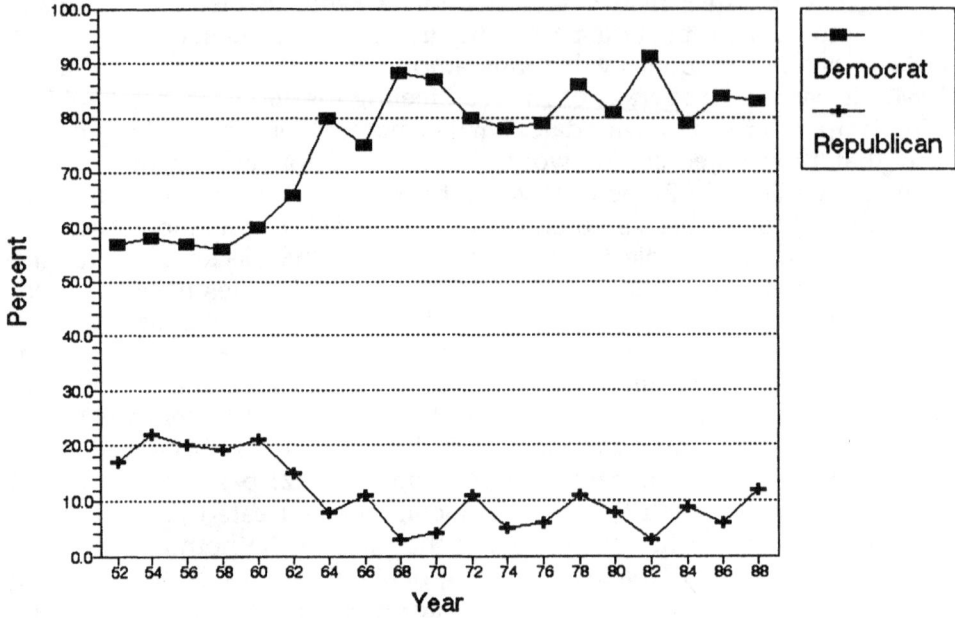

Note: Data were taken from the CPS' 1952–1988 National Election Studies; percentage of black political independents not shown.

oned the cause of the poor and the unemployed, Roosevelt held a dismal record on race. Of the more than 150 civil rights bills introduced in Congress during his administration, not one passed into legislation. It was only much later, in Roosevelt's third term in office, that he issued an executive order making discrimination in government employment illegal and establishing a Committee on Fair Employment Practices to enforce a nondiscrimination policy in defense programs (Carmines and Stimson, 1989:31).

Although a new and growing majority of blacks voted Democratic during the New Deal era, the Republican party remained an attractive political alternative for many blacks. In the 1952, 1956, and 1960 presidential elections, blacks remained slightly independent of the Democratic party, dividing their votes between the two parties (Walters, 1988:28). Dwight Eisenhower, for example, received 40 percent of the black vote in 1956, while Richard Nixon netted one-third in 1960 (Huckfeldt and Kohfeld, 1989:11). Moreover, it was not until the 1964 presidential election that the overwhelming majority of blacks began to identify themselves as Democrats. From 1952 to 1962, somewhere between 56 to 66 percent of blacks identified themselves as Democrats or political independents leaning toward the Democratic party. By 1964, however, a full 80 percent identified themselves as Democrats or as independents favoring the Democratic party (See Figure 1).

The surge in black identification with the Democratic party in the 1964 election was largely the result of the new racial liberalism of the party and, more specifically, the enactment of civil rights legislation in the Kennedy-Johnson era. President Kennedy, like Roosevelt before him, had initially chosen the strategy of ignoring the call for civil rights legislation. For example, he refused to endorse a civil rights bill introduced in May 1961 that he himself had asked be drafted (Lawson, 1976:288). Democratic presidential contenders had learned during the Truman years that they could not afford to respond to blacks' civil rights demands, because it would antagonize their white southern supporters. When, at the end of his first administration, Truman sent to Congress the first civil rights bill since Reconstruction, southern Democrats walked out of the national convention. Although he was reelected, Truman's action cost him the electoral votes of Alabama, Mississippi, Louisiana, and South Carolina (Carmines and Stimson, 1989:34–35). Kennedy's own strategy might have worked, but the civil rights movement had emerged, elevating civil rights from a regional interest or special interest of blacks to the national issue. In February 1963, in response to widespread racial violence, demonstrations, marches, and boycotts, Kennedy submitted a civil rights bill to Congress that was intended to protect blacks' voting rights in the South.

In their book, *Issue Evolution*, Edward Carmines and James Stimson attribute Kennedy's inability to keep the issue of race off the political agenda and the transformation of the party from racially conservative to racially liberal to a number of factors. They point out that by World War II, southern black migration to the North meant that northern Democrats, especially those in large urban centers, had become dependent upon black votes. Suddenly "[f]or a Democratic presidential nominee to win Illinois meant, in other words, that he had to win big in Chicago, which meant he had to do very well among black voters in the city" (Carmines and Stimson, 1989:33). The civil rights movement was another politically destabilizing factor. As the civil rights movement pushed forward, whites' attitudes on race had become more sympathetic toward blacks' demands for equal rights. Senator Barry Goldwater was also instrumental. Between 1950 and 1960, race was a nonpartisan issue. Although not a racist himself, Goldwater was on the the six Republican senators who voted against the 1964 Civil Rights Act. In doing so, and as the Republican party's choice for president in 1964, Goldwater made race into a highly partisan issue, with Democrats now squarely occupying the pro–civil rights side and Republicans the anti–civil rights camp. The public, who until 1964 had seen no real difference between the parties on racial matters, now recognized the Democratic party as the more racially liberal of the two.

Carmines and Stimson, however, overlook the critical role of blacks as agents of change *within* the Democratic party. At the center of their thesis is their belief that party elites, operating largely independently of blacks, managed to transform the Democratic party's position on race and their belief that this, in some sense, was accidental. They note that until 1958, racially liberal Republicans had always outnumbered racially liberal Democrats. In that year, Senate elections altered the mix of liberal Republicans and liberal Democrats when eleven Republicans were replaced by Democrats, ten of whom were racial liberals. Because race was not yet an elec-

188 Ethnic Politics and Civil Liberties

tion issue in 1958, this replacement, according to Carmines and Stimson, cannot be accounted for other than as evidence that 1958 was simply a bad year for Republicans in the Senate. The 1968 elections brought the next big wave of liberal Democrats, both in the House and the Senate. In these elections, race, which was now a major political issue, did affect the outcome. Yet blacks themselves had always maintained a role in effecting the transformation of the Democratic party from the conservative to the liberal party on race issues. From the 1920s to the present, the political influence of blacks within the Democratic party grew, and by the mid-1960s they were able to push the Democratic party toward the left on racial issues.

The Development of Black Political Power

The watershed year in black politics is often identified as 1965, when the voting rights bill was enacted. The Voting Rights Act enabled blacks to move away from direct-action techniques and protests to electoral political activities and involvement in party politics (Rustin, 1964; Smith, 1981). Passage of this act led to a dramatic increase in black voting power, with black registration in the South increasing from less than 31 percent in 1965 to approximately 60 percent by 1980 (Lawson, 1985). It also resulted in an explosion in the number of black elected officials across the country. The number of black political officeholders increased from an estimated 500 or so in the early 1970s to well over 6,000 by the late 1980s (Williams, 1987).

However, black political empowerment efforts predate the 1965 Voting Rights Act (Walton, 1972). These efforts could be felt within the Democratic party structure as early as the 1920s. As Carmines and Stimson note, blacks' migration to the North altered their political status, giving them more influence within the party. However, the black vote in the North was also highly concentrated. In his work on the development of the civil rights struggle, Doug McAdam notes that between 1910 and 1960, 87 percent of the total number of black immigrants from the South settled in seven key industrial states in the North: New York, New Jersey, Pennsylvania, Ohio, California, Illinois, and Michigan (1982:79). Moreover, northern black political power was not without its negative consequences. Newspapers of the day attributed both the failure of the Senate to confirm Hoover's Supreme Court nominee, John J. Parker, and the defeat of several senators who had supported Parker to the black vote (McAdam, 1982:80).

The three decades preceding the civil rights struggle were marked by a steady accumulation of black political resources. Not only did many blacks relocate from the South to the North, enjoying the franchise for the first time as well as freedom from the coercive control of the sharecropping system, but black organizational strength improved as well. Black college enrollments increased sharply, particularly after 1940, and local NAACP chapters expanded rapidly throughout the 1930s, 1940s, and 1950s (McAdam, 1982). Furthermore, during the civil rights movement blacks began to use their newly acquired power to play an even larger role within the

Democratic party at the national level. Until the mid-1960s, blacks in the South were effectively locked out of the Democratic party and of politics in general. But as the 1964 national elections approached, the Mississippi Freedom Democratic party (MFDP), an offshoot of the Council of Federated Organizations (COFO), a multiracial civil rights organization, was formed to challenge the all-white primary delegation from Mississippi to the National Democratic Party Convention. At the convention, the all-white delegation retained its seats as representatives of the state of Mississippi, while the MFDP was offered two at-large seats and promised future party rules that would prevent the seating of groups that discriminated against minority groups. Most political observers and activists outside the MFDP, including Martin Luther King, welcomed these steps as a fair compromise (Lawson, 1976). But, even though the Democratic party later initiated important reforms to increase minority and black participation at convention, there remained the perception that blacks were still locked outside the party.

Accordingly, blacks began to reassess their relationship with the Democratic party, even while black voting for Democratic presidential candidates remained consistently high. Indeed, in the 1980 presidential election, Ronald Reagan was elected with the lowest percentage of black votes of any previous Republican presidential candidate (Carmines and Stimson, 1989:54). In addition, identification with the party remained constant at or above 80 percent throughout the 1970s and 1980s. However, as happened with white voter turnout, black voting in presidential and off-year national elections fell successively throughout the 1970s, even while the gap between blacks and whites in registration and turnout closed (Williams, 1987; Wolfinger and Rosenstone, 1980). Furthermore, blacks' frustration with the party and their perception that their vote was being taken for granted grew during this period.

The frustration with the limits of their voting power has been a constant theme in black politics. As a minority voting bloc in national elections, black leaders have wrestled with the problem of how to best exploit the strategic value of the black vote (Walters, 1988). Their political liberalism has often put them in situations where neither of the major-party candidates supported their interests. Furthermore, their status as members of a racial minority has meant that despite loyalty to the Democratic party, they were not in a position to extract political goods or to participate in the selection of national leaders. In 1972, black political leaders, intellectuals, and elected officials met in Gary, Indiana, to discuss the possibility of forming a national black party to counter both the Democratic and Republican parties (Walters, 1988). However, this idea has held only limited appeal within the black community, particularly among black elected officials. In 1984, only 25 percent of blacks in the National Black Election Study favored a national black political party, and in a 1980 national survey of black Americans, approximately 40 percent expressed support for such an idea. In contrast, though, a majority of black Americans have consistently favored the idea of a black presidential candidate (see Walters, 1988:45).

By the time Jesse Jackson appeared on the national political scene in 1983, black political discontent with the Democratic party had intensified. While Reagan was elected through a crush of support by white Americans, enjoying some of the highest popularity ratings since Eisenhower, fewer than one out of every ten black voted for him. The Reagan administration proved to be disastrous to black economic interests, and the Democratic party had failed to serve as an effective counter to the administration during this period. When he made his bid to run for the presidency, many saw Jackson as a candidate who would speak to those outside national politics, and especially to black Americans (Barker, 1989). Furthermore, since the civil rights struggle of the 1960s, blacks had become an important and formidable voting bloc. The defection to the Republican party of white, southern Protestants, who had been the largest and most important constituent-group member of the New Deal coalition, sharply increased the party's dependence upon the black vote. Although blacks still represented a minority voting power, the Democratic party stood to lose every presidential election if it did not receive the lion's share of the black vote in each election year. Moreover, just as the Supreme Court's *Brown* decision had encouraged early black civil rights activists, the successive gains in the number of black elected officials, and in particular the election of black mayors in cities like Chicago, helped generate widespread feelings of new political optimism among blacks. Blacks felt more politically effective. In the 1948 National Black Election Study (NBES), a large majority (72 percent) strongly agreed with the statement "If enough black vote, they can make a difference in who gets elected president." Fewer than 11 percent disagreed.

The new black voting bloc that emerged by 1984 was an entirely different entity from the one that had participated in the New Deal coalition having returned FDR to office three additional times, despite the fact that he had refused to support any of the 150 civil rights bills sponsored in Congress. The black electorate had clearly matured. Indeed, in 1983, it was their new voting clout that served as the trump card in Jesse Jackson's hand.

The Impact of Jackson on the Black Electorate

While many believe that Jackson's candidacy led to white flight from the Democratic party, its impact on the black electorate is less clear. Contrary to claims that it had only a negligible effect (for example, Reed, 1986), his candidacy further intensified the already high engagement of the black electorate in presidential politics. In the first place, black interest in the presidential election increased. While 51 percent said that their interest remained the same, 46 percent of blacks claimed to be more interested in the presidential election because of Jackson's candidacy. And although many assumed that Jackson's candidacy would damage blacks' ties to the party, his 1984 candidacy actually strengthened blacks' affiliation with the party in 1988. Between 1984 and 1988, the percentage of strong Democrats within the sample increased from roughly 44 percent to approximately 60 percent. As Table 1 displays, black Democrats who more strongly favored Jackson in 1984 were more likely to become strong Democrats in 1988. Among those who rated Jackson 76 or higher on a scale from 0 to 100 in 1984, 72 percent of those who were weak Democrats in 1984 claimed to be strong Democrats in 1988. In contrast, among weak Jackson supporters (ratings of 51–75) and those who rated Jackson unfavorably (ratings of 0–50), the percentages of weak Democrats who became strong Democrats in the 1988 reinterview were 35 and 34 percent, respectively.[3] His 1984 candidacy, therefore, had the same sort of revitalizing effect on blacks' Democratic commitment that Roosevelt and Johnson had had on past generations of blacks.

Jackson's effect on black participation has garnered mixed reviews. Some claim that Jackson boosted black participation in 1984, while others state that Jackson depressed black participation in 1988. Still others have asserted that Jackson had no effect on black participation. In *The Jesse Jackson Phenomenon*, Adoph Reed remarks that the relationship between support for Jackson and black voter registration is "at best, ambiguous" (1986:17). Reed attributes the increase in black registration in 1984 to the steady growth in black registration rates in the South throughout the 1970s and 1980s. Furthermore, he adds the Reagan's reelection bid may have itself stimulated black turnout because of blacks' uniform opposition to his administration.

Given that Jackson was not on the ballot in the presidential election, his candidacy as a primary presidential contender may have had no discernible effect on black voter turnout in the presidential election. Research has found that prenomination preferences are unrelated to voter turnout in the general election (Stone, 1986; Kinney and Rice, 1988). Voters who supported candidates who lost the party's nomination are no less likely to vote in the general election than those who favored the nominee during the primary season. Prenomination preferences, nevertheless, have effects on other forms of voting behavior. Voters whose candidate lost the party's nomination tend to be more critical of their party's nominee and less critical of the opposing party's candidate. They are also less likely to participate in campaign activities such as contributing to the nominee's election funds or campaigning on behalf of the nominee.

Nevertheless, since Jackson ran in both the 1984 and 1988 primaries, the cumulative effect of his candidacies could be greater than their effects taken singly. Most important, Jackson's protracted struggle with the party leadership may have undermined blacks' allegiances to the Democratic party. It could be argued that Jackson's second bid for the Democratic presidential primary was somehow related to the drop in black voter turnout in 1988. In the long run, his supporters may eventually become less enchanted with the party.

Of the blacks interviewed over the telephone in the NBES, 76 percent voted for president in 1984, while 83 percent of those reinterviewed voted in the 1988 presidential election. The percentages of blacks who reported voting in the 1984 and 1988 surveys are much higher than the figures

Table 1. Cross-Tabulation of Blacks' Strength of Identification with Democratic Party in 1984 and Partisanship in 1988 by Jackson Rating in 1984 (Black Democrats in 1984 Only)

1984 Democratic Strength	1988 Partisanship						
	Strong Democrat	Weak Democrat	Independent Democrat	Political Independent	Republican	Total Percent	N
Jackson Ratings							
(100–76)							
Strong	80.4	14.0	1.3	0.0	4.3	100.0%	107
Weak	71.7	18.3	7.5	0.0	2.0	100.0%	33
Independent	47.3	23.5	10.8	5.3	13.2	100.0%	20
(75–51)							
Strong	83.2	15.0	1.8	0.0	0.0	100.0%	44
Weak	35.3	54.9	7.0	0.0	2.8	100.0%	24
Independent	49.0	11.3	23.9	11.8	4.0	100.0%	16
(50–0)							
Strong	84.8	7.8	5.4	0.0	2.1	100.0%	40
Weak	34.3	28.5	18.2	19.1	0.0	100.0%	21
Independent	22.1	0.0	11.5	27.0	39.3	100.0%	12

Note: Given their small numbers within the black community, self-identified strong Republicans, weak Republicans, and independent Republicans were combined to form a single Republican category. Weighted Percentages.

Table 2. Effects of Jackson Primary Support and Reagan Evaluations on Black
Voter Participation in the 1984 and 1988 Presidential Elections
(Logit Coefficients)

	Voted for President, 1984		Voted for President, 1988	
	B	SE	B	SE
Primary Support (Jackson)	.52[a]	(.26)	−.58[a]	(.66)
Reagan/Bush Rating	−.22[a]	(.10)	−.03[a]	(.01)
N	529		209	
Predicted Correctly	84%		88%	

[a]$p<.05$
[b]$p<.01$
Note: Logit analysis was performed using SST Version 2.0 (Dubin and Rivers). Control variables that were included but not presented are the following: education, income, age, gender, region, system responsiveness, political trust, political interest, race identification, membership in a politically active church, partisanship, and home ownership. In the 1988 model, "voted in 1984" and "media use by respondents" were added as additional control variables. For a full account of the results, see Tate 1990b.

released by the U.S. Census Bureau, which estimated black turnout in 1984 and 1988 to be 52 and 56 percent, respectively (U.S. Census Bureau, 1989). The high levels of voter participation found in the NBES are no doubt due to the fact that this is a telephone survey.[4] Although these respondents' levels of voter participation may not be representative of black participation in 1984 and 1988, it is still expected that the determinants of black participation remain unbiased.[5] The effects of Jackson and Reagan on black electoral participation were estimated using logit analysis. The results are presented in Table 2.

Jackson's effect on black electoral participation was largely positive in 1984. Primary participation by blacks in some states increased from 14 to 87 percent in 1984 (Cavanagh and Foster, 1984), and black Democrats who favored Jackson were more likely to vote in the 1984 presidential primaries (see Tate, 1990b, for analysis). Although he did not have a discernible effect on black voter registration in 1984, as Table 2 demonstrates, those who favored Jackson in the primary were slightly more likely to vote in the 1984 presidential election than those who favored Mondale or some other candidate. Reagan had a strong effect on black participation in the 1984 presidential election as well. Blacks who strongly disapproved of Reagan's performance as president were more likely to vote than those who approved of Reagan's performance. Therefore, both Jackson and Reagan proved to be equally strong stimuli to the black vote in 1984.

In 1988, preliminary analysis revealed that approval of Reagan was unrelated to black participation in the presidential election, but Bush ratings were linked to black participation. Blacks who evaluated Bush negatively were more likely to vote. Given that negative sentiment toward Reagan and Bush was associated with black voter participation, it may be anti-Republican sentiment, not specifically antiparty to Reagan or Bush that motivates blacks (who, after all, are overwhelmingly Democratic) to vote. In stark contrast to 1984, those who favored Jackson in the 1988 presidential primary were much *less* likely to vote than those who favored Dukakis.

There are essentially two reasons why many Jackson supporters may have refused to go to the polls for Dukakis in 1988. First, Jackson's supporters may have sat this election out to express their dissatisfaction with the Democratic party. The disappointment felt by blacks over Jackson's second failed attempt may have been much greater than the disappointment felt over his initial failure in 1984, and Democratic leadership may have been held accountable. However, rather than viewing this refusal to vote as an attempt to punish the party for its treatment of Jackson, it is more likely that decision not to vote Jackson supporters was a *strategic* decision. Mondale was an established political figure within the black community, and Jackson supporters turned out for him. Dukakis, in contrast, was not. Moreover, Dukakis presented himself not as a liberal (even though the Bush camp effectively labeled him as such), but as a political moderate, someone who would more effectively manage government. Because of this, Dukakis may have been less acceptable to Jackson supporters as an alternative to Jackson. They desired a more progressive and personally dynamic leader. Furthermore, the drop in white voter turnout in 1988 suggests that neither presidential candidate was especially attractive to the voters. Thus, had a more attractive and dynamic Democratic candidate been nominated, Jackson supporters might have come forth.

Blacks and the Democratic Party: 1992 and Beyond

A review of the history of blacks' political activity in the twentieth century reveals a marked growth in political power and influence in national politics. Black migration to the North, beginning in the 1920s and continuing unabated up to World War II, as well as the accumulation and concentration of their political resources during the civil rights struggle, fundamentally altered their political status. Blacks no longer played a quiescent role within the Democratic party. As more blacks became Democrats, their activism also helped to transform the Democratic party from a racially conservative to a racially liberal one.

Having facilitated its transformation, blacks also became more politically active both within and outside the Democratic party. They emerged as the progressive wing of the party. Although Jackson's 1984 candidacy played a significant part in promoting the growth of black political activism, that factor alone cannot account for the new power that blacks possess within the Democratic party. Even without Jackson, black Democrats would probably still have pushed for greater visibility as well as more responsiveness from the party. Furthermore, even without Jackson in the race, black political aspirations are headed toward a black presidential candidate, or at least, a candidate who more clearly articulates and supports their interests. Blacks' new influential position within the Democratic party has created concern among Democratic party leaders. The Jackson candidacies, and blacks' support of his candidacies, have made it more difficult for the Democratic party to manage its unstable coalition of blacks, white liberals, and Southerners. A return to their past, quiescent state in electoral and party politics, however, is possible, though highly unlikely. The Democratic party must find a way to manage its coalition, taking full account of the new political clout that blacks now wield.

At this point, it is highly likely that Jackson will manage a third attempt for the presidential nomination in 1992, although it is doubtful that he will have the same positive effect on black voter turnout in 1992 as in 1984. In 1984, Jackson had the historic significance of his candidacy to activate black voters. And as Gerald Austin, Jackson's campaign manager in his second bid, remarked prior to the Super Tuesday primary in 1988, "There's always less enthusiasm the second time" (Toner, 1988). In his third bid, Jackson must campaign even harder to build up black enthusiasm. But even with a new and strong appeal to blacks by Jackson, black voter participation in the 1992 presidential election will be most strongly affected by the type of Democratic candidate that is nominated and how that candidate campaigns within the black community. Although they are hugely supportive of Jackson, black Democrats, as strategic voters, still operate relatively independently of him. If the party eventually chooses not to nominate Jesse Jackson in 1992, then in order to mobilize the black vote, it should nominate a progressive substitute to Jackson. To do otherwise is to ignore the preferences of a large and fully mobilized segment of the party.

Notes

1. The 1984–1988 National Black Election Study. For its description, see note 2.
2. The 1984–1988 National Black Election Study is a longitudinal study of black political attitudes and electoral behavior during the 1984 and 1988 presidential elections. The study was conducted by the Program for Research on Black Americans, the Institute for Social Research at the University of Michigan. The 1984 preelection interviews were conducted from late July through 6, November, while reinterviews followed immediately after the election. The 1988 preelection reinterviews were held from August through 8 November, reinterviews began immediately after the election. A total of 1,150 voting-age blacks were obtained in the first wave, 872 in the second wave, 473 in the third wave, and 418 in the fourth and final wave. Because the sample for the first wave was derived using a disproportionate Random Digit Dial Design, the sample requires weighting. The 1988 sample also requires a corrective weight to offset sample attrition. The 1984 data set is currently available through the Inter-University Consortium for Political and Social Research, Ann Arbor, Michigan. For a summary of the 1984 data in tabular format, see Tate et al., 1987.
3. The causal direction between Jackson evaluations and black partisanship is unclear. In an analysis reported elsewhere (Tate, 1990s), a cross-lagged structural-equation model was developed, which revealed that partisanship in 1984 had

no effect on Jackson evaluations in 1988, while Jackson evaluations strongly affected the direction and strength of black partisanship. Furthermore, the positive effect of Jackson evaluations in 1984 on black partisanship in 1988 remained constant even after controls were introduced.

4. In contrast to face-to-face surveys, telephone surveys generally obtain respondents with a higher socioeconomic profile, individuals who are then more likely to vote. Furthermore, the 1988 figure is especially high in large part due to survey attrition; respondents less likely to vote were lost. The high turnout in 1988 may also be a reflection of the politicizing effect of the 1984 interview. These 1988 respondents may have registered and voted in higher numbers as a result of their participation in the 1984 interview.

5. The extent of overreporting, a problem for all voting studies, cannot be ascertained. Blacks, in fact, may be twice as likely to overreport voting as white (Abramson and Claggett, 1984). Sigeiman (1982) found, however, that voting data that contained overreporters and data purged of overreporters yielded similar results.

References

Abramson, Paul, R. and William Claggett. 1984. "Race-related Differences in Self-Reported and Validated Turnout." *The Journal of Politics*, 46:719–38.

Barker, Lucius J. 1989. "Jesse Jackson's Candidacy in Political-Social Perspective." In Lucius J. Barker and Ronald W. Walters, eds. *Jesse Jackson's 1984 Presidential Campaign*. Urbana and Chicago: University of Illinois Press.

Carmines, Edward G., and James A. Stimson. 1989. *Issue Evolution*. Princeton, NJ: Princeton University Press.

Cavanagh, Thomas E., and Lorn S. Foster. 1984. *Jesse Jackson's Campaign: The Primaries and Caucuses*. Washington, DC: The Joint Center for Political Studies.

Huckfeldt, Robert, and Carol Weitzel Kohfeld. 1989. *Race and the Decline of Class in American Politics*. Urbana and Chicago: University of Illinois Press.

Kinney, Patrick J., and Tom W. Rice. 1988. "Presidential Prenomination Preferences and Candidate Evaluations." *American Political Science Review*, 82, no. 4: 1,310–19.

Lawson, Steven F. 1976. *Black Ballots*. New York: Columbia University Press.

_____. 1985. *In Pursuit of Power*. New York: Columbia University Press.

Lewis, I. A., and William Schneider. 1983 "Black Voting, Bloc Voting and the Democrats." *Public Opinion*, 6, no. 5: 12–15,59.

McAdam, Doug. 1982. *Political Process and the Development of Black Insurgency, 1930–1970*. Chicago: University of Chicago Press.

Reed, Adolph, Jr. 1986. *The Jesse Jackson Phenomenon*. New Haven: Yale University Press.

Rosenstone, Steven J., Roy L. Behr, and Edward H. Lazarus. 1984. *Third Parties in America*. Princeton, NJ: Princeton University Press.

Rustin, Bayard. 1964. "From Protest to Politics: The Future of the Civil Rights Movement." *Commentary*, 65:25–31.

Sigelman, Lee. 1982. "The Nonvoting Voter in Voting Research." *American Journal of Political Science*, 26, no. 1: 47–56.

Smith, Robert C. 1981. Black power and the transformation from protest to politics. *Political Science Quarterly*, 96, no. 3: 431–43.

Stone, Walter J. 1986. "The Carryover Effect in Presidential Elections." *American Political Science Review*, 80, no. 1: 271–79.

Tate, Katherine. 1990a. "Bloc Voters, Black Voters, and the Jackson Candidacies, 1984–88." Paper presented at the 1990 annual meeting of the American Political Science Association, San Francisco, CA, 30 August–2 September.

_____. 1990b. "Black Participation in the 1984 and 1988 Presidential Elections." *American Political Science Review.* Forthcoming, Dec. 1991.

Tate, Katherine, Ronald E. Brown, Shirley J. Hatchett, and James S. Jackson. 1987 *The 1984 National Black Election Study Sourcebook.* Ann Arbor, MI: Institute for Social Research.

Toner, Robin. 1988 "Battle for the Black Vote Is Over before It Started." *The New York Times*, 28 February, 28, p. 28.

U.S. Bureau of Census. 1989. "Voting and Registration in the Election of November 1988 (Advance Report)." Current Population Reports, Series P-20, no. 435, February.

Walters, Ronald W. 1988. *Black Presidential Politics in America: A Strategic Approach.* Albany, NY: State University of New York Press.

_____. 1988. "The Emergent Mobilization of the Black Community in the Jackson Campaign for President." In Lucius J. Barker and Ronald W. Walters, eds., *Jesse Jackson's 1984 Presidential Campaign.* Urbana and Chicago: University of Illinois Press.

Walton, Hanes, Jr. 1972. *Black Politics: A Theoretical and Structural Analysis.* Philadelphia. Lippincott.

Weiss, Nancy J. 1983. *Farewell to the Party of Lincoln.* Princeton, NJ: Princeton University Press.

Williams, Linda F. 1987. "Black Political Progress in the 1980s: The Electoral Arena." In Preston, Michael B., Lenneal J. Henderson, Jr., and Paul L. Puryear, eds., *The New Black Politics.* 2d ed. New York: Longman Press.

Wolfinger, Raymond E., and Steven J. Rosenstone. 1980. *Who Votes?* New Haven: Yale University Press.

Two Political Traditions: Black Politics in the 1990s

Ronald Walters

Howard University

T he November elections of 1989 ushered into office a class of black elected officials who had campaigned and won in majority white districts (see Appendix 1). Immediately, this even was hailed as the "new" black politics by a consensus of press, politicians, and even some of the victorious candidates, who themselves began to tout the phenomenon of "crossover," or "mainstream" politics as the wave of the future.

To begin with, it is possible to dismiss the claim that "mainstream/ crossover" politics is a new phenomenon, since even a cursory look at the data yields the understanding that since at least 1968 black politicians have been elected in a variety of political jurisdictions where blacks constituted a minority of the population (See Appendix 2). Indeed, a surprising fact is that a review of thirty-four cities with populations of more than 50,000 reveals that in 1988, twenty-two (63 percent) had white populations greater than 50 percent (see Appendix 3). Considering the fact that there were 300 black mayors in 1989, the accumulation of black mayoral seats in white-majority political jurisdictions means that today they constitute approximately 10–15 percent of the total.

What appears, then, to have made the elections of November 1989 appear new is that so many black politicians were elected from various white-majority political jurisdictions simultaneously.

Black Politics and Black Politicians

What emerges in the crossover paradigm is a strongly favorable bias for moderate politics operationalized by blacks. This raises the questions of whether the emerging trend should even be identified as "black politics" and whether, consequently, the raw expansion in the number of black elected officials from white-majority districts is necessarily a net gain for "black progress."

Defining Black Politics

We begin with the understanding that the distinction between the recently elected black moderate politicians and the first generation of politicians who emerged from the civil rights movement era is more than a distinction between professions and background; it is a profound distinction in political strategies that could evince an even more profound difference in political socialization and, thus, in political values. Even though the civil rights strategy was relatively moderate and its ends were thoroughly consistent with putative American ideals of equal rights, those who attempted to legitimize crossover political leadership appear to attack the civil rights legacy. (WETA-TV, 1990). This appeared to signal a greater willingness on the part of whites to vote for certain kinds of black candidates. In addition, the nature of the offices added to the drama: in addition to the breakthrough victories by black mayors in Cleveland, Seattle, and New Haven, there were the history-making first elections of blacks to the mayoralty of New York City—the nation's second-largest city—and to the governorship of Virginia.

More important, analysts seemed to imply that this was the *preferred way for all blacks* to campaign for office in majority-white political jurisdictions. The essence of this issue, according to this consensus, was that black elected officials had been elected to office in black-majority districts by basing their campaigns on a strong racial appeal, which sometimes had the effect of alienating whites from biracial coalitions. The crossover black politicians, in contrast, had specifically attempted to neutralize the race issue altogether by refraining from making strong racial appeals, eschewing a racial identity, and seeking to identify strongly with the issues favored by the majority white populations. Thus the two political traditions:—which will prevail in the 1990's?

The essence of the problem is that the aggressive legacy of the civil rights movement contains the inherent notion of confrontation and pressure as a methodology for forcing major American institutions to legitimize black demands for justice. On the other hand, *the intent of those now rushing to rationalize crossover politics appears to be to "normalize" black politics, or to subordinate black demands to the normal workings of the political process and, thereby, to denude it of its urgency and oppositional character.*

The ethic of resistance to oppression as the basis for making strong demands for justice is a part of the black political tradition that was articulated early in this century by W. E. B. Du Bois as a result of his work with the Niagra and NAACP organizations:

> This program of organized opposition to the action and attitude of the dominant white group includes ceaseless agitation and insistent demand for equal-

ity; the equal right to work, civic and political equality, and social equality. It involves the use of force of every sort: moral suasion, propaganda and where possible even physical resistance. (Du Bois, 1940:193)

In the late 1930s, Professor Ralph Bunche of Howard University suggested that the Negro vote might play a role in the "development of full integration" and give blacks a new sense of "responsibility and civic dignity" by forming a coalition with "that small band of perspiring Southern liberals who are doggedly working for broad social reform" (Grantham, 1973:88.) He went on to say that

> it does seem that the vote could be traded for improved facilities and services where the Negro vote in any significant numbers. *In those areas* in which the Negro is able to wield the stick of political power, his requests are much more attentively listened to and complied with [my emphasis]. (Grantham, 1973:88.)

Martin Luther King, Jr., took up this theme both practically and analytically in attempting to define the concept of black power. He observed that although black voting power in the South was not developed, even in the North blacks were alienated from participation. He asserted that blacks needed "responsible militant organization . . . [in their] struggle" and that when "they learn that united and organized pressure can achieve measurable results, [they] will make [their] influence felt. . . . and the political power of the aroused minority will be enhanced and consolidated" (Washington, 1986:307).

King observed one further, crucial problem: that black political leaders were ineffective, in the first instance, because they "did not ascend to power on the shoulders of mass support," but through the largess of white political machines. He then continued:

> Tragically, he is in too many respects not *a fighter for a new life* but a figurehead of the old one. Hence very few Negro political leaders are impressive or illustrious to their constituents [my emphasis]. (Washington,1986:308)

As a result, King said, black leaders are hampered in their bargaining with white party leaders and find themselves in a vacuum, unable to build leverage or sustain influence. So, he suggested, blacks would have to "create leaders who embody virtues we can respect . . . who are political warriors on our behalf." (Washington, 1986:308)

At the same time, with regard to political coalitions, he counseled that blacks should establish alliances with "white *reformers* and independent political groups" [my emphasis], suggesting that a true alliance was based "upon some self-interest of each component group and a common interest into which they merge." The nature of the allied interests King had in mind were those that would embody "structural changes in the society" (Washington,1986:308).

King, then, appeared to believe that the kind of political leaders who participate in politics would not be moderated but, would be, in his words, "political warriors," and that if the black masses did exercise militant action to mobilize in support of black political leaders and if such leaders were accountable, these leaders would have the influence and power necessary to bargain successfully in pursuit of black objectives. Finally, in fashioning political coalitions with whites, the objectives sought should be directed toward *structural changes* in society. These expectations appear to be quite different from those that have emerged in the 1990's.

Bayard Rustin, who was a theoretician of the civil rights movement, buttressed the feeling that the aim of the movement should be to form a coalition inside the Democratic party that could become an "effective vehicle for social reconstruction." He continued:

> The role of the civil rights movement in the *reorganization of American political lifes* is programmatic as well as strategic. We are challenged now to broaden our social vision, to develop a functional program with concrete objectives. We need to propose alternatives to technological unemployment, urban decay, and the rest. We need to be calling for public works and training, for national economic planning, for federal aid to education, for attractive public housing — all this on a sufficiently massive scale to make a difference [my emphasis]. (Rustin, 1971:122)

It is revealing that, in the period of black power, part of the deficit of white power was that it often failed to make viable political coalitions with blacks based on fair equity in return; rather, blacks usually functioned as exploited subordinate parts of an urban machine. Thus, the concept that emerged out of the 1960's was that it was necessary as a symptom of the equitable sharing of power, to enter into political coalitions with whites.

Chuck Stone also supports the view that the black vote had traditionally been used to elect white liberals or to support the urban machines for patronage, but that with the advent of the black power concept this changed. He said that the coming of black mayors in 1967 in Gary, Cleveland, and Washington signaled the emergence of a "group of politicians . . . proclaiming (their) ability to govern both whites and blacks." (Stone,1968:25). Stone opines that in many places where white ethnic groups had governed, they did so out of all proportion to their strength in the population. (Stone,1968:23). He further demonstrates that, in many cities under white control, white ethnics in white-majority coalitions governed without much regard for the interests and needs of blacks, and that, in most cases, the myth of the "melting pot has been used as a cover for the attainment of [white] group power, while paying lip service to the American creed" (Stone,1968:22). Clearly, the implication is that the democratic pluralist political system that works to empower white ethnics does not function as well to incorporate black racial politics.

Thus, even in the political thought of civil rights integrationists, the value of political change through challenging institutionalized racism was strong. But it became even stronger when the movement changed to adopt an explicitly black identity and ideology. Reginald Gilliam, Jr., observes that despite the confusion that existed among leaders and organizations

concerning the meaning of "blackness," there was a push to institution-
alize it in some form, since its power derived in part from the fact that it
was a norm that was antithetical to prevailing norms and political behavior. Gilliam states that "such institutionalization is clearly a political process in that it directly challenges the dominant society to change"
(Gilliam,1975:261–62).

In summary, what is striking here is that both radical leaders and the
most moderate thinkers and activists appeared to have developed great
expectations of electoral politics as represented by the following propositions:

1. The ends of Black politics, as it emerged through the strategies and
    tactics of grass-roots community organizations, were designed to chal-
    lenge institutionalized practices of racism and to foment the necessary
    changes in behavior that would result in the fair dispensation of goods,
    services, and principles.
2. A major goal of black politics was to develop institutionalized political
    power, transferring the values of changes from the movement into
    institutional channels such as supporting various candidates and hold-
    ing office.
3. The resulting leadership established in American political institutions
    should be strong, progressive, and change-oriented.
4. Interracial political alliances and coalitions should be made with a bias
    toward progressive, reform-oriented whites, in keeping with the needs
    of the black community.
5. In the governing of cities and other political jurisdictions, black lead-
    ers should attempt to see that all who were under their perview ben-
    efited, but certainly black needs were to be attended to as a priority.

Although the above statements, upon which the resulting concepts are
based, are selected in a random and subjective fashion, nevertheless, they
are explanatory in that they characterize black expectations from the electoral process. As such, these factors have implications for how one must
campaign in black-majority districts, and they also set the standard for
what black populations, of whatever size, might expect from black candidates and elected officials. That is to say, even though the black candidate
may be limited in his or her appeal to the black population, that population must enter freely into the competition for the attention of whoever
presents him or herself for office—black or white. Thus, these factors
imply that a candidate's style, issues, and strategy must honestly comport
with the racial demography of the black-majority population.

The Normalization of Black Politics

Given the focus on the crossover phemonenon, some observers feel that
the debate about the conceptualization of black politics is urgent, because
the increasing moderation of black campaigners leads, in many cases, to

the migration of blacks into major political institutions and to the acquisition by blacks of significant institutional roles. These blacks' successes may represent a strategy that is not solidly devoted to creating the kind of tension that would strongly raise issues from the perspective of black interests. State of California Assemblywoman Maxine Waters evokes this sentiment when she says that there is a veritable conspiracy by some media analysts to create "a neutered black official that's been 'mainstreamed' [and] who would not be an advocate for the poor and disenfranchised" (Barnes, 1990:263). Likewise, a former mayor of Gary, Indiana, Richard Hatcher, was reported to feel that "today, a growing number of Black candidates don't feel that obligation to do something about the terrible conditions in which black people live, or at least don't show it" (Barnes, 1990:263). Hatcher himself said that "It appears that some of the more prominent black candidates in the last few years are willing to make that kind of concession" and that "I don't think that we can afford to concede bits and pieces of that [black agenda] for expediency's sake" (Barnes, 1990: 263).

There is, then, underneath this debate about political style, the barely audible debate about the impact of institutionalization upon black leadership in producing moderate, nonconfrontational politics, and about, whether or not it makes much difference in terms of absolute resources or whether black politicians would be much better than white politicians. Some of what is intended by those who favor crossover politics is clear, as Linda Williams analyzed their meaning for Jesse Jackson: "the message of the successful Blacks to Jackson is that 'he'll have to moderate [his campaign tactics] even more and change his campaign style' if he wants to get as much white support as Wilder or Dinkins" (Williams, 1989:A47).

Those who are posing this moderate, nonconfrontational style as the correct and future path often do not relate style to substance; they also, by implication, suggest that blacks demands upon the political system for the eradication of racism and for greater distribution of the wealth of society should be extremely moderate as well. They dismiss the fact that what is polarizing about authentic black politics is not merely its style but *its responsiveness to the already polarized conditions in society between blacks and whites and between rich and poor.* They appear to have found a convenient tool, in the elections of November 1989, to make their case, suggesting that greater political office and, thus, responsibility for all levels of politics may be acquired through moderate politics, and that such politics should have little to do with substance.

Two Political Traditions

We have been addressing the evaluation of the meaning of the crossover politics, and it is clear that we have been discussing, not one, but two political traditions—black politicians representing majority-white political jurisdictions and black politicians representing majority-black political jurisdictions. Each of these traditions has its own integrity and raison d'être.

The confusion in this, and the reason why some analysts have extended the meaning of "black politics" to cover this growing crossover phemonenon, is that both sets of leaders are black. However, *in terms of the meaning of black politics as it emerged from the civil rights/black politics movements, black leadership of white majorities is not properly speaking to be regarded as black politics.* Thus the press's need to evaluate one tradition in terms of the other and to place a higher value on moderate, nonconfrontational style and deracialized politics is consistent with their expectations of white political representation, and, in effect, they are demanding that blacks who win in such districts conform to this model. As such, this is a reasonable expectation.

It is unreasonable, however, to devalue black politics—to demean the kind of demanding leadership and focus on black issues that emerged from the special history of blacks and that has, thus, shaped their political mobilization. This reaffirms the view that the theory blacks have fashioned to give potency to the political strategies they might employ in the achievement of their objectives is valid. It is a theory that is based on the urgency of the black condition that transcends the normal incremental workings of institutions; it is a theory that is based on the necessity for change in the way institutions and political processes function and therefore, on the need to bring pressure upon those institutions; it is a theory that is unashamed or unafraid to describe and project the black agenda; it is a theory that involves positing the persistence and virulence of racism as a basic cause of black subordination; and even though tactics of compromise are often useful, it is an uncompromising theory in the basic sense that the goal is to enhance black progress. In short, blacks have a right to demand a useful product from the political system in exchange for their participation and to evaluate the worthiness of politics on that basis. Thus, it is valid for them to ask "What difference does it make?"—to the satisfaction of their interests—that blacks are elected in majority-white districts.

The attempt to "normalize" or "mainstream" this theory of social change is paramount to divorcing the rationale for black demands from their political strategies. It is important to understand this because black politics, or the activity of black politicians representing majority-black populations, will probably remain the major genre of politics in the black community for the foreseeable future. Thus, even though black politicians who represent majority-white political jurisdictions may choose to function as a valid part of the collective leadership, the distinction between these two categories of politics should be clear.

Appendix 1

Position and Jurisdiction	Winner	Percent of Vote
Governor, Virginia	Doug Wilder	50.6
Mayor, New York	David Dinkins	51
Mayor, Seattle	Norman Rice	58
Mayor, New Haven	John Daniels	70
Mayor, Cleveland	Michael White	55
Mayor, Durham	Chester Jenkins	53

Sources: the *Washington Post* and the *New York Times.*

Appendix 2
Black Representation of Minority-Black Districts

Name	Office	State/City	Year	% Blk
Ed Brooke	U.S. Senate	Massachusetts	68	3
Mervyn Dymally	Lt. Gov.	California	74	7
George Brown	Lt. Gov.	Colorado	78	3
C. Delores Tucker	Sec. State	Pennsylvania	71	—
Roland Burrus	Comptroller	Illinois	77	13
Richard Austin	Sec. State	Michigan	72	12
Vel Phillips	Sec. State	Wisconsin	77	3
Henry Parker	Treasurer	Connecticut	76	3
Andrew Young	U.S. House	Georgia (5th)	72	44
Ronald Dellums	U.S. House	California (8th)	70	21
Yvonne Burke	U.S. House	California (28)	72	40
Barbara Jordan	U.S. House	Texas (18th)	72	44
Harold Ford	U.S. House	Tennessee (8th)	74	47
William Clay	U.S. House	Missouri (1st)	68/88	54/46
Alan Wheat	U.S. House	Missouri (5th)	82	20
Warren Weidener	Mayor	Berkeley, CA	72	21
Herbert White	Mayor	Pittsburg, CA	71	—
Benjamin Day	Mayor	Leavenworth, KS	72	—
Hilliard Moore	Mayor	Lawnside, NJ	72	—
Clarence Bridgers	Mayor	Carson, CA	74	—
Tom Bradley	Mayor	Los Angeles, CA	74	17

Source: compiled from annual volumes of *The Almanic of American Politics, National Journal,* and *The National Roster of Black Elected Officials,* Joint Center for Political Studies. William Clay's district was 54 percent black in 1968 and 46 percent black by 1988.

Appendix 3
Black Mayors and Percent of Black Population in the City
(for cities of over 50,000 population)
(compiled January 1990)

City, Mayor, and Political Affiliation	% Black	% Hispanic
1. Birmingham, AL (Richard Arrington, D)	55.6	—
2. Oakland, CA (Lionel Wilson, D)	46.9	—
3. Richmond, CA (George Livingston, D)	47.9	—
4. Compton, CA (Walter Tucker, D)	74.8	21.1
5. Inglewood, CA (Edward Vincent, I)	57.3	19.6
6. Los Angeles, CA (Tom Bradley, D)	17.0	27.5
7. Lynwood, CA (Paul Richards, I)	34.8	43.2
8. Thousand Oaks, CA (Lawrence E. Horner, I)	.8	5.8
9. Hartford, CT (Carrie S. Perry, D)	33.9	20.5
10. New Haven, CT (John Daniels, D)	31.9	8.0
11. Washington, DC (Marion Barry, D)	70.3	—
12. Pompano Beach, FL (E. Pat Larkins, D)	17.9	2.2
13. West Palm Beach, FL (James O. Peele, D)	27.9	8.6
14. Tallahassee, FL (Dorothy Inman, D)	31.8	1.8
15. Atlanta, GA (Andrew Young, D)	66.6	—
16. Rockford, IL (Charles E. Box, D)	13.9	2.9
17. Gary, IN (Thomas V. Barnes, D)	70.9	—
18. New Orleans, LA (Sidney Barthelemy, D)	55.3	3.5
19. Baltimore, MD (Kurt Schmoke, D)	54.4	—
20. Detorit, MI (Coleman A. Young, D)	63.1	—
21. Pontiac, MI (Waltomore L. Moore, I)	37.2	6.5
22. Camden, NJ (Melvin R. Primas, Jr., D)	53.0	19.2

Appendix 3 (Continued)
Black Mayors and Percent of Black Population in the City
(for cities of over 50,000 population)
(compiled January 1990)

City, Mayor, and Political Affiliation	% Black	% Hispanic
23. East Orange, NJ (John C. Hatcher, Jr., D)	83.2	—
24. Newark, NJ (Sharpe James, D)	58.2	18.6
25. Mount Vernon, NY (Ronald A. Blackwood, D)	48.7	4.8
26. New York, NY (David N. Dinkins, D)	25.2	19.9
27. Cleveland, OH (Michael White, D)	43.8	3.1
28. Dayton, OH (Clay Dixon, D)	36.9	—
29. Springfield, OH (Timothy S. Ayers, D)	17.2	—
30. Philadelphia, PA (W. Wilson Goode, D)	37.8	3.8
31. Newport News, VA (Jessie M. Rattley, D)	31.5	—
32. Suffolk, VA (Jonnie E. Mizelle, D)	47.6	—
33. Roanoke, VA (Noel C. Taylor, R)	22.0	—
34. Seattle, WA (Norman Rice, D)	9.5	2.6
		*(Asian—7.4)

Source: County and City Data Book, U.S. Census Bureau, Department of Commerce, May 1988.

References

Barnes, James A. 1990. "Into the Mainstream." *National Journal*, 3 February.
Du Bois, W. E. B. 1940. *Dusk of Dawn: An Essay Toward an Autobiography of a Race Concept*. New York: Harcourt, Brace.
Gilliam, Reginald. 1975. *Black Political Development: An Advocacy Analysis*. Port Washington: Kennikat.
Grantham, Dewey, ed. 1973. *Ralph Bunche: The Political Status of the Negro in the Age of FDR*. Chicago: University of Chicago Press.
Rustin, Bayard. 1971. *Down the Line*. Chicago: Quadrangle Press.
Stone, Chuck. 1968. *Black Political Power in America*. Indianapolis: The Bobbs-Merrill Company.
Washington, James M. 1986. *Testament of Hope: The Essential Writings of Martin Luther King, Jr.* San Francisco: Harper and Row.
WETA-TV. 1990. "Politics: The New Black Power." WETA-TV Special, aired 26 February 1990.

Williams, Linda. 1989. "Blacks Show Ability to Win in Mostly White Areas."
The Washington Post, 9 November, p. A47.

Review Essays

New Directions in
Eastern European Research

Kathie Stromile Golden

University of Colorado at Colorado Springs

The unfolding of events in Eastern Europe during the latter half of 1989 surprised both Westerners and non-Westerners. The collapse of Eastern European communist systems was related in part to Mikhail Gorbachev's rise to power in the Soviet Union. Unlike his predecessors,[1] Gorbachev did not just give lip service to the need for far-reaching societal reforms directed at increasing economic efficiency in the Soviet Union and throughout the Soviet bloc; he also initiated policies crucial to the achievement of economic efficiency. Equally significant, Gorbachev demonstrated a willingness to loosen control over Eastern Europe for the sake of successfully reforming the Soviet economy.

Although there is a voluminous amount of research seeking to assess the "spillover" effects of Gorbachev's policies of glasnost (openness) and perestroika (economic restructuring) on Eastern European political systems, a substantial amount of such research presents a less-than-optimistic view of the extent to which the Soviet leader would demonstrate his commitment to economic reforms and liberalizations that could ultimately undermine Soviet bloc cohesiveness. In short, researchers were and still are cautious in making predictions about Gorbachev's democratization program and about the postcommunist systems of Eastern Europe. Such caution is predicated on the past behavior of Soviet and Eastern European leaders who advocated reforming their economic systems. History shows that during the post–World War II era, Soviet and Eastern European leaders have often vacillated between extreme repression, liberalization, and sophisticated forms of repression. Thus, it is not surprising that scholars of Eastern European politics did not foresee the impending collapse of communism. The uncertainty about the depth of Gorbachev's reforms, coupled with the fact that Communist party dominance throughout the region did not end until December, with the Romanian citizens' overthrow of the Ceauşescu regime, means that there is a dearth of published scholarly literature on postcommunist Eastern Europe. There is, however, a substantial amount of literature focusing on developments in Eastern Europe during the last five years.

While time and space constraints preclude an exhaustive treatment of literature published since 1985,[2] a brief sampling of research addressing widespread changes during the last three years will increase our understanding of the extent to which internal factors contributed to the diminution and eventual demise of Communist party rule in Soviet bloc countries. Additionally, this sampling will suggest directions for future research endeavors.

The following discussion focuses on several works that include analyses of some of the radical developments in Eastern Europe during 1988 and 1989. Of the research providing the focus for this essay, five are books and two are journal articles. These seven works are divided into three broadly defined, but not mutually exclusive, categories: dissent and opposition, economic reform and political change, and Soviet–Eastern European relations.

Dissent and Opposition

Political dissent and opposition are not phenomena new to Eastern Europe. From the inception of Communist party rule until the events of 1989, Eastern European citizens engaged in organized as well as spontaneous activities directed at weakening or ending the party's monopoly on power. In fact, the history of Communist party rule reveals ebbs and flows in citizen resistance, rebellion, and political opposition to such rule. The Polish people's opposition to party rule is, perhaps, better known by outsiders than that of other Eastern European citizens. Citizens challenges to communist rule have, however, occurred persistently throughout the Soviet bloc, although some have been more visible than others.

Bugajski and Pollack (1989) present an especially comprehensive analysis of oppositionist trends in the states of contemporary Eastern Europe. The authors trace the development and growth of dissent and opposition campaigns throughout Eastern Europe. Dissent and opposition campaigns are likened to a series of well-developed geological fractures crisscrossing the earth's surface. Bugajski and Pollack posit that cracks in the landscapes of Eastern European communist systems render the party vulnerable. That is, the persistence of rebellion, dissent, and other forms of political activism and Eastern European leaders' inability to effectively address challenges to their rule created situations in which the very fabric of party domination could at any time be torn apart.

The uniqueness of this volume lies in its comparative focus and the authors' attempts to differentiate between dissent strategies and orientations—revolutionist and evolutionist strategies—and the various forms of government repression. The attention given to both large and small, highly visible and not so visible, dissent and oppositionist campaigns contributes to the uniqueness of this book. Finally, Bugajski and Pollack's research suggests that Gorbachev's willingness to loosen control over Eastern Europe was a necessary but not sufficient condition for the collapse of communism in the region. In the absence of persistent opposition, rebellion, and dissent, it is probable that some communist regimes would remain intact today.

In a similar manner, Skilling (1989) examines the distribution of uncensored (samizdat) writing throughout Central and Eastern Europe. Although the author is careful to note that the term *samizdat* is without precise meaning, he distinguishes between various national forms. Skilling elaborates on the importance of samizdat as an instrument of dissent and opposition, thereby establishing its connection with efforts to diminish the Communist party's stranglehold on Central and Eastern Europe. The author's research makes clear Central and Eastern European citizens' commitment to fostering the development of "civil societies," that is, societies less restrictive of individual freedoms, especially freedom of expression.

A third volume, although not explicitly focusing on dissent and opposition, seeks to illuminate the correlation between dissent movements and the development of a post-totalitarian mind. Goldfard (1989) provides a theoretical analysis of political, economic, and social changes in the Soviet bloc that is directed at increasing Westerners' understanding of such changes. The author posits that Western scholars' inability to differentiate between traditional and modern tyranny has prevented them from recognizing the various forms of totalitarianism that have existed in Soviet bloc countries. This inability, in turn, affects our understanding and appreciation of political and social changes in contemporary Eastern Europe.

Goldfard's main goal is to identify political and cultural alternatives to modern tyranny. To this end, he illuminates the connections between force and reason and between truth and violence as they define contemporary totalitarianism. The author's extensive discussion of the emergence of cultural language and sociopolitical activities outside official purview substantiates the existence of a totalitarian order that has been rejected by Eastern European people, especially Polish people. This brings to the forefront the extent to which contemporary political theory hampers our ability to understand and appreciate the notion that Eastern European dissent movements were perhaps more crucial than Mikhail Gorbachev's glasnost in creating an alternative system (civil society). The scholarly research discussed in this section, although similar in focus, is different in scope and approach. Each book, however, establishes that the political systems imposed on Eastern European citizens were always tenuous, in that they were never accepted fully by the citizenry of the region.

Economic Reforms and Political Change

At various times since World War II, Eastern European leaders recognized the need for economic reforms, but their commitment to initiating and implementing such reforms appeared more as attempts to pacify discontentment among the citizenry than as deeply held convictions relevant to economic efficiency. Most, if not all, communist leaders understood that the proper implementation of economic reforms, such as decentralization in production, greater self-management, and privatization, would seriously undermine Communist party control over society. This awareness accounts, in part, for the unwillingness of some communist leaders to initiate and implement far-reaching reforms. As long as Soviet leaders provided economic and political support for Eastern European communist regimes, they could avoid making necessary economic reforms. Gorbachev's assumption of power and his emphasis on perestroika (economic restructuring) had an impact on the leadership of each Soviet bloc country. In effect, Gorbachev made it clear that the Soviet bloc countries had to stand on their own economic feet. This, then, came to mean that far-reaching economic reforms would be necessary throughout most of the region.[3]

Milanovic's (1989) comparative analysis of the process of economic reforms in the East and West provides useful insights into recently enacted policies in several Eastern European countries. In setting the tone for the analysis, Milanovic devotes several chapters to explicating differences and similarities between capitalist and socialist economies. He delineates the advantages of both systems' methods of production. He argues that, not unlike economic liberalization in the West, reduced state interference in economic life is the core of economic reforms in the East. Milanovic also alludes to the lack of uniformity in moves toward liberalization in the East. The absence of uniformity is then an indication of the Soviet leader's willingness to allow each country to pursue its own strategies.

Chapter 5 of this volume includes a discussion of the loosening of state regulations and greater opportunities for private-sector expansion in Poland, Czechoslovakia, and Hungary.[4] After a brief discussion of the forms of liberalization that have been tried recently (1987–1988), Milanovic concludes that liberalization in the agricultural sector provides the greatest opportunity for private-sector growth in these countries. His analysis of the potential for conflict at various levels and sectors of socialist production substantiates his argument.

Cochrane (1990), in an examination of reforms in agricultural prices in Poland, notes that many of the countries of Eastern Europe began to introduce market reforms prior to the recent political upheavals. Although Cochrane's analysis primarily focuses on Poland's 1989 liberalization measure and its 1990 economic program, her analysis also has implications for other Eastern European countries.

Her cogent longitudinal analysis of changes in Polish producer prices, in retail prices (nominal and real), and in subsidies paid to the agricultural and food industry, coupled with an examination of the state's continued control over purchasing, production, and the supply of inputs, illuminates the problematic nature of introducing market reforms in centrally planned economies. Like Milanovic, Cochrane identifies Hungary and Czechoslovakia, as well as East Germany, as countries in which price reforms and liberalization have the greatest potential for immediate success. This article is significant because it demonstrates that the most recent political changes in Eastern Europe will neither single-handedly nor without tremendous difficulty ensure the successful implementation of badly needed economic reforms. Unlike communist political systems, centrally planned economies cannot change and produce successful economic programs overnight.

Soviet–Eastern European Relations

Key questions arising in relation to Gorbachev's reforms and the loosening of control over Eastern Europe are, What will be the impact of these reforms on Soviet–Eastern European relations? Does this mean that the Soviet Union is willing to forego its position of dominance for the sake of the success of Soviet reforms? How will these reforms impact on Soviet–Eastern European military relations? Prior to the radical political changes of 1989, the prevalent view held by Western scholars and policymakers was that the Soviet leadership was not likely to seriously risk its status in the region for the sake of greater economic efficiency. Thus, the loosening of control over the region was viewed with caution. While most scholars and policymakers need to be somewhat optimistic about the economic aspects of Soviet and Eastern European reforms, few were optimistic about the Soviet leader's willingness to relinquish Soviet dominance relative to the Warsaw Pact. At present there remains a great deal of uncertainty about Gorbachev's intentions and perception in the military sphere. It is, however, well established that he is very concerned regarding a unified Germany's membership in the North Atlantic Treaty Organization (NATO).

A major attempt to assess Soviet–Eastern European relations in the era of perestroika and glasnost is undertaken in a volume edited by Aurel Braun (1990). The Braun volume posits explanations regarding Soviet and Eastern Europeans' political and ideological perceptions of each other. Using a multidimensional approach, the authors elucidate the historical bases for Eastern European leaders' and citizens' distrust of and hostility toward the Soviet Union. Collectively, the chapters comprising this book reveal cross-national variations in political/ideological, economic, military, and cultural relations with the Soviet Union. The data presented in this volume are critical to understanding cross-national differences in Eastern European leaders' willingness to embrace Soviet reforms, as well as to understanding variations in citizens' enthusiasm about the prospects for meaningful change.

The Collapse of Communism

The literature discussed so far suggests that Mikhail Gorbachev's policies of perestroika and glasnost had a significant impact on the demise of Communist party rule in Soviet bloc countries. Undoubtedly, Soviet reforms had spillover effects, but there is substantial evidence that other factors were equally important. One of the earliest, if not the earliest, scholarly works addressing the events of late 1989 (Schopflin, 1990) examines various factors that had significance for the collapse of communism in Eastern Europe.

Schopflin's investigation indicates that economic deprivation, criticism from intellectuals, and divisions within the Communist party leadership coalesced to bring down the communist system. The author's in-depth analysis of the shortcomings of Soviet-type systems—their divergence from the ideals of socialism—substantitates that these systems effectively created sociopolitical environments that ultimately led to their collapse. In other words, the communist systems' growing inability to create viable economies, to mobile the citizenry (that is, to gain legitimacy), or to settle internal disputes, coupled with Gorbachev's hands-off policy, resulted in the events of late 1989.

Conclusion

The literature examined in this essay is neither definitive nor necessarily representative of scholarly work on the subject. It does, however, encompass much of the data that are presented in a substantial amount of the research in this field. Moreover the interpretations of data utilized in these works are indicative of the cautiousness exhibited in other scholarly works. Additionally, this literature provides clues that can enable us to more fully understand how various factors converged to bring about the end of Communist party domination in Eastern Europe. Several telling statements concerning the nature of Western research on Soviet bloc countries also emerge from the literature.

First, Western scholars' inability to foresee the rapidity with which the transformation of Eastern European political systems would occur indicates that we were possibly lulled to sleep by the outcomes of past movements towards reform in both the Soviet Union and Eastern Europe. Second, it appears as though Western scholars summarily dismissed the potential effectiveness of persistent dissent and opposition to political leadership (communist or otherwise). In this respect, Eastern European dissidents appear to have had a much better understanding of their abilities to effect change than did Western scholars. At the very least, these dissidents had greater confidence than did Western scholars in the usefulness of various forms of political activism. Finally, it can be argued that Western scholars, even in the face of compelling evidence, were unwilling, if not afraid, to risk making predictions that contradicted the wait-and-see syndrome, which was and still remains somewhat prevalent among students of Eastern European politics.

On the positive side, the literature providing the focus for this essay can inform future research. The literature on dissent and opposition suggests that our understanding of cross-national differences in the collapse of Communist party domination would be enhanced by research focusing on national variations in citizens' challenges to party rule. Research on economic reforms indicates national differences in how easily the centrally planned economies of Eastern Europe can be transformed into capitalist or mixed economies. Therefore, future research in this area will, partially out of necessity, focus on each country's prior experiences with various forms of liberalization and with the present citizenry's readiness to bear short-term hardships for the sake of long-term economic viability. Perhaps the most interesting of all research will be that pertaining to the future of Soviet–Eastern European relations. Research in this area will possibly attempt to discern the extent to which Eastern European countries will continue to identify with the Soviet Union, particularly in terms of foreign policy and military security. At any rate, we now have the opportunity to engage in many exciting research activities utilizing much more reliable data. Simply stated, research in this area can be less speculative.

Notes

1. For an elaboration of the extent to which Gorbachev's commitment to economic reforms, democratization, and openness in communication differs from that of his predecessors, see Ross, 1987; and Adam, 1989.
2. The body of literature focusing on changes in Eastern Europe since Gorbachev's rise to power is quite enormous. This author has examined more than sixty scholarly books, published between 1987–1990.
3. For a full elaboration of Gorbachev's position on Eastern Europe and the need for economic reforms, see Dawisha, 1988.
4. Milanovic alludes to the 1987 Soviet law that enabled individuals to engage in economic activities that were previously banned, the 1988 Polish law that allowed for private-sector operations in almost all areas of activities, and the 1988 Czechoslovak law that also allowed for private sector operations in all services (Milanovic, 1989:65).

References

Adam, Jan. 1989. *Economic Reform in the Soviet Union and Eastern Europe Since the 1960s*. New York: St. Martin's Press.

Braun, Aurel, ed. 1990. *The Soviet-East European Relationship in the Gorbachev Era*. Boulder, CO: Westview Press.

Bugajski, Janusz, and Maxine Pollack. 1989. *East European Fault Lines*. Boulder, CO: Westview Press.

Cochrane, Nancy. 1990. "Reforming Agricultural Policies in Eastern Europe: The Case of Poland." *Problems of Communism*, 39, no. 1: 64–73.

Dawisha, Karen. 1988. *Eastern Europe, Gorbachev, and Reform: The Great Challenge.* Cambridge: Cambridge University Press.

Goldfard, Jeffery. 1989. *Beyond Glasnost: The Post-Totalitarian Mind.* Chicago: University of Chicago Press.

Milanovic, Branko. 1989. *Liberalization and Entrepreneurship.* New York: M. E. Sharpe, Inc.

Ross, Dennis. 1987. "Where Is the Soviet Union Heading?" Pp. 660–78 in Henry Rowsen and Charles Wolf, eds., *The Future of the Soviet Empire.* New York: St. Martin's Press.

Skilling, H. Gordon. 1989. *Samizdat and Independent Society in Central and Eastern Europe.* Columbus: Ohio State University Press.

Schopflin, George. 1990. "The End of Communism in Eastern Europe." *International Affairs*, 66, no. 1: 3–16.

The Problem of Preconceived Perceptions in Black Urban Politics: The Harold F. Gosnell, James Q. Wilson Legacy

Hanes Walton, Jr.
Leslie Burl McLemore
C. Vernon Gray

Savannah State College
Jackson State University
Morgan State University

R ooted in one's perception is the very essence of one's idea of universal realities, and inherent in one's perception is one's vision of reality,
which in the intellectual community, often-times gets translated into the
academic and scholarly equivalent of the real world. Essentially, it is one's
perceptions that are the key to fashioning one's intellectual grasp and
understanding of one's worldview. The problem arises, however, when
one's perceptions seem prejudged and predetermined. It is with these a
priori assumptions and presuppositions that bias and distortions are born
and then offered up to the academic community as political and social
truths. Thus, the *problem of perception is in its prior beliefs and attitudes that are
inaccurate.*

Such a problem arose in black urban politics with the pioneering works
in the area (Walton, McLemore, and Gray, 1990). This is nowhere better
seen than in the contrast between the works of two of the pioneers in the
field, Professors Harold R. Gosnell and James Q. Wilson. The differences
in their works (and their perceptions), which draw upon the same city,
Chicago, provide an excellent set of insights into the problems of perception when it comes to black urban politics.

The Role of Preconceived Perceptions in Conceptualization

One of the critical problems that has faced blacks, and the appraisal and evolution of their experience—political, social, economic, and otherwise—is that many evaluators have arrived at the door of the black experience with preconceived ideas and notions. Hence the black experience could teach or tell or reveal nothing to them. They merely selected aspects of the experience to fit their preconceived notions. Thus, the die was cast.

Gosnell and Wilson in their approaches to black urban politics reveal that they had two different sets of perceptions when they designed their studies. Gosnell designed his study based upon what he found inside the black community. Therefore, he spent five years studying the black political community before he wrote his book (Gosnell, 1934). Wilson, on the other hand, brought to his study the notion of "civic leaders" as developed by Peter B. Clark, Norton Long, E. C. Banfield and Peter Rossi, and the idea of "administrative leadership and public planning" from Chester Barnard, David Riesman, Philip Selnick, and Martin Meyerson and E. C. Banfield (Wilson, 1960).[1] To take these ideas, particularly the notion of "civic leadership" (it is central to his book) that was born in the Progressive Era during the struggle between good government reformers and corrupt and machine politicians, and apply them uncritically to black politics in a tightly segregated city is highly questionable. This was merely applying a view of civic leadership that was developed for an unfettered majority to a segregated racial minority. At the very least, a minority view of civic leadership should have been developed. However, Wilson arrived at his subject matter with already-developed perceptions.

But if Wilson had preconceived academic concepts that he judged to be essential and necessary tools for analyzing the black community, he also had a preconceived ideology for guiding the use of those tools. He wrote early in the book: "The classic and most widely accepted statement of the nature of race relations in America has been that of Gunnar Myrdal. To Myrdal, race relations are not a 'Negro problem.' There is no Negro problem in America. Rather, it is a 'white man's problem'" (p. 6). Wilson disagreed with this position. He wrote

> Whatever the ultimate cause of the race problem, the present question concerns what is being done about it today. The answer to this question indicates that in addition to the "white man's problem," there is also a "Negro problem" [and] that problem is the difficulty in generating vigorous and prolonged civic action around race goals. The civic life of a community, the raising, agitating, and disposing of issues is carried on by civic leaders. Negro civic leaders in Chicago have not been able, by and large, to create and sustain a vigorous civic life. In some sense, Negro critics of their own leaders may be right. There may well be a scarcity of able and creative leadership. (p. 7)

He continues: "It will be argued here that the ghetto has a life and a logic of its own, apart from whatever whites might do to create and maintain the outer walls of it" (p. 7). He had commented earlier "the Negro may live in prison, . . . but the prison is vast, and there is plenty of space" (p. 6). Thus, with these opening remarks (set in place by page seven) Wilson was ready to account for whatever "weaknesses of conflict might be found" in Negro civic and political leadership. Hence, with a concept borrowed from the white community and with a desire to lay bare the "Negro problem," Wilson was set to explain the search for leadership in Negro politics.

This then is the difference, and it is a crucial one, between Gosnell and Wilson. Gosnell derived his ideas and concepts from the black political experience, both nationally and in Chicago, and he used black assistants. Wilson developed his concepts externally to the black community and then imposed his externally derived concepts to find and explain the "Negro problem." Therefore, their resultant portraits and conceptualizations of black urban politics (Negro politics, as they labeled it) were destined to be in sharp contrast.

Gosnell, in effect, defines Negro politics as something done and undertaken by Negro politicians, hence the title of his book (Gosnell, 1935). Wilson, on the other hand, conceptualized Negro politics as something done and not done by Negro "civic leaders." Although he says he plans to include Negro political leadership, (p. 7), they never appear anywhere in the book. Thus, the book really only focused upon "Negro civic leaders" as seen from the white community. In comparing and contrasting white civic leaders, in both an overt and covert fashion, to black civic leaders continually throughout the book, Wilson made *normative* judgments that white civic leaders were the "best," the norm, and the ones to be valued. He, therefore, arrived at the second part of his conceptualization of the Negro politics—the search for leaders. Wilson's comparison led him to see black leaders as weak and ineffective, so that the black community was constantly looking for an effective and strong leader. To this he added another factor. "What is meant [by the remark that there is no Negro leadership], of course, is that there are no 'good' Negro leaders, leaders who are selflessly devoted to causes which will benefit Negroes as a race and as a community" (p. 30). Thus, the search meant for both successful as well as committed leaders.[2] Such a definition of leaders in a tightly segregated society not only defies logic, but it places a burden on these leaders when they are unsuccessful.

In sum, Wilson conceptualizes Negro politics as the internal struggle in the black community for civic leaders who are both committed *and* successful. Not only does this conceptualization lean toward the apolitical and a narrowly circumscribed view of things, but it contrasts sharply with that of Gosnell. Gosnell, at least, conceptualized the "politics" in his study by focusing on black political leadership, while Wilson focused on the "civic leaders" outside of the political arena.

The Preconceived Perceptions and the Methodologies

If Gosnell lacked and Wilson had systematically structured preconceived perceptions on launching their separate studies of Negro politics in Chicago, it is obvious that such prestudy orientations would help to shape the methodologies in the two studies. Since Gosnell had to learn about the Negro community, his work shows a rich diversity of research techniques and procedures. Gosnell wrote, "Before discussing the Negro in the politics of a Northern metropolitan community, it is therefore necessary to review the history of Negro participation in American politics" (Gosnell, 1935:1). Thus, Gosnell began with a historical analysis of Negroes in national politics, and then he moved to a demographic analysis to locate Negro politics in the *specific* locale of Chicago politics. After having moved from the general to the specific, he then used detailed case studies to further illuminate Negroes in Chicago politics. He explored the major political figures of that era (Edward Wright and Oscar DePriest) and explained political outputs to the community as a result of this political activity.

To develop this scheme, Gosnell used, besides the historical analysis, demographic (census) analysis, case studies, numerous interviews, content analysis of Negro newspapers, participant observation (both by himself and by several black assistants) of numerous black political meetings, tabular and statistical analyses and references, selected analysis of commissioned studies, and five personally drawn facsimile portraits of black elected and appointed individuals. It was indeed unusual for a political scientist to illustrate his own work, to say the least. In fact, Gosnell's methodological techniques ran the gamut. Even Wilson wrote, "Gosnell and his research assistants worked for five years gathering their materials primarily by interviewing Negroes and attending their meetings" (Wilson, 1967a; ix).

This rich diversity of research techniques and procedures is not present in Wilson's work. Wilson's methodological procedures were one-sided. He relied, as he erroneously claimed that Gosnell did, on interviews only. In Chicago, he identified 105 community leaders, and

> of 105 on the list, 95 were interviewed at length. These interviews were loosely structured explorations of the "civic" issues and the involvement of the respondent with the civic issues. No fixed interview schedule was employed, each interview was designed to elicit from the particular individual the activities and issues that most concerned him and in which he played some role . . . The interviews ran, in length, from forty-five minutes (in a few cases) to more than twenty hours (in one case). The average interview consumed about an hour and a half. (p. 11)

This is what Wilson tells the reader about Chicago. Little or nothing is given the reader about the interviews he conducted in the other northern cities. In fact, Wilson put the comments on the other interviews in a note on page 17. He wrote, "The research in Chicago took place during 1958–

59. Research in other northern cities (Detroit, Los Angeles, and New York) was conducted during the summer of 1959, and consisted of a number of interviews with selected civic and political leaders in each city. My analysis of the situation in each city was then circulated to the people interviewed, as well as to others, for comments." Later in an introduction to Gosnell's book, Wilson reveals in another note that he interviewed one of Gosnell's former research assistants (Wilson, 1967a). Thus Negro politics, as conceived by Wilson, meant locating and talking with "Negro civic leaders," as determined by himself.

Fundamentally, Wilson's methodology may be viewed as a *personal document approach*, a technique developed by the University of Chicago's Department of Sociology in the 1930s, his own institution at the time. This approach involves the random interviewing of people in selected sites over a set of far-ranging issues to determine their viewpoints, social outlooks, and values in a less-than-quantitative manner, but in a more descriptive framework (see Bulmer, 1984:52–55, 90; Gottschalk et al., 1947). In writing up the data analysis, the author could then draw upon any of the personally documented interviews to support his findings or interpretations. No standards or procedures were necessary or had to be devised to guide one in the use of these documents. Such an approach was not only methodologically unsound and controversial, it was later discredited (Bulmer, 1984:52–55, 90; Gottschalk et al., 1947). Knowingly or unknowingly, Wilson employed such a scheme in his work. But the flawed methodology was not the only shortcoming of Wilson's book. The other problem was that it lacked perspective, particularly on Chicago black protest or civic leaders in the local NAACP.

Wilson's search for black civic leaders led him to interview members of the Chicago NAACP during the late 1950s and to draw conclusions in part about black civic behavior based on what he found in this time frame. However, Professor Christopher Reed's mammoth and exhausting history of the Chicago NAACP reveals that Wilson had seen the NAACP and its black civic leaders at the wrong point in time. In the 1950s, the branch was quiescent and ineffective. Thus Wilson got the wrong impression. Reed writes:

> By the Kennedy years, at the dawn of the Civil Rights Revolution, University of Chicago political scientist James Q. Wilson published his research findings on the character and scope of black civic leadership of the past decade in *Negro Politics* (1960). Wilson offered a ringside view to the world of local black politics in 1958 just as the branch was neutralized by south side machine leader, Congressman William L. Dawson. The study, however, overlooked the high level of protest advocacy of the previous three decades. Readers were left with the impression that before the fifties the branch was without victories in the struggle for racial equality. It was left to two scholarly works that appeared in the mid-1960s to redeem the branch historically. This was the manner in which the branch was presented in the written pages of history. (Reed, unpublished manuscript: 3).

Thus, Wilson's personal documentary approach, which left him so much latitude in evaluating black civic leaders, left him equally unprepared to grasp a perspective on black protest leaders. Any student of black civil rights knows that the history of such activity has been uneven and non-linear. Evidently Wilson brushed such consideration aside and noted that what was happening in the 1950s had always happened.[3] Such a leap in logic is, for balanced and scholarly works, unfathomable. But Wilson's work made the leap. Even in the subsequent paperback release of the work, when better research had surfaced, Wilson failed to make the corrections and revisions.

However, Gosnell listed in his notes people that he interviewed (at least at times); Wilson did not. For reasons unknown, Wilson's data sources were deliberately obscure, ill-defined, and poorly reported to the reader. There was no list of persons interviewed and no breakdown on the data in three cities. This was crucial, given his methodological approach. Even when Wilson quotes freely from his interviews, as he does in the middle and latter sections of the book, he does not reveal to the reader where these people are, their positions, nor any indication of why these quotes were chosen over others. In point of fact, the only basic criterion or standard used to select and place quotes seems to be that they support Wilson's notion or ideological posture of the existence of a "Negro problem" that highlights Negro individual or group weaknesses and shortcomings.

Taken together, Gosnell's methodologies spring not from his preconceived perceptions, but from a need to learn about the community, while Wilson's dominant methodology coincides well with his concern for civic leadership and the Negro problem. Conceptualization determined methodological techniques.

The Preconceived Perceptions and Findings

Gosnell's findings not only arose out of his black community study, but offered a balanced interpretation of events. Of Gosnell's efforts, even Wilson wrote, "Gosnell was clearly egalitarian in his own sentiments. . . his book has a tone of detachment and open curiosity that suggests less an author's struggle to be impartial . . ." (Wilson, 1967a:ix).

Gosnell's book is about Chicago. Wilson's book is about Negro politics in the North, and it uses Chicago as a supposedly empirical case study to bolster his remarks about blacks in New York, Detroit, and Los Angeles. Gosnell's book is descriptive and analytical; Wilson's book offers sweeping generalizations, broad conclusions that rest in neither fact nor fiction. Gosnell's book portrays his subject matter—the Negro politician; Wilson's book claims to be about the black search for leadership, but he never develops or conceptualizes how a minority community can search for political and civic leadership in a tightly segregated urban area. Wilson does not give the faintest hint of this in his work, but instead writes at length about the differences between political leaders and civic leaders and offers a strange normative set of typologies—welfare and status ends, militant and moderate political styles and prestige, token organizer, and "new" Negro types of leaders. These typologies are so poorly integrated and unconnected either to each other or to the cities under study that the whole of Part III of the book leaves the reader in a blur of discontinuity, but very clear about the conservative postures and proclivity in the black community, based on class cleavages and differences as Wilson sees them.

In the chapters of Wilson's book, one finds broad generalities and theoretical propositions at various points that are unrelated to the paragraph or the logic of the arguments themselves. For example, he writes, "there is the general conservatism of Negro leaders . . . Negro leaders tend to be conservative, and to share . . . the values of white conservatives. Few felt that there is anything at stake important enough to warrant an attack on the status quo and the political party which controls and supports existing arrangements" (Wilson, 1960:47). He continues, "There is a distinct and evident aversion to politics among Negroes of the middle and upper classes" (p. 57).

He begins his final insights by noting, "One of the most important constraints on effective leadership in the Negro community is lack of agreement among leaders as to what they want" (p. 169). In one place in the book, Wilson defines the legislative strategy of black pressure groups as a force. He writes, "The tendency to seek politico-legal solutions to race problems may be merely a special case of a general disposition to favor compulsion or force in handling problems" (p. 222). In a country of laws, not men, and one where the system is straining under legal challenges, blacks' use of legalism is somehow portrayed as being endemic to black culture.

Next Wilson moves to his insights about militant and moderate black leadership styles. "The militant leader," in his words, "values protest over access" (p. 224). He finds "agitation to be intrinsically worthwhile, apart from all considerations as to the immediate results of such effect" (p. 224). He continues, ". . . the Negro moderate tends to share the political value system of the white conservative" (p. 233). In addition, "the moderate . . . displays less confidence in the efficacy of legislative solution than does the militant" (p. 238). "A moderate is concerned with the value of access to white influentials, and is reluctant to sacrifice access to protest or policy" (p. 243). He concludes by saying that "in Chicago [read, the North] far more persons tend to be moderates than tend to be militants" (p. 253).

Finally, we hear that, "Negro civic life attracts ideologues: this can make compromises hard and dispassionate discussion difficult" (p. 286). Therefore, "here [read, in the North], when Negroes fail to act effectively, it is more often the case of failure internal to the Negro community than of constraints imposed by the larger community" (p. 289). (This conclusion is a simple repeat of his opening statements—some 283 pages earlier.) Wilson closes his book on northern Negro politics by indicating explicitly that the problem lies in "Negro culture." "An investigation," he asserts, "into the ethos of the urban Negro might very well begin with the sense of limitation, of inadequacy, of an absent or uncertain future, as the central theme" (p. 294). Later, he repeats himself. Black political powerlessness and ineffectiveness "lie in the halls of the northern Negro ghetto itself" (p. 307). He makes a similar statement earlier on page 159: "only a thorough inquiry into the ethos of the Negro at its most fundamental levels could provide any certain answers" (p. 159). In short, not the segregationist politics and its system, but black (Negro) people are their own worst problem.

All of the preceding quotations were presented so that the reader may see, not only that these words and sweeping ideas were not and could not be empirically based, and that they had no substantive base in fact or reality, but also that they were apparently preconceived notions that Wilson had set out in the very beginning of the book. The book merely confirmed his own bias about race. At best, statements such as those above may be characterized as little more than assumptions and assertions that support particular views of public policy and philosophy. Thus Wilson's book developed an academic portrait of urban black politics that by and large supported the views and thinking of the neoconservatives and black conservatives of the 1980s. In sum, it may suggest that Wilson's *Negro Politics* is a conservative political dictionary on race in the city. It is clearly quite different from Gosnell's view of black politics.

Indeed, Gosnell's findings were not derived from a comparison and contrast syndrome like Wilson's, and thus did not carry negative value-laden conclusions. Preconceived notions led Wilson to lay bare the basic characteristics and features of the "Negro problem" as seen through the eyes of white civic leaders. Thus, Wilson demonstrates in his "findings" that Negro politics were fraught with shortcomings because of problems in Negro culture. Yet Wilson never divulges to the reader, explicitly or implicitly any notion of what constitutes the black culture.

Wilson's negativism, however, does not mean that Gosnell did not find some negative things about Negro politics, for he did. But since these findings did not flow from a comparison and contrast syndrome, they do not in the context of Gosnell's book take on such great proportions. A reading of Gosnell will reveal both negative and positive things. A reading of Wilson will reveal his findings to be so negative that few, if any positive things come to light. This is probably why Wilson, in the final analysis, showed little regard for Gosnell's book, which predated his by twenty-five years.[4]

The Preconceived Perceptions and the Legacies

What then did these books portend for black politics in general and black urban politics specifically? What academic and scholarly legacies did these two men leave for the study and analysis of the fledgling area of black urban politics?

Beyond his pioneering study on black politics in Chicago, Gosnell would pen only two more articles on the subject, and one of these would be with his former student and colleague, Professor Robert Martin. The first article looked at black voters in northern cities and tried to describe, as clearly as possible, their voting behavior in the 1940 presidential election

(Gosnell, 1941). The coauthored article, coming more than twenty years later, offers a careful look at the increases in black officeholders at the local, state, and congressional level, particularly the five new congressmen. Moreover, the vicissitudes in black voting behavior are examined using both the available survey data and aggregate election returns (Gosnell and Martin, 1963).

Both articles continued Gosnell's careful and balanced approach to the subject matter and attempted to evaluate the subject from data within the community, that is, using the community efforts as the basic yardstick. Perhaps most important of all, Gosnell did not arrive at his conceptualization and data analysis of the subject with preconceived ideas and notions. In addition, Gosnell used several methodological techniques to provide the most comprehensive portrait as possible. Thus, with such an approach, each of Gosnell's articles enriches the data base of the fledgling field.

Wilson, on the other hand, pressed on, making the area one of his major focuses for at least another six years. During that time he attempted to establish himself as an "expert" on the subject matter, or in the words of Professors Mack Jones and Alex Willingham, as a "custodian" of the black political experience (Jones and Willingham, 1970). Whatever the reality, Wilson would, after the publication of his book, deliver a paper at the American Political Science Association convention in September 1960, on "Negro Civic Leadership." This would be followed by two book chapters (one for an anthology and one for a black reference book) and five articles for various publications on the subject (for his article on the black riots, see Wilson 1967b).

The outpouring of articles would go on from 1960 through 1966; the anthology chapter came out in 1964 and the reference book chapter in 1965. Yet, when he finished his single-focused works on the black political experience, he would continue to write on the subject by devoting chapters or partial chapters to the experience. For instance, in his book, *The Amateur Democrat*, Chapter 9 reflects on the subject; Chapter 20 in his coauthored *City Politics* and Chapter 9 in his book *Political Organizations*, look at a black civil rights organization. Even when he shifted his focus to police behavior, crime, and criminality, he continued to temporize on the black experience. While Wilson continued to put the black experience in all aspects of his work, one reality stands out, and that is the continuity between his *Negro Politics* and the subsequent five articles and two chapters.

Although Wilson carefully divorced his work from Gosnell's, he actually modeled him in several other respects. His first article, "How the Northern Negro Uses His Vote," appears to follow Gosnell's 1941 article. In sum, Wilson's short and tentative steps into the new area seem to be modeled on the earlier work of Harold Gosnell. His third article, "The Strategy of Protest: Problems of Negro Civic Action," (Wilson, 1961), was based on his book and continued the ideas and findings therein.

The article, "Two Negro Politicians: An Interpretation," (Wilson, 1960) not only continued the theme and ideas launched in *Negro Politics*, but looked at black politics for the first time by focusing upon the only two black congressmen in the country and on the differences in their style. For Wilson, leadership and style were more important than legislative efforts and achievements. The focus on style left the implication that style was more important than substance and that certain types of black leaders were more valuable and useful than others. The article clearly promoted a specific concern and suggested that black politics in white institutions had little to offer the black community except very limited tangible benefits. Wilson would return to one of those congressmen when he was under attack in 1966 in "The Flamboyant Mr. Powell" (Wilson, 1966).

In his article "The Negro in Politics" (Wilson, 1965a), Wilson would not only continue but would add to his conservative approach, as newer concepts of conservatism as reaction to black progress in the 1960s took the offensive. In this article, he turned to the neoconservative Nathan Glazer for scholarly guidance. He wrote, "The Negro's demand for economic equality is no longer, as Nathan Glazer pointed out, simply a demand for equal opportunity, it is a demand for equality of economic *results*" (Wilson, 1965a:964). Not only did Wilson accept this inaccurate interpretation of Glazer,[5] he would incorporate this new negative neoconservative assumption into his other works. In this work, he asserted, "American politics has for long been accustomed to deal with ethnic demands for recognition and opportunity; it has never had to face a serious demand for equal economic shares. Thus, in the North as well as the South, the principal race issue may become a conflict between liberty and equality" (Wilson, 1965a:964).[6] Thus, with Wilson's help, this false dichotomy was under way and being dropped quietly into writings on black politics, even though the article did not address the issue.

Wilson continued to denigrate black leadership. He wrote, "The Northern Negro Community, lacking a simple clear objective and a well-organized and unified leadership will continue to be volatile" (Wilson, 1965a:965). Of Southern blacks, he said, "Negro politics in the South has yet to be professionlized . . . [and] to say that the Southern Negro political leadership is unprofessional does not mean that it is either unskillful or unsuccessful" (1965a:952). Yet, he nowhere tells the reader what he means by the term unprofessional, causing the negative ascription to stand.

Outside of the major southern cities, Wilson thought he saw in the rural black belt regions the rise of radical black leadership as exemplified by the Mississippi Freedom Democratic Party. But he quickly offered a way to defuse such "radical" black leadership. He suggested, "Early and measured accommodations to Negro political demands has, in many Southern cities, led to the emergence of relatively moderate Negro leaders and of a Negro strategy emphasizing limited objective" (1965a:954). Once again, we see Wilson's preference for moderate black leadership.

Of evolving black politics, Wilson concluded his article by saying "Negroes, in short, will increasingly be able to play marginal politics. But this approach rarely produces wholesale or fundamental changes in the life chances of large numbers of people" (p. 969) and "because of the structure of America politics as well as the nature of the Negro community, Negro politics will accomplish only limited objectives" (p. 970).

This article was pivotal, however, for it raised the specter of "criminal behavior among lower-class Negroes" (p.963), which presages his future work on crime and the police. On this issue, he opined, "What is remarkable is that so few candidates for mayor or governor are openly exploiting white fears of crime, particularly Negro crime. In part this is because too many of them must face Negro voters who would immediately interpret such views as anti-Negro prejudice even if, in fact, prejudice had nothing to do with it" (p. 963). Thus, with these insights Wilson was on his way to study police and criminal behavior.

In the final analysis, Wilson's version of black politics leaves a legacy that is a dark and brooding portrait encased in a conservative ideology. Or, put another way, Wilson's work at its very best is a negative conservative approach to black politics and, from this conservative analysis, little that is useful, meaningful and "professional," to use his own words, arises from black political activity.

His legacy, then, is one of bringing to his subject matter a set of preconceived ideas and theses. His first step was to conceptualize, from a ideological point of view, key concepts and ideas from the majority political experience and to apply it uncritically to the black experience, and then to weave in and out of this conceptualization fact and a criterion based upon the majority community. As black politics evolved, he continued to assert that limited objectives are all that can be had, implying that political efforts should not be made.[7] Finally, Wilson appears critical both of black political leadership officials and of black efforts to empower themselves.

Conclusions

Gosnell left a body of work that is conceptualized and formulated from within the community's experience. Its data gathering was meticulous and comprehensive and its data analysis employed a variety of methods and techniques. Moreover, Gosnell's findings are not evaluated on norms and criteria established outside of the political community under scrutiny. This is Gosnell's legacy, a body of balanced scholarship to succeeding generations.

Wilson left an essayistic body of work that is a prime example of conservative reflection. It was formulated and conceptualized from outside the community's political experience. The data gathering remains largely obscure. Wilson's data seem guided by conservative and neoconservative ideas and appear more to be interpretation than scholarship. Scholarship follows basic guidelines, method, and approaches, whereas interpretation is less structured and constrained. Wilson's work may be viewed as a broad mosaic of ideas developed within certain normative value context. As Professor John Strange argued earlier, Wilson treats his subject, "Negro Politics" without ever delimiting or defining it.[8]

Professor Samuel D. Cook is even more telling: "The miseries and trag-
edies of blacks have been obscured and moralized by mythology, ethos
and rhetoric" (Cook, 1971:xxxi). Armed with Professor Cook's insights,
one can clearly see that Wilson's mixture of facts and conservative ideology left an unbalanced legacy about the black political experience in urban
America.

Notes

1. Wilson (1960) addresses these in various places: Peter B. Clark: p. 318 n. 8 and
   p. 385, n. 1; Norton Long: p. 321, n. 1 and p. 333, n. 5; E.C.Banfield: p. 331, n.1;
   Peter Rossi: p. 333, n. 5; Chester Barnard: p. 320, n. 14; David Riesman: p. 327,
   n. 3; Philip Selnick: p. 332, n. 3; Martin Meyerson and E. C. Banfield: p. 325,
   n. 6; p. 329, n. 37; p. 330, n. 44; p. 331, n. 5; and p. 34, n. 2.
2. For Wilson's ambivalence toward King's leadership, see pages 327–32. The
   reader should see his remarks about black inspirational leadership on pages
   175, 176, and 277. Wilson also denigrates and disparages King's leadership in
   note 10 on page 327, based on information from on unnamed black informer.
   He further deflates King's leadership in note 3, page 332, when he seeks to
   show the conflict that existed between the NAACP and King, as if to suggest
   that conflict between black leaders is a given without explaining why. Wilson's
   overall approach is to use King's leadership as a tool with which to criticize
   other black leaders in the North, and then to attack King's leadership.
3. Reed's work reveals that in the early years, the NAACP branch was led and
   staffed by white civic leaders, yet it accomplished little and blacks had to
   wrestle control from whites so that the organization could make even nondis-
   criminatory advances (Reed, unpublished manuscript: Chapter 2).
4. For an extended discussion of why Wilson's works fails to build on Gosnell's
   see Walton, McLemore, and Gray, 1990.
5. See Walton, 1988:116–70, for a clear-cut discussion of this argument voiced by
   Wilson, Glazer, and other neoconservatives as a public opinion thesis to un-
   dercut the civil rights gains of the 1960s.
6. Also in the Bicentennial issue of *Public Interest*. Wilson and Glazer argue the
   issue and make the point of the alleged conflict between liberty and equality
   (Wilson, 1988: p. 166).
7. In his introduction to the paperback edition of *Negro Politics*, which came out
   five years later, Wilson wrote, "Dramatic as some changes have been, the
   major dimensions of the political system have remained to same . . . the division of leaders, differences in goals and tactics continue to be operative"
   (Wilson, 1956b:vii).
8. Quoted in Walton, 1972:11.

References

Bulmer, Martin. 1984. *The Chicago School of Sociology: Institutionalization, Diversity
    and the Rise of Sociological Research*. Chicago: University of Chicago Press.
Cook, Samuel DeBois. 1971. "The American Liberal Democratic Tradition, the
    Black Revolution and Martin Luther King, Jr." In Hanes Walton, Jr., ed., *The
    Political Philosophy of Martin Luther King, Jr*. Connecticut; Greenwood Publishing
    Co.

Gosnell, Harold F. 1934. "Political Meetings in the Chicago Black Belt." *American Political Science Review*, April: 254–58.

_____. 1935. *Negro Politicians: The Rise of Negro Politics in Chicago*. Chicago: University of Chicago Press. (Paperback edition: Chicago: Phoenix Books, 1967).

_____. 1941. "The Negro Voter in Northern Cities." *National Municipal Review* 1941: 264–67.

_____. 1967. *Negro Politicians: The Rise of Negro Politics in Chicago*. Paperback edition. Chicago: Phoenix Books.

Gosnell, Harold F., and Robert E. Martin. 1963. "The Negro as Voters and Office Holders." *Journal of Negro Education,*, Fall: 415–25.

Gottschalk, Louis R. et al. 1947. *The Use of Personal Documents in History, Anthropology and Sociology*. New York: Social Science Research Council

Jones, Mack H., and Alex Willingham. 1970. "The White Custodians of the Black Experience." *The Social Science Quarterly*, June; 31–35.

Reed, Christopher R. unpublished manuscript. *The Chicago NAACP: Its Internal Development and External Relationships, 1910–1960.*

Walton, Hanes, Jr. 1988. *When the Marching Stopped: The Politics of the Civil Rights Regulation Agencies*. New York: State University of New York Press.

_____. 1972. *Black Politics*. Philadelphia: J. B. Lippincott.

Walton, Hanes, Jr., Leslie Burl McLemore, and C. Vernon Gray. 1990. "The Pioneering Books on Black Politics and the Political Science Community, 1903–1965." *National Political Science Review*, 1990:196–218.

Wilson, James Q. 1960. *Negro Politics: The Search for Leadership*. Illinois: The Free Press. (Paperback edition: New York: The Free Press, 1965).

_____. 1961. "The Strategy of Protest: Problems of Negro Civic Action." *Journal of Conflict Resolution*, September: 291–303.

_____. 1960. "Two Negro Politicians: An Interpretation." *Midwest Journal of Political Science*: 365–369.

_____. 1965a. "The Negro in Politics." *Daedalus*, Fall: 949–71.

_____. 1965b. "Introduction" to the paperback edition of Wilson, 1960.

_____. 1966. "The Flamboyant Mr. Powell." *Commentary*, January: 31–35.

_____. 1967a. "Introduction" to the paperback edition of Gosnell, 1935.

_____. 1967b. "Black and White Tragedy." *Encounter*, October: 63–68.

The Political Reincorporation of Southern Blacks: The Case of Birmingham

Huey L. Perry

Southern University

Jimmy Lewis Franklin, 1989; **Back to Birmingham: Richard Arrington, Jr., and His Times,** (Tuscaloosa: University of Alabama Press,) xi + 363 pp. ISBN 0-8173-0435-5 (cloth).

Back to Birmingham is a biographical account of the rise of Richard Arrington, Jr., from a humble upbringing in rural Alabama to become one of the most powerful local public officials in the United States. The author, Jimmy Lewis Franklin, a professor of history at Vanderbilt University, has produced a well-researched chronicle of the life of the thrice-elected mayor of Birmingham, Alabama. The book is a cross between popular history and scholarly history. Franklin tells a masterful story of Arrington's life, a feat that is greatly facilitated by the absence of the heavy documentation of traditional scholarship. Although the book is not characterized by heavy documentation, the author has carefully researched his subject and knows him very well. The author is apparently personally close to Arrington. A normal concern about a work produced by an author close to the subject is the question of objectivity. The book rates well on this dimension. Overall, Franklin's book is an objective, well-written account of Arrington's rise to political power in Birmingham.

The first two chapters focus on Arrington's family and educational background. The middle chapters (Chapters 3–7) focus on Arrington's development as a political actor in Biringham, first as a city council member and later as mayor. These middle chapters, along with the two final chapters (Chapters 9 and 10), which focus on his reelection and second mayoral term respectively, are the chapters of greatest interest to political scientists. Chapter 8 focuses on Arrington's political, religious, and family values. Chapter 10 also includes a brief discussion of Arrington's reelection for a third term in 1987.

Arrington's entry into politics in Birmingham was influenced by the killing of a young black woman by a white Birmingham police officer. More than any other single event in the tragic history of race relations is Birmingham, including the 1963 bombing of the Sixteenth Street Baptist Church, in which four black girls were killed, the Carter killing unleashed forces of change in the city that led to a dramatic reordering of blacks' place in politics and society in Birmingham. Although an eight-member blue-ribbon committee appointed by then-mayor David Vann voted 7 to 0 with one abstention, that the Carter shooting had been unjustified, the mayor refused to dismiss from the police force the officer who had committed the shooting. This decision exacerbated the anger of the black community and led to Richard Arrington's decision to run for mayor against his liberal ally Vann.

Franklin's account of the factors leading to Arrington's decision to run for mayor is reminiscent of the factors leading to Harold Washington's decision to run for mayor in Chicago. Arrington, like Washington, was virtually drafted by the black leadership in the city to run for mayor. The city's handling of the killing was a major factor in decision calculus throughout this process of political recruitment. Arrington had long been an outspoken critic of police brutality against blacks in Birmingham. As was the case with the black community in general, for Arrington the Carter killing produced a bitter feeling that demanded that some ameliorative action be taken to avenge this affront to the black community.

The 1979 mayoral election results demonstrated just how deft black voters can be in punishing politicians who they believe betray their trust. Just as they had failed to support Mayor George Seibels in 1975, (had not supported affirmative action in municipal hiring and the allocation of municipal contracts), blacks did not support Vann in 1979, as they had done in 1975, because of his handling of the Carter shooting. In the election, 55 percent of the city's voters turned out to vote. Arrington led the field, receiving 31,521 votes (44 percent of the vote). Mayor Vann's 11,450 votes not even enough to place him in a runoff. Although Vann had received overwhelming black support in his mayoral race in 1975, a factor crucial to his election, in 1979 Vann did not win a single black voting box in the city.

The 1979 mayoral election casts important light on an ostensibly new and important development in black and American politics—the issue of black candidates running so-called deracialized campaign, in which black issues and concerns are deliberately downplayed by these black candidates in order to attract white voters (see Perry, 1990b). About half of the major black candidates who won elections in the 1989 elections ran deracialized campaigns. Many analysts speculate that this is a new phenomenon in black and American politics. However, a close analysis suggests that black candidates have long been pragmatic in their realization of the necessity to win some white votes in order to win elections. This was certainly true of Arrington in the 1979 mayoral race. Confident of his support among blacks, Arrington spent the last days of the general election campaign focusing on issues that appealed across racial lines: economic concerns, streamlining government to ensure more effective services, developing an effective mass-transit system as a cornerstone of progressive economic development, assistance for small businesses including minority businesses, and international trade. Arrington won the election, receiving 44,798 votes to Frank Parson's 42,814 votes, which constituted a winning margin of 2.2 percentage points. Arrington's 73 percent of the black vote represented an increase of 10 percentage points over the 63 percent he received in the primary. Arrington received 10 percent of the white vote.

Placing Arrington's 1979 mayoral campaign and election in a larger framework of black electoral experience illustrates both continuity and change in the black political experience. It is possible to identify three phases of successful black electoral activity in contemporary black politics, and all three phases are characterized by an understanding on the part of black candidates of the importance of winning a certain proportion of the white vote to winning the election, and pragmatic approach by black candidates toward achieving that end. In the first phase of successful black electoral activity, successful black candidates running against white opponents in majority-white jurisdictions generally could expect to receive no more than 10–20 percent of the white vote. In his 1979 campaign, Arrington avidly sought support from sections of the white population in Birmingham that he thought would be most receptive to his candidacy. The same pattern is true of Ernest Morial's first campaign for mayor of New Orleans in 1977 and Harold Washington's first campaign for mayor of Chicago in 1983.

More recently, a second phase of black electoral success consists of blacks winning office against opposition from a black candidate in majority-black jurisdictions or districts. In this phase, the white electorate usually is able to determine the winner of the election, and the successful black candidate will usually have strong majority support from whites. In the race for Georgia's Fifth Congressional District (centered in Atlanta) in 1986, John Lewis was able to defeat Julian Bond by attracting a significant minority of the black vote and successfully appealing to the white electorate (Jones, 1988: 7). Lewis received 40 percent of the black vote and 80 percent of the white vote. The Fifth Congressional District in 1986 has a black population proportion of 65 percent and a black voting-age population proportion of 60 percent. Lewis won the race with 52 percent of the vote to Bond's 48 percent. Lewis's winning coalition was apparently comprised of low-income blacks and upper-income whites (Davis and Willingham, 1986: 9). Similarly, in Sidney Barthelemy's first campaign for mayor of New Orleans in 1985, Barthelemy sought and received white voter support, winning 83 percent of the white vote.

The third and most recent phase of successful black electoral activity is the current deracialization phase, in which black candidates run in majority-white jurisdictions, usually against white opponents. As the 1989 elections indicate, white support for black candidates in this phase ranges from strong minority support to majority support.

This section indicates two important observations about contemporary black politics in the United States. First, a deracialized approach to campaigning by black candidates is not per se a new development in black politics. Second, the development of contemporary black politics over their three phases has been characterized by increased white support of successful black candidates. The latter is a very important development in black and American politics, a development probably best explained by a generation of black elected officials' demonstration that they could carry out the duties and responsibilities of their offices as well as other occupants of public office. This was certainly true of Arrington, who realized several major accomplishments during his first term.

One of Arrington's major accomplishments during his first term was in the area of providing fiscal leadership to address the city's budget-deficit problem. Arrington inherited a projected $2.5 million shortfall in the city's income for the last quarter of 1979. By taking cost-cutting measures, which included the reorganization and consolidation of departments; the coordination of efforts between economic development and community development, the use of a more sophisticated date-processing system to administer federal grants; and the continuation of the city's self-insurance system for buildings, equipment, and employees, Arrington was able to solve the city's deficit problem. Another of Arrington's major successes during his first term was in the area of economic development. A $27 million bond issue, supported by Arrington, made possible the building of a high school sports facility and a jail, and commercial revitalization projects. Some eight thousand additional jobs for Birmingham's citizens were created as a result of these projects.

Another of Arrington's accomplishments during his first term included crime reduction. For the ten year period before Arrington came to office, crime in Birmingham had increased, compared to the nation as a whole. It began to decline in 1980 and at a pace that exceeded the national average. By mid-1982, crime in Birmingham was declining at an 8 percent rate, compared with 5 percent nationally. Another area of significant achievement for Arrington was the professionalization of the police force. Given Arrington's historic and intense opposition to police brutality, the professionalization of the police department was a high priority for him during his first term. Arrington's efforts were apparently successful, for police officers used less deadly force in making arrests, and charges for resisting officers and for assaults decreased. Also, police brutality complaints dropped by 75 percent during Arrington's first term. Unfortunately, the author does not provide empirical data to support these accomplishments. This is generally true throughout the discussions of Arrington's accomplishments, this is one aspect of the book in which the popular history genre results in a diminution of the product from the scholarly standpoint.

Arrington's major failure was in the area of economic development. A public-private plan of economic development for downtown Birmingham called Block 60, which would have constructed a major office-building complex, a large convention-quality hotel, and 130 units of residential housing, faced considerable opposition from black and white small-business owners, and the project never got off the ground. When some of the small businesses in the Block 60 area refused to sell their property to the city to make room for Block 60, the city turned to condemnation as a strategy for obtaining the property needed for construction. While condemnation was eventually overturned by a state court in a lawsuit filed by a disgruntled property owner, challenging the legality of the municipality's action the project failed principally because one of the largest property owners in the area demanded that he get a 50 percent increase in the selling price for his property, after he had agreed to terms with the city, and that he become the owner and developer of half of Block 60. These terms were unacceptable to Arrington, in part because a decision to pay the increased price would have meant a renegotiation with all the other businesses that had agreed to terms with the city.

Clarence Stone provides valuable insight as to why the Block 60 project failed in terms of the inherent difficulty involved in managing complex urban redevelopment activities: "In order to pursue a program such as redevelopment, a governing coalition must be able to sustain efforts by a variety of actors and to ensure that the high level of coordination needed for complicated projects is achieved, sometimes in the face of controversy" (Stone, 1989: 188). However, Paul Peterson's observation that municipal developmental policies are generally characterized by minimal conflict within municipalities, and that if any important opposition arises to such policies it is likely to come from sources external to the city promulgating the policies, misses the mark substantially in terms of it applicability to Block 60. In explaining the sources of opposition more significant than the minimal opposition that may be generated within the municipality, Peterson observes: "If there is more important opposition, it is usually generated by agencies or organizations external to the local political system— perhaps by a competing city or by a federal agency or by a private firm trying to achieve better terms in its negotiation with the city" (1961: 132). In general intracity opposition to Block 60 was significant, and specifically, the firm that tried to negotiate a better deal for itself with the city, and whose efforts in this regard resulted in scuttling the entire project, was a local firm rather than a nonlocal firm as Peterson suggests.

Perhaps the best analysis in the book centers on the topic of organizational replacement in the structure of black politics in Birmingham. The most important political organization in Birmingham from the 1930s through the 1970s was the Jefferson County Progressive Democratic Council. Founded in the 1930s by veteran black leaders such as Arthur Shores, W. C. Patton, and Odie Hancock, the Council worked to increase black voter registration and black political unity. In the 1930s, 1940s, 1950s, and 1960s, the organization worked for a unified black vote and for the election of racially moderate white candidates. The Council grew significantly in the 1960s, but began to decline in the 1970s. In the eyes of its critics the black leadership of the Council became too conservative in its pursuit of political and social change for blacks. One of the Council's severest critic was the late Emory O. Jackson, the editor of the *Birmingham World*. Among several criticisms leveled at the Council, Jackson charged that the Council made no demands upon politicians who received its endorsements.

Curiously, a similar indictment of black political organizations was made by former New Orleans mayor Ernest Morial, on the basis of his experience as mayor. Morial indicated that black organizational leaders asked him for individual benefits but seldom for group-based benefits. In his study of the impact of black political participation in six Florida communities, James Button (1989:225) found that black organizations were not directly instrumental in improving the benefits that blacks received in municipal employment and municipal services. The question of black political organizations working to make public officials who receive their support accountable to these organizations is an area that is worthy of additional research by political scientists.

The Jefferson County Citizens Coalition was organized by Arrington in 1977, hastening the demise of the Democratic Council. The Coalition soon became not only the most powerful black political organization in the city but the most powerful organization generally for controlling the routes to public office (Perry, 1990s: 142–43). Arrington was once a member of the Council. He broke with the Council and formed the Coalition primarily because he wanted more young blacks to become involved in political activity and leadership, and by and large the Council was not supportive of such.

Franklin shows that black political activity in Birmingham is capable of operating at high levels. In Arrington's 1979 mayoral race, blacks turned out to vote at a higher rate than whites. In the 1981 city council race, in which the Coalition endorsed an all-black slate for the city council, blacks also turned out in a higher percentage than whites (48 percent to 43 percent, respectivity). This incidence of racial political behavior seems to be applicable to most elections in which a viable black candidate seeks election against a white opponent to a visible public office (Perry and Stokes, 1987:236). Arrington was subjected to heavy criticism for the all-black slate endorsed by his organization. There was a backlash by white voters in the general election, for four of the five blacks who made the ten-person runoff were defeated. Edward LaMonte, Arrington's chief of staff at this time, thought that the all black slate had been a poor decision on Arrington's part that had cost him much political support among whites who had previously supported him. As a result of the 1981 election, there was one less black on the city council than there was before the election.

Chapter Eight focuses on Arrington's personal values. Although important for understanding Arrington's personality, this chapter in all likelihood will not be of great utility to most political scientists because it does not help to explain political behavior and event in Birmingham. The chapter focuses on Arrington's divorce from his first wife and his subsequent remarriage, his family and religious values, and his political and social values.

Chapter Nine focuses on Arrington's reelection campaign. Franklin makes a very important point in the beginning of the chapter relative to the social impact of blacks serving in important governmental positions. The more blacks serve with distinction in important governmental positions, the more they will be accepted by whites as full participants in the political process. This will eventually translate into increased white electoral support for black candidates. This phenomenon clearly manifested itself in the 1989 elections, in which a number of blacks, including Douglas Wilder in Virginia and David Dinkins in New York City, won election to important governmental positions with substantial white support.

Arrington's primary opponent in the 1983 election was the white Harvard-trained lawyer John Katopodis. Arrington easily won reelection, receiving 60 percent of the vote to Katopodis's 39 percent. Arrington received 12 percent of the white vote. The Coalition endorsed the reelection of four of the five incumbents—two blacks and two whites—and all four made the primary cut. The Coalition also endorsed two nonincumbent blacks for the council. The four incumbents and one of the two black nonincumbents endorsed by the Coalition won election to the city council.

One of Arrington's major defeats during his second term was the defeat in 1986 of a $65 million bond referendum that Arrington had proposed to fund school and museum construction, park and neighborhood development, drainage projects, parking facilities, sanitary sewers, and industrial parks—projects the city could not afford out of the existing budget because of dramatic cutbacks in federal financial assistance to the city. Although Arrington had an impressive record in passing previous bond measures, this one suffered a resounding defeat. Arrington's anticipated high turnout among blacks, who stood to profit substantially from the improvements in the school facilities and symbolically from the civil rights museum that the bond measure would have funded, did not materialize; blacks turned out to vote at only slightly over 21 percent. White turnout was almost double black turnout.

In the city council race in 1985, blacks elected a majority on the council, and that majority elected William Bell the first black president of the council. In 1985 all of the successful council candidates were endorsed by the Coalition. In 1987 Arrington stood for reelection for a third time. Arrington handily defeated his opponent Chester McKee, an eastside white businessman, who had led the fight against Arrington's 1986 bond measure. Arrington received 51,909 votes to McKee's 28,825. Arrington won 64 percent of the total vote and 10 percent of the white vote. In the 1987 election the black majority on the council was increased to 6–3. In 1987, as in 1985, all of the successful council candidates were endorsed by the Coalition.

While *Back to Birmingham* is an account of the rise of Richard Arrington, Jr., to a position of political authority in Birmingham, it is more than that. It also represents the general reincorporation of southern blacks into the political process and their development as a substantial component of the political process in the South. In its presentation of the political life of one man, this book says a lot about how far we have progressed as a society to open up the political process to all citizens. Students of blacks politics, southern politics, and American politics alike would profit from reading this book.

References

Button, James. W. 1989. *Blacks and Social Change: Impact of the Civil Rights Movement in Southern Communities*. Princeton: Princeton University Press.

Davis, Marilyn, and Alex Willingham, 1986. "Taking the Fifth." *Southern Changes*, 8:7–9.

Jones, Mack H. 1988. "Black Mayoral Leadership in Atlanta: A Comment." Paper presented at the annual meeting of the National Conference of Black Political Scientists, Washington, DC, March.

Perry, Huey L. 1990a. "The Evolution and Impact of Biracial Coalitions and Black Mayors in Birmingham and New Orleans." In Rufus P. Browning, Dale Rogers Marshall, and David H. Tabb, eds., *Racial Politics in American Cities*. New York: Longman.

_____. "Black Electoral Success in 1989." *PS: Political Science & Politics*, 23:141–62.

Perry, Huey L., and Alfred Stokes. 1987. "Politics and Power in the Sunbelt: Mayor Morial of New Orleans." In Michael B. Preston, Lenneal J. Henderson, and Paul Puryear, eds., *The New Black Politics: The Search for Political Power*, 2 ed. New York: Longman.

Peterson, Paul E. 1981. *City Limits*. Chicago: University of Chicago Press.

Stone, Clarence N. 1989. *Regime Politics: Governing Atlanta, 1946–1988*. Lawrence, KS: University Press of Kansas.

Book Reviews

Rufus P. Browning, Dale Rogers Marshall, and David H. Tabb, eds. *Racial Politics in American Cities* (New York: Longman, 1990) x + 243 pp.; ISBN 0-8013-0178-5 (paper).

In his novel *Coningsby*, Benjamin Disraeli wrote, "the more I think, the more I am perplexed by what is meant by representation." In their 1984 book *Protest Is Not Enough: The Struggle of Blacks and Hispanics for Equality in City Politics*, Browning, Marshall, and Tabb argued that political incorporation of ethnic and racial minorities through an electoral coalition with white liberals was the key for minority access to power in urban areas of the United States. Political incorporation meant more than representation; it meant becoming part of a dominant coalition, usually through electing a minority mayor. In this volume, the editors have attempted to gather material relevant to their earlier thesis by extending the investigation beyond the the northern California cities where the original work was done to an additional eleven cities across the Untied States. What is the status of, conditions of, and results of political incorporation there?

In order to ascertain this, the editors call upon a team of academic specialists in the politics of the different cities, Raphael J. Sonenshein (Los Angeles); Richard A. Keiser (Philadelphia); John H. Mollenkopf (New York); Robert T. Starks and Michael B. Preston (Chicago); Toni-Michelle C. Travis (Boston); Clarence N. Stone (Atlanta); Huey L. Perry (Birmingham and New Orleans); Christopher L. Warren, John G. Corbett, and John F. Stack, Jr. (Miami); and Carlos Muñoz, Jr., and Charles P. Henry (San Antonio and Denver). In addition, the editors update their findings on the ten northern California cities. Unlike many edited collections that lack even one concluding chapter, this volume has two, one by Sonenshein comparing coalitions in New York, Chicago, and Los Angeles, and another and more general one by the editors. The perceptive reader may note that earlier versions of some of the essays first appeared in an edition of *PS* in 1986.

The strengths of the volume are that it presents basic descriptive material on political incorporation from several U.S. cities, and that some of the individual essays go beyond that to put the descriptive findings in theoretical perspective. Unfortunately, the theoretical perspectives are not always the same. Apparently the authors of the individual chapters were not held to any common list of theoretical concerns beyond "political incorporation" in general. Thus some of them, such as Sonenshein on Los Angeles, Stone on Atlanta, Mollenkopf on New York, and Warren, Corbett, and Stack on Miami, give empirical and at times theoretical consideration to the problems of maintaining coalitions containing minorities in their cities; others, however, give short shrift to the question of differing interests and trade offs. It is empirically evident from the individual chapters that black-Latino cooperation is probably more difficult to achieve than black–white liberal cooperation. Some analysts, such as Keiser on Philadelphia and Perry on Birmingham and New Orleans, focus on careful evaluation of what minorities have gained from their participation in coalitions.

A major shortcoming of the book is, simply stated, that, the findings do not come together. Coverage of cities, even by reference, is less than comprehensive. Cities with minority mayors, such as Washington, DC, Baltimore, Detroit, Cleveland, Gary, and Newark, are mentioned only in passing, if at all. Some of the essays are concerned only with their particular city or cities and make little or no attempt to relate these findings theoretically either to those of Browning, Marshall, and Tabb's original work or to other cities, even those contained in this volume. Even two concluding chapters do not remedy this situation; the first is only concerned with the three major cities of the United States although there are some useful generalizations developed about how the roles of ideology, interests, and leadership affect the position of minorities. Leadership, in particular, seems to be of crucial importance in the development and decline of minority-based coalitions, but a focus on such successful individuals as Tom Bradley and Harold Washington needs to be complemented by a comparative, theoretically based treatment of the role of leadership. In their own conclusion, the editors mention several points for comparison, but they are largely content to cite what others in the volume have already stated, supplemented with several direct quotations from Anthony Downs and Adolph Reed.

There are two fundamental problems with this approach. The first is that urban analysts need to be clear about what they mean by representation. In *The Concept of Representation*, Hanna Pitkin argues that there are two substantive types of representation, passive — descriptive and symbolic representation — and active, including policy

representation. What does it mean to have political incorporation? Is the desired representation descriptive ("There were also losses in this period. The mayor's office in Berkeley, which was held by two successive black mayors in the seventies and eighties, was won by a white woman in 1987")? Is it symbolic (hence the emphasis on minority control of the mayor's office, irrespective of whether the mayor really has much power)? Is it policy representation? And, if so, in what areas? One would think that increasing minority access to housing, health care, and library and recreational facilities would be important concerns on which minority administrations could be evaluated. Instead, the chapters in the book give much more attention to minority access to city jobs and contracts, even though most of the contributors argue that minorities are better off politically by forming coalitions outside urban political machines or party regulars.

The more careful conceptual and empirical work that needs to be done would be enhanced by greater attention to recent literature on minority representation (outside of the mayor's office), urban reform, and urban public administration. It would also be improved by some theoretical treatment of the nature of coalitions, which might be gained from studying the vast literature on party coalitions in European democracies, especially those deeply divided by political cleavages. The relative roles of class and race in urban representation also need to be addressed; only Stone's essay on Atlanta really develops this perspective here. There also needs to be systematic investigation of the constraints on minority representation through urban coalitions — what are the roles of the federal and state governments, of the differing structures of city governments, judicial interpretations, and private economic interests? Only the last is more than minimally covered in this volume. In short, analysis of contemporary racial politics in U.S. cities needs to consider systematically both internal and external influences on what minority-inclusive coalitions can be expected to achieve, and then to consider what they actually achieve.

Probably nobody who reads this journal would disagree with the normative view that there ought to be more representation for minorities in urban politics. Browning, Marshall, and Tabb's previous book was a pioneering effort in showing how this could be done. Despite the insights and occasional brilliance of some of the individual contributions, the current volume is more of a sequel than an advancement of the theoretical perspective developed earlier. Even in a book aimed largely at undergraduate courses, more could have been done, especially considering the talents of the contributors. As the urban predicament in the United States worsens, political scientists need to do some hard and systematic thinking about the consequences of different patterns of political institutions, mass political behavior, and leadership.

Donley T. Studlar
Oklahoma State University

Charles P. Henry, *Culture and African American Politics* (Bloomington and Indianapolis: Indiana University Press, 1990.) ix + 140 pp.; ISBN 0-253-32754-7 (cloth).*

We share certain mythologies. A history. We share political and economic systems and a rapidly developing, if suspect, ethos . . . We are an African people who have been here since the early 17th century. We have a different way of responding to the world. We have different ideas about religion, different manners of social intercourse. We have

*Winner of the 1991 NCOBPS Best Book Award.

different ideas about style, about language. We have different esthetics. (August Wilson, *The New York Times*, 26, September 1990)

Charles P. Henry's *Culture and African American Politics*, part of an Indiana University Press series on Blacks in the Diaspora, tackles the very difficult task of identifying the elements of culture, such as language, style, religion, music, and leadership, that arise out of African and African-American culture and examines these factors as they operate within, shape, and ground black political life. In a wide-ranging examination of music, language, social organization, political leadership, and philosophical meaning, Henry argues that "Black politics, then, may be distinguished. . . by its inclusion of a wider variety of political expression and by its dependence on rhetoric and charisma, and by its rootedness in a black church tradition that blends sacred and secular vision." (p. 107).

African-American culture is only demarcated from politics in the larger society, where the separation of church and state is implicitly enshrined in the first amendment to the United States Constitution, by the fact that the joining of sacred and secular is fundamental. Henry significantly enlarges the meaning of the word *race* beyond its use by those of us who talk about its significance, whether alone or in combination with class or economic, to refer to racial politics; he shows how distinctive African-American cultural development had been in colonial America and how that distinctive development has continued into the contemporary era in the United States.

This work should be required reading for scholars, black and white alike, in political science, history, sociology, psychology, African-American studies, and education who want to understand African-American politics. It will also be useful for upper-level undergraduate and graduate courses.

This is a very subtle and complex work, which joins two developing bodies of literature, one pursuing and identifying the existence of a distinctive slave or African-American culture (for example, work by Stuckey and Harding), and the other (including work by Preston, Morris, Williams, Barker, and Morris) describing and developing theoretical categories for black political behavior. The two areas have not previously been joined in so explicit a fashion. The work is simultaneously pathbreaking and complementary to many recent publications, and it will generate considerable debate, criticism, and discussion. The remainder of this review focuses on topics raised in specific chapters.

Chapter 2 and 3, "Black and Blue," and "Afro-American Style and Lower Class Behavior," address the questions of what basic elements of culture and cultural differences have evolved from the African origins of the black population and within that relatively isolated group in the centuries in which it has resided on the North American continent. Henry notes, for example, that conflicts over the mastery of cultural styles, forms, and techniques more closely related to Europeans arise in the evolution of music and language. Other research on densely concentrated black populations in South Carolina and Georgia, where the most distinctive forms of African-American speech (Geechee and Gullah) exist, shows that the vocabulary is English, although untranslated African names for specific objects are often incorporated, while "African" grammatical patterns and accents remain intact. In parallel fashion, Henry shows that African-Americans submerge identifiably African substance under a European exterior: the evolution of gospel music early in the twentieth century, for example represented a musical and structural return to Africa, while the lyrics and message moved away from a sacred universe such as that found in the spirituals.

Henry's discussions of music, which permeate the book in a nonsegmented fashion, parallel music's dominant role in all sectors of African and African-American life. In Africa, music is distinguished by its task-related complexity, and its social, controlling, and psychological functions are very important. In American, music becomes communal psychoanalysis, social control, social reorganization, and political reorganization. Aldon Morris, for example, has described the role of music in the civil rights movement in maintaining group spirit in jail, on the picket line, when being or having been beaten, or in convincing people to change their accepting behavior into challenging behavior.

The models of leadership that appear in political science studies of black politics have focused on style, most frequently on whether the incumbents were "militants" or "moderates." The deinitional components that distinguished such behavior centered on whether the individuals encouraged or discouraged adaptation to the larger political environment: namely to the existence and the legitimacy of racial hierarchy and to the political and economic inequality that resulted from that structure. "Bad Black Men" who elevated the mores and values of the black community, who emphasized political and social equality, were and are militants to white society, but were and are "potent symbols of focused Black rebellion." Within this context, Jesse Jackson and Marion Barry and others like them, whose individual and institutional "leadership" remains immoral, illegitimate, and fundamentally incomprehensible to whites, although sometimes controversial to blacks nonetheless touches on potent, traditional, legitimate political themes in the African-American political cosmos.

Henry addresses this fusion of the

sacred and the secular in his analysis of the jeremiad, of the political sermon, of an explanation of the collective suffering of black people, in his discussion of the complex religious significance of the Garvey movement, although it was apparently secular, and in his notation that King, although a religious leader, made public justice his goal and civic religion his domain.

Chapter 5, "Cultural Politics and the Jackson Campaign," thus has a context within which to discuss the criticisms of Jackson and of this religious institutional base, offered by Adolph Reed in his work on the 1984 Jackson campaign. Reed faults Jackson for his charisma, for an antidemocratic character, for the ritualistic nature of his campaign, and for his use of rhetoric. Henry notes "it is not so much antidemocratic as it is charismatic. And it *is* ritualistic, but in the sense that it affirms black dignity and selfhood that have been denied by racism." Quoting Wildavsky, Henry notes that charismatic leadership most often arises in sectarian cultures that emphasize equality and non-hierarchically structured relationships. By contrast, "a hierarchical political culture favors *equality before the law* so as to adjudicate differences. . . . in order to maintain social differences (emphasis added, p.87).

The book is not without its faults. Many of the topics are not discussed as thoroughly as their importance merits. Chapter 5, for example, includes an analysis of a number of Jackson's sermons and a description of sermons by other black ministers; these need a more a structured discussion. Despite these small lapses the author has accomplished the very challenging task that he set for himself.

Henry has integrated work in a variety of fields to create a distinctive analysis of African-American culture and politics. His work significantly enriches the field of political science, and enriches the political scientist's understanding of the behavior of a critical segment of the American population, and therefore of the society as a whole. I will end with Henry's beginning: "[B]lack politics contains the possibility of a synthesis between selfish individualism and group responsibility that could provide an instructive moral vision for the entire society" (p. 11).

Dianne M. Pinderhughes
University of Illinois, Champaign-Urban

Frank R. Parker, *Black Votes Count: Political Empowerment in Mississippi after 1965* (Chapel Hill: University of North Carolina Press, 1990.) xv +254 pp.; ISBN 0-8078-1901-8 (cloth).

Books about Mississippi or by Mississippians have a special place in understanding American society and politics. In the pervasiveness of its tyrannical oppression of its huge population of African Americans, V.O. Key, Jr., said it was "in a class by itself." Martin Luther King, Jr., in his oration at the 1963 march on Washington called it a "desert state, sweltering with the heat of oppression." Books, such as Frank R. Parker's, that deal with the transformation of the political culture and institutions of this, the most brutally racist of the American states, should therefore be of interest to those enamored of the "Mississippi Mystique," but also the scholars with interests in American, southern and black politics.

Parker's book deals with the role of litigation in this transformation. He is eminently qualified to write it. Currently director of the Washington-based Lawyers Committee for Civil Rights under Law, Parker spent more than a decade in Mississippi leading the fight in the courts for effective enforcement of the Voting Rights Act. But this is no mere dry, technical legal treatise. Unlike many lawyers, Parker writes well; more important, he locates his analysis of the constitutional and legal issues within broad historical and theoretical perspectives derived from the recent literature on southern and black politics. Thus, both legal and social science scholarship are informed by the book, a rare feat in today's Balkanized academy. It is a product, in part, of the symbiotic relationship between social scientists and lawyers in voting rights as an area of law and research. Parker might have given more attention to this relationship in writing this book.

When, as a result of mass movement protests in Mississippi and elsewhere in the South, Congress enacted the Voting Rights Act in 1965, Mississippi reacted with the same massive resistance that had met the Supreme Court's 1954 school desegregation decree. First, there was an effort to deny the state's huge population of blacks (more than a third of the population) the simple right to cast a ballot. When this was overcome by the dispatch of federal registrars, the state shifted from a strategy of vote denial to one of vote dilution. For more than fifteen years Mississippi legislature attempted to dilute the effectiveness of black votes through such devices as racial gerrymandering, at-large election, multimember districting, abolishing elective offices, and increasing the qualifications for offices. Parker recounts in great detail Mississippi's strategy and the counter-strategy employed by the civil rights community to combat it and make black votes count. Two points are clearly established in these early chapters: (1) the centrality of structural barriers in inhibiting the effective exercise of the ballot by black Mississippians, and (2) the importance of litigation as a tool to remove these barriers and to facilitate political changes.

In subsequent chapters Parker deals with the impact of the Mississippi voting rights struggle on the state and the nation. First, he shows that in Mississippi it led to a substantial increase in the number of black elected officials, from 64 in 1965 to 664 today—the largest number of any state in the nation.

However, at approximately only 7 percent of the total number of elected officials, this number is still far below what equitable representation would require, given that blacks constitute about one third of the state's population. A second impact was the election of more moderate, reform-oriented white officials who have put aside overt racist rhetoric and practices. Thus black ballots in Mississippi have resulted in the transformation of this bastion of white supremacist politics, so that today among the southern states it is no longer in class by itself. A final consequence of the voting rights struggle in Mississippi and elsewhere in the nation was the forging of the national standard of minority-vote dilution bases on results-oriented rather than intent-oriented test (now codified in Section 2 of the Voting Rights Act as amended in 1982). In recounting in great detail and richness how this standard emerged out of the long court battles, Parker offers a thorough empirical rebuttal to the largely ideological arguments of Abigail Thernstorm (*Whose Votes Count?*) and other neoconservative scholars who contend that voting rights law has evolved into an affirmative action, race-based entitlement of political office by the law of proportional representation.

Without the legal struggle in Mississippi and elsewhere since 1965 it may well have been that the gains won in the voting rights area after decades of painful and bloody struggle would have been rendered near meaningless. Parker, as an attorney, is therefore rightfully proud of the role the legal fraternity played in blunting this attack on the achievements of the civil rights protest movement; indeed on the role litigation has played in the struggle for racial justice since Reconstruction. Yet litigation is inherently limited as an instrument of social change, especially change in the racial hierarchy. For example, after long years of costly struggle, blacks in Mississippi and the nation today constitute only a miniscule proportion of elected office holders, and fair and equitable representation, at the present rate of growth, is decades away. Second, while litigation and lobbying have been effective in removing overtly racist, discriminatory barriers in voting and other areas, they have had little impact on the social and economic consequences of these barriers. On the contrary, in Mississippi and generally in the United States, between one-third and one-fifth of African Americans find themselves mired in Third World–like conditions of poverty and deprivation. And these conditions, in many instances, have grown worse as the number of black elected officials has increased.

Finally, the courts historically (except for the brief era of the "Warren Court" from the 1950s to the late 1970s) have been indifferent or hostile to the legal aspirations of blacks. In the post-Reconstruction era the Supreme Court gave a narrow and crabbed reading to the provisions of the Civil War amendments and to congressionally enacted civil rights statutes and, if its 1988–1989 term is an indicator, the newly emerging conservative majority on the current Court may do the same thing with respect to voting and other civil rights legislation. The standards of the 1982 amended Voting Rights Act are already under attack in the lower courts and may be effectively undermined as the 1990 reapportionment cases reach the Supreme Court.

Thus, litigation while useful must now be approached with caution. Justice Thurgood Marshall in his 1989 address to First Circuit Court of Appeals judges accused his bethren on the Court of a "deliberate retrenching of the civil rights agenda" and urged civil rights lawyers to look beyond the Court to state legislatures and the Congress to protect civil rights. In all likelihood blacks will have to go beyond the Congress and legislatures as well if black rights are to be protected and the institutional constraints to socioeco-

nomic equality are to be removed. But that's a question for another book and another time. Meanwhile *Black Votes Count* is an important contribution to the literature on the African-American freedom struggle.

Robert C. Smith
San Francisco State University

Carlos Muñoz, Jr. *Youth, Identity, Power: The Chicano Movement* (London: Verso Press, 1989) xi + 216 pp.; ISBN 0-86091-197-7 (paper).

Professor Muñoz presents us with a critical work that fills an intellectual void on minority political movements. *Youth, Identity, Power: The Chicano Movement* allows us to understand the significance of the Chicano movement of the late 1960s and early 1970s, as well as to place it in its historical context. Muñoz's work represents the first substantive and systematic examination of this political movement, which remains largely obscured by the black civil rights movement.

This work employs a historical and analytic style. Muñoz lets us know in his introductory section that his analysis will revolve around cultural, class, and ideological themes that are historically based. This sets Muñoz's work apart from much of the literature on political movements in the United States that employs traditional paradigms, which tend to severely limit discussions of class, ideology, and historical context. He argues that in order to understand the Chicano student movement and the Chicano power movement "which it generated," we need to place it in the proper historical and analytic context.

In his initial chapter, Professor Muñoz offers a colonial setting by which to understand the sociopolitical oppression and economic exploitation of the Chicano (Mexican American) in the twentieth century. The post–U.S.-

Mexican War setting has had, according to Muñoz, a "profound impact" on Mexican-American political and intellectual development. Thus, not only were Mexican Americans victims of imperialism like people in other Third World countries experiencing the "bite" of the Yankee, but they,

> (l)ike the Native American peoples,. . . were subjected to a process of colonization which, in addition to undermining their culture, relegated the majority of them to a permanent pool of cheap labor for US capital. As a "conquered" and nonwhite people, they were never the beneficiaries of the fruits of capitalist development. (p. 19)

Muñoz effectively argues that segregation, educational deprivation, cultural repression, and inculcation of revisionist U.S. hegemonic indoctrination have been historically damaging outcomes of such subjugation for Mexican Americans. This has had an additionally profound historical impact in that it has prevented the formation of a significant Mexican-American middle-class intellectual sector (p. 20). Few Mexican-American youth were able to break away from such strong socialization molds, although some, like labor organizer (and Ph.D.) Ernest Galarza were successful. In fact, Muñoz begins his discussion of the origins of Mexican-American student activism with Galarza in the late 1920s.

Professor Muñoz rounds out the first chapter by offering an analytic assessment of the assimilationist roles played by institutions such as the YMCA in providing political indoctrination and social training for middle-class intellectual "melting" (integration) for selected Mexican-American youth in the 1930s and 1940s. A positive spin-off of such training was the formation of a small Mexican-American middle-class intellectual sector, which taught value in education and pride in culture to Mexican-American youth. However,

given its support and tradition of liberal capitalism, this "Mexican American Generation" was limited in its approach to fundamental problems such as poverty and low educational levels in Mexican-American communities.

The second chapter revolves around a discussion of "The Chicano Generation" of the 1960s. This youthful generation of Mexican Americans was significantly affected by the turmoil of that decade. Whereas the development of Mexican-American middle-class organizations in the 1950s were for the most part assimilationist and either conservative or "apolitical," the 1960s witnessed the development of Viva Kennedy Clubs, the Farmworkers Movement, and the "increasing discontent of the leadership of LULAC (League of United Latin American Citizens), MAPA (Mexican American Political Association), and other middle-class organizations" that would come to have "a significant impact on student activists associated with those organizations" (p. 55).

The development of Chicano student activist organizations began by 1966 and 1967 in the forms of MAYO (Mexican-American Youth Organization), UMAS (United Mexican American Students), and others (p. 58). However, Muñoz contends that ideologically these new organizations were much akin to the Mexican-American movement of the 1940s—emphasizing themes of progress through education and recruitment to and retention in college.

By the late 1960s both the black power movement and the antiwar movement had begun to influence some Chicano student leaders into a more militant posture. Muñoz could have strengthened his work through further elaborations on such influence, However, he argues that what formed the real basis of the fledgling Chicano movement was a continuing search for identity:

> To a large degree, the movement was a quest for identity, an effort to recapture

what had been lost through the socialization process imposed by US schools, churches, and other institutions. (p 61).

In order to break out of that identity crisis, the more militant student leaders began to realize that the processes of socialization must be taken on.

Muñoz contends that the catalytic event in the rise of Chicano student militancy was the high school "blow out" (walk outs) of 1968. Over 10,000 Mexican-American Los Angeles high school students went on strike for a week-and-a-half over issues ranging from racist school policies and teachers, to freedom of speech, to the hiring of Mexican-American teachers and administrators and to classes on Mexican-American history and culture. Muñoz contends that

> the strike was the first major mass protest explicitly against racism undertaken by Mexican-Americans in the history of the United States. As such, it had a profound impact power on the Mexican American community in Los Angeles and in other parts of the country, and it generated an increased political awareness along with visible efforts to mobilize the community. This was manifested in the revitalization of existing community political organizations and the emergence of new ones. . . (pp. 64–65).

The strike moved student activism beyond the politics of accommodation and integration which had been shaped by the Mexican-American Generation and the community's middle-class leadership. (p.65).

These "walk outs" of 1968 had a profound effect on what would become known as the Chicano movement, inasmuch as it represented the first loud cry for Chicano power and self-determination.

In chapter 3, Muñoz discusses both the rise and integration of the Chicano student movement and the Chicano power movement. He traces the founding of MECA (Movimiento Estudiantil Chicano de Aztlan) and argues that it was crucial to the development of both. MECA's role was to encourage students.

> to see themselves as a part of the new Chicano generation that was committed to militant struggle against US institutions that had historically been responsible for the oppression of Mexican-Americans. Adamant rejection of the label "Mexican-American" meant rejection of the assimilationist and accommdationist melting pot ideology that had guided earlier generations of activists. (p. 80).

A major part of MECA's goals were directed toward the creation of Chicano Studies programs on college and university campuses, and building and maintaining links between such programs and the broader Chicano-Latino community. However, by the early 1970s these goals had been largely achieved, and internal ideological conflict would begin to fundamentally weaken the organization.

In Chapter 4, Muñoz attempts to place the rise (1970) and fall (1975) of La Raza Unida Party in the context of the Chicano movement described and assessed in the two previous chapters. He discusses the extent to which the "Chicano student movement played a major role in the development of La Raza Unida Party" (p. 113). In assessing the party's strengths and limitations. Muñoz argues that ultimately the party became "a nationalist, independent third party, with no regard for class differentiation" (p. 117). It became a political party based on the time-bound ideology of Chicano nationalism that could not survive the movement.

The fifth chapter of Muñoz's work focuses on the quest of Chicano student and faculty activists for an alternative paradigm as well as for the creation and coordination of Chicano

Studies programs. He assesses and applauds the movement forces that came together to develop the seeds for such programs. They

> reasoned that a focus on a specifically Chicano experience would contribute to the student's discovery of Mexican cultural traditions and thereby provide a better understanding of themselves and their people. This understanding, in turn, would generate a dialectical process that would somehow join together a new identity and a new culture. . . with the political action necessary to produce change in Mexican American communities (p. 140)

His discussion of the formation of NACS (National Association of Chicano Studies) in 1974 takes place in this light. NACS was envisioned as the national vehicle that would provide direction for Chicano Studies programs. The initial vision and basis for its creation was "the general agreement that the dominant paradigms of the social sciences had failed to meaningfully address themselves to a proper interpretation of the Chicano experience" (p. 153). It never lived up to the vision. The founding of this organization came at a period when both the Chicano student movement and the broader Chicano power movement were in permanent decline.

The final chapter of this significant work reflects some retrenchment and regression over the past decade, symbolized by the turn from a "Chicano" identification to a "Hispanic" identification. In arguing that a skeletal MECA is all that remains of the Chicano movement and of the 1960s student activist groups generally, his assessment of the prospect for a rekindling of the Chicano movement is not optimistic as the Reagan-Bush agenda carries into the 1990s. He concludes that a lesson not well-learned is that the 1960s are over, as are the specific issues that gave rise

to the Chicano movement. A new movement must be predicated on new issues.

James A. Regalado
California State University, Los Angeles

Emile Sahliyeh, *In Search of Leadership: West Bank Politics since 1967* (Washington, D.C.: The Brookings Institution, 1988) x + 201 pp.; ISBN 0-8157-7698-5 (cloth)/0-8157-7697-7 (paper).

Scholarly attention to politics in the West Bank and Gaza Strip is a very recent phenomenon, dating to not much earlier than the 1970s. That is why this book should be considered a pioneering work about a region that has historically been the political center of the Palestinians, and that would become so again if a two-state solution to the Palestinian question was implemented. The West Bank and Gaza Strip, occupied by Israel in 1967, are the western and southern regions of historic Palestine. Their population, with the exception of Israeli Jewish colonists, is Palestinian Arab. West Bank political life under the occupation has remained largely invisible to the Western eye until the popular uprising (*Intifada*, in Arabic) that began in December 1987.

The primary sources in this book are interviews, pamphlets, and leaflets gathered during 1978–1984, when Sahliyeh taught at Bir Zeit, the oldest and most well-known university in the West Bank. Sahliyeh recounts historic developments during 1967–1987 in which the West Bank leadership was transformed from a leadership by a small traditional elite from the commercial and landowning classes to a leadership by more ideologically and socially diverse groups. The turnover in leadership accompanied rising education and income, and the entry to the political arena of new political actors, mainly the Palestine Liberation Organization (PLO) and Israel. In eight chapters, the book

traces the rise in power of new leadership groups, their political loyalties, their
political agendas and strategies, and the
obstacles that hinder their survival and
autonomy.

Sahliyeh concisely and clearly describes decade-long developments in
West Bank politics. The first decade following the occupation witnessed the
rise of urban elites to prominence. They
sat alongside the traditional elites as
mayors and council members and as
members of region-wide political resistance committees, the National Palestine Front and the succeeding National
Guidance Committee. The new urban
elite was not socially or economically
distinct from the notables who constituted the traditional elites. Their outlook, however, was more mobilizational
and openly supportive of the Palestine
Liberation Organization. In the 1980s,
the makeup of the political elites again
changed and became broader. The current leadership is varied and consists
of intellectuals, professional, and leaders of organizations representing students, labor, women, and Islamists.

Sahliyeh singles out students and Islamists as the main social movements
of the 1980s and allocates two chapters
for their discussion. These two new
movements are much more ideological
in their rhetoric, and their competing
nationalist and Islamist young male fol-
lowers have already engaged in confrontation, which have sometimes been
violent. In contrast, Sahliyeh mentions
women's organization only in passing.
Thus, he overlooks the budding wom-
en's movement that began with the first
women's work committee in 1978. This
is a serious oversight in the book and
an example of how women's political
contributions are kept invisible. Fortu-
nately, the Intifada has brought unprecedented visibility to West Bank and Gaza
Strip women, which has made their contributions evident to the indigenous
population and also to audiences in the
West. The Palestine Liberation Organization has also become more vocal about
recognizing women's political work in
the Intifada.

The main thesis of the book is that
political leadership in the West Bank
has been dominated by what Sahliyeh
calls "outside players." He places developments in West Bank leadership in
the context of relations to three dominant political forces: the Jordanian government, the Palestine Liberation
Organization, and the Israeli government. Saudi Arabia also entered the political arena when it began to finance
Islamic universities and other Islamist
enterprises. The story of West Bank elite
politics, as Sahliyeh sees it, is about a
leadership that has not had its own independent voice. Instead, local leaders
have been manipulated by material and
political rewards, first by the Jordani-
ans and then by the Palestine Liberation Organization, to serve those actors'
political agendas. Israel's primary impact on West Bank leadership has been
the depletion of their ranks through
constant persecution, especially the policy of deporting both leaders and those
activists who show leadership potential.

The assumption that pervades Sahliyeh's argument is that indigenous West
Bank leaders are conceptually a political entity distinct from the Palestine Liberation Organization. The model in
which the Palestine Liberation Organization is an outside player belongs to
Menachem Milson, the first Israeli ci-
vilian administrator of the occupied territories. The outlook is in sharp contrast
to the attitude held by most Palestinians (see also Cobban, 1990). The idea
of the West Bank political identity that
stands apart from a national Palestinian identity has little historical basis outside of the fact that the area was
separately administered by Jordan from
1948–1967. Neither can it be supported
by current West Bank sentiments. In a
recent survey of West Bank and Gaza
Strip residents, the leadership of the

Palestine Liberation Organization received 72.2 percent support, while King Hussein received only 3.3 percent. Of the respondents 95 percent subscribe to the national consensus that the Palestine Liberation Organization is the sole and legitimate representative of the Palestinian people (Shadid and Seltzer, 1988). There is no evidence that West Bank residents (with the exception of some Islamists) consider the Palestine Liberation Organization anything but their national government-in-exile.

The relationship between the Palestine Liberation Organization and West Bank leaders is also bolstered by extensive social and family ties, including those created when deportees were added to the PLO's ranks. Nakhleh (1988) and Cobban (1990) also point out that the Palestine Liberation Organization listens closely to the needs of the indigenous leadership. Furthermore, it was the Palestine Liberation Organization's Khalil al-Wazir who was responsible for the broad political infrastructure of mass-based organizations that have sustained the Intifada till now. The relationship between the Palestine Liberation Organization and the West Bank leadership is interactional, complex and institutionalized.

While Sahliyeh succeeds in capturing the spectrum of political opinions and rhetoric of West Bank elites, he rarely ventures into common threads that have conceputally formed political events since the beginning of the occupation. Sahliyeh is correct in identifying pan-Arabism as a dominant thought among the pro-Jordan traditional elites prior to the middle 1970s. But he fails to address steadfastness (*sumud* in Arabic), the central concept that has permeated West Bank political behavior since the Israeli occupation began. Sumud is the idea that Palestinians under Israeli occupation must remain on the land and fight to protect their identity and their political, economic, legal, and cultural rights. Sumud is the conceptual framework that can best explain West Bank politics, whether the rhetoric is pan-Arabist or Palestinian nationalist (see also Nakhleh, 1988).

In Search of Leadership: West Bank Politics since 1967 was published in 1988 and, therefore, predates the political developments that accompanied the Intifada. These include the historic decisions by the Palestine Liberation Organization to recognize Israel and reject terrorism. This does not detract from its value as a good introductory text on Palestinian politics in the West Bank. For those interested in books that focus on the Intifada, I recommend: *Intifada: The Palestinian Uprising against Israeli Occupation*, edited by Zachary Lockman and Joel Beinin (South End Press, 1989); *Land before Honour: Palestinian Women in the Occupied Territories*, by Kitty Warnock (Monthly Review Press, 1990); and *Intifada: The Palestinian Uprising—Israel's Third Front*, by Ze'ev Schiff and Ehud Ya'ari (Simon and Schuster, 1990).

Amal Kawar
Utah State University

References

Cobban, Helen. 1990. "The PLO and the Intifada." *Middle East Journal*, 44, no. 2: 207–233.

Nakhleh, Emile A. 1988. "The West Bank and Gaza: Twenty Years Later." *Middle East Journal*, 42, no. 2: 209–26.

Shadid, Mohammed, and Rick Seltzer. 1988. "Political Attitudes of Palestinians in the West Bank and Gaza Strip." *Middle East Journal*, 42, no. 1: 16–32.

Linda S. Parker, *Native American Estate: The Struggle over Indian and Hawaiian Lands* (Honolulu: University of Hawaii Press, 1989) vii + 260 pp.; ISBN 0-8248-1119-4 (cloth).

This book tells the historical saga of how native American Indians and Hawaiians were separated from most of their land base by Anglo settlers. To my knowledge it is the only book that covers both of these indigenous groups. Not surprisingly, the author finds many parallels in the way these two sets of native peoples were treated. The book also points out the basic contradiction between native and Anglo concepts of land use and ownership: "the Indian and Hawaiian valued land for its products rather than the land per se. They maintained a metaphysical relationship with the land and neither conceived of land in terms of absolute ownership" (p. 23).

The initial chapters of the book describe how native lands were taken by Anglos', often through unscrupulous or violent means. The author then describes efforts to restore some of the lost lands, and to protect the remaining native land base from further encroachment. This reviewer is quite familiar with the literature on American Indians but not with the history of Hawaiian natives. Thus I learned a great deal from the passages dealing with the island state. Anyone interested in American Indians, or any indigenous people, will profit from the material on native Hawaiians.

The material covering native Americans on the mainland is in the form of a general historical survey. Much has been written on this subject, and an overview of all the different elements can only provide an introduction. The strength of this book lies, not in the presentation of new information (there is little of that), but rather in the comprehensiveness of the narrative. The book provides glimpses of numerous case studies on land disputes, water and hunting and fishing rights, and struggles over Indian sovereignty. None of the case studies goes into great detail, but when read together they provide a clear picture of the pattern of abuses that has persistently marred our policy toward native peoples.

This is not a detached, empirical tome.

The author has a strong affinity for the Indian point of view (she is Cherokee) and is not hesitant to use valued-laden language. The litany of abuses cited in the book are no doubt accurate, but the author does not always provide substantiation for her accusations. For example, the author writes "The Department of Reclamation [sic], the Bureau of Land Management, and the U.S. Army Corps of Engineer. . . persistently have taken Indian land and water rights for dams, irrigation projects, forest reserves, and other economic or recreational programs" (p. 55). Regarding the Corps of Engineers and the Bureau of Reclamation, I think this statement is true, but I know of no instance where the Bureau of Land Management has taken Indian land or water; if there have been such instances, I would like to see the substantiating information. The author's mistaken identification of the Bureau of Reclamation in the Department of Interior (the error is repeated on p. 79) leaves one wondering if the author is truly familiar with that particular facet of native/Anglo relations. The book can best be described as a polemical indictment of our policy regarding native Americans and Hawaiians. Some Anglo policymakers, especially those at the state and local level, will object vehemently to her interpretation of events; native Americans and their Anglo allies will react differently. Both sides would probably agree, however, that Indian tribes, once characterized as a vanishing race, are still very much an enduring cultural and political entity: "Native Americans in recent decades, particularly in the last twenty years, have shown a resurgence of nationlistic sentiment and demand for their traditional rights in the exploitation of land and its resources. Hawaiians and Indians increasingly have sought to restore and affirm historic water, fishing, hunting, gathering and access rights" (p. 192).

This book will provide an introductory foundation for anyone delving into the intricacies of Indian law and policy. It is especially important that such a book be available now, given recent events concerning Indian policy. There is now a coordinated movement under way to undermine Indian treaty rights. There is nothing new about that, but recently the movement has become more systematic and intensive. For example, the Wisconsin Counties Association is leading an attempt to set up a national lobbying organization to "modernize" Indian treaty rights. Wisconsin has been the scene of racist protests against Indians' exercising off-reservation fishing rights. Indian tribes are now organizing to fight back; if one wonders why Indian people feel so threatened, a close reading of this book will help provide the answer.

Daniel McCool
University of Utah

Garcia, F. Chris, ed., *Latinos and the Political System* (Notre Dame: University of Notre Dame Press, 1988) v + 501 pp.; ISBN 0-268-01285-7 (cloth).

Chris Garcia has made a valuable contribution to the literature in political science and the subfield of ethnic politics by publishing this collection of articles on the Mexican-American, Cuban, and Puerto Rican political experience. This book is the successor to his previous edited work, *La Causa Politica* (1974). That classic text brought together a number of important works on the radical and nationalistic politics of the Mexican-American community during the 1960s. This volume reflects a shift toward an increased participation by Latinos in the governmental process. As the author states in his preface, this represents an effort to illustrate primarily "conventional or accommodational politics." While I would have liked to see an emphasis on radical and nonconventional politics, what Chris Garcia has done is provide the scholarly com-

munity with one of the few textbooks on the market that gives the reader a comprehensive overview of Latino politics. The book is divided into five sections: history and demography, input into the political system, the conversion process, outputs of the political system, and feedback or outcomes and reactions.

One of the most important features of the book is the number of articles that appear in print for the first time. Oftentimes, new articles published in edited books are little more than reviews of existing data or hastily written compositions, but many of the new works found in *Latinos and the Political System* are important contributions to the literature in their own right. Richard Santillan's work on the Midwest is a good example of the growing body of work on Mexican Americans living outside of the Southwest. John Garcia's and Carlos Arce's article on political attitudes and political participation draws data from the underutilized 1979 National Chicano Survey. Tatcho Mindiola's and Armando Gutierrez's work on the Texas legislature's sixty-seventh session (1981) is one of a handful of works on Mexican Americans that attempts to draw links between ethnicity, issue content, and political representation. Finally, the essay by de la Garza, Wrinkle, and Pollinard on attitudes toward immigration offers some survey research data to the growing debate concerning the relationship between Mexican Americans and immigrants from Mexico. These articles offer challenges to the conventional wisdom employed in a field where more sensitivity to the complexity of minority politics is called for.

Previously published articles in this collection are also a part of the new directions that research on Latino politics has taken since the 1960s. Harry Pachon's work on Hispanic representation in the federal bureaucracy, Angelo Falcon's work on black and Latino politics in New York, Welch's and Hibbing's analysis of Hispanic representation in the U.S. Congress, and the essay by Fraga, Meier, and England on Latinos and educational policy are works that attempt to come to grips with the vexing problems of race and political representation. While not all the reprinted essays are as strong as these, the book itself offers a wide overview of Latino politics that is useful both as an introduction to the topic and as an important data source for researchers.

What can be learned from a perusal of these works? To begin with, great effort is made to emphasize diversity within the Latino population itself. Not only are three major Latino groups (Mexican Americans, Puerto Ricans, and Cubans) covered in this volume, several papers focus on the ideological, income, and cultural differences within each of these groups. If anything, *Latinos in the Political* system emphasizes the unwieldly nature of the concept "Latino" and forces the reader to take note of the conflicts and differences within each major national category. Nevertheless, some common themes among the groups are analyzed. A history of discrimination and conflict with the Anglo population is discussed in the historical introduction. Furthermore this history of conflict is related to the social and economic status of contemporary Latinos. Discrimination and the lack of community resources continue to act as barriers to more effective participation in the political process. Special attention is given to other factors, such as the low rates of naturalization among Latinos, conflicts between Latinos and blacks, conflicts between generational cohorts and income segments within the Latino subgroup, and political manipulation (for example, gerrymandering), that thwart the growth of Latino political strength.

As the authors in the first section on participation show, the community is not without an active political culture. Political organizing is a vital force in a community that continues to develop new and innovative organizational responses to social problems. Carlos Muñoz, Mario Barrera, Joseph Sekul, and Avelardo Valdez document the effort to better the social and economic condition of the Latino people through community organizing. Other essays document the growing strength of the Latino community in the policy-making process. One notable work is that of Susan Welch and John R. Hibbing in which the voting patterns of Mexican Americans are analyzed in relationship to the election of progressive public officials. Latinos have also made great strides in the courts. Karen O'Connor and Lee Epstein reveal that, despite some setbacks, the Mexican American Legal Defense and Educational Fund serves as a dynamic representative of Latino interests in the courts. These last two essays, and that of Joseph Sekul on community organizing, are some of the best in the "outputs" section, insofar as they relate political activity to specific public policy outputs. Although drawing causal links between action and social change is difficult, each of the articles included in this volume would have benefited from a detailed discussion of the impact that political organizing, representation, or electoral participation have on the everyday life of the Latino community. The last three essays on outputs and feedback tend to be overly general and ponderous.

Perhaps these problems could have been avoided if a section on theory had been included. Only a few authors attempt to tie their research to larger questions in political science. This is a serious omission in light of the growing interest in integrating social theory with data on racial and cultural minorities. For example, the text contains some strong essays on Latino representation in Congress, the behavior of Latino representatives in the Texas legislature, and the Mexican American Legal Defense and Educational Fund, but the implications of their findings for the interactions of race and class are left unexplored. We learn of the cultural and political divisions within the three major Latino groups covered, but the question of ethnicity as a concept is left unexamined.

Some articles touch on the question of black politics in relationship to the Latino community, and it is here that a solid theoretical grounding is most necessary in order to understand the points of conflict and convergence between the black and Latino community. Angelo Falcon's piece on politics in New York City touches on the problem of minority group conflict, but no model of group conflict is addressed or developed. Another theoretically interesting question that needs exploration is the existence of a conservative political agenda within the Cuban-American community in Florida and elsewhere. Recent political events reveal that, not only do Cubans tend to be conservative in their political outlook, but they often come in direct conflict with the traditional goals of the African-American as well as the Mexican-American and Puerto Rican communities.

Serious questions about the nature of race relations in the United States need to be asked. Are all Latinos subject to equally severe discrimination? Does cultural assimilation have a political impact? What are the racial attitudes held by members of the Latino community itself, and can they promote or hinder multiracial coalitions?

There are many demands that could be made of any text, but they should not detract from the contribution that this fine collection of readings makes to the discipline.

Benjamin Marquez
University of Wisconsin-Madison

Gabriel Kolko, *Confronting the Third World: United States Foreign Policy 1945–1980* (New York: Pantheon Books, 1988) xiii + 332 pp.; ISBN 0-394-57138-X (cloth)/0-394-75833-8 (paper).

In his latest contribution to the international relations literature, Kolko assesses U.S. foreign political, economic, and military policy in the Third World from 1945 to 1980, notably in Africa, Asia, Latin America, and the Middle East. His main hypothesis is that the role of Third World nations as exporters of raw material generally defines their structural relationship to the United States. He refers to "structural relationships" vaguely as "[economic] inter-relationships between America's business interests and economy and those of poor nations" (p. 227). Kolko asserts further that the "economic component [is] always inextricable with all the motives of U.S. [foreign policy]," and often, as in Latin America (p. 37) and Africa (p. 113), the economic component is its primary objective.

A second hypothesis that Kolko makes is that the continuity in U.S. foreign policy since 1945 has been a function of both the background and socialization of U.S. decision makers. For example, he states that U.S. decision makers have consistently applied the "capitalist credo" in dealing with the Third World (p. 117). He attributes this to the fact that America has preeminently been an economic civilization, and all those who have succeeded in it have been products of its culture, absorbing its instinctive values and premises without reservation.

Kolko divides the postwar–1980 era into four distinct periods: Foundations (1945–1950), Post–Korean War (1950–1960), Democratic Party (1961–1968), and the Decade of Perpetual Crisis (1969–1980). Kolko's views about the consistency of how postwar American foreign policies have been managed are found throughout the text. The record indicates that, as the two major powers of the postwar era (the United States and the U.S.S.R.) disagreed over which form of political system was best, they built competing spheres of influence and, to a limited extent, left the management of the individual Third World countries in the hands of the locals in the *"region."* ("Spheres of influence" refers to a grouping of states over which a major power wields authority or hegemony to such an extent that the influenced states usually give up some degree of their sovereignty to the influencing nation.) The record also indicates that postwar American military policy has been consistently *antirevolutionary*. That is, the United States has generally (though there are some exceptions) chosen to play it safe by siding with the existing power structure, no matter how antidemocratic, rather than with the forces of social change. This has occurred most frequently in Latin America.

A third characterization that Kolko makes has to do with the way in which American foreign-policy makers have approached the management of the economies of Third World countries. According to Kolko, profits, not peace, have been the nation's top priority.

Moreover, America's political and military actions in the Third World are taken for the purpose of addressing economic problems. These are what are known as tenets of *economic imperialism*.

Preoccupation with establishing the superiority of the "economic imperialism" view affects Kolko's ability to make concrete policy recommendations. The author also does not address in any thorough manner some of the crucial historical factors that have had an impact upon American policymakers' attitudes toward decision making in the international context. Otherwise, the book is strongly argued and well documented. Future debates on the pattern of U.S. foreign policy in the Third World will definitely have to take in into account.

Harold W. Moses
Southern Illinois University at
Carbondale

The *National Political Science Review (NPSR)*, a publication of the National Conference of Black Political Scientists, invites authors to submit manuscripts for its next volume. The NPSR welcomes contributions on any important research problem in political science but is particularly interested in theoretical/empirical research that focuses on politics and policies that advantage or disadvantage groups by reasons of race, ethnicity or sex, or other such factors.

Contributions should be no longer than 30 typewritten pages double-spaced, and should follow guidelines of the *Chicago Manual of Style*. An abstract of no more than 150 words should appear just beneath the title and before the text begins. Author's names should be placed on a separate cover sheet. Five copies of each manuscript should be sent to Matthew Holden, Jr., Editor, Department of Government and Foreign Affairs, 232 Cabell Hall, University of Virginia, Charlottesville, VA 22901.

Requests for book reviews should be sent to Paula D. McClain, Book Review Editor, Department of Government and Foreign Affairs, 232 Cabell Hall, University of Virginia, Charlottesville, VA 22901. Inquiries about standing orders should be addressed to Transaction Publishers, Rutgers—The State University, New Brunswick, NJ 08903.

For Product Safety Concerns and Information please contact our EU
representative GPSR@taylorandfrancis.com
Taylor & Francis Verlag GmbH, Kaufingerstraße 24, 80331 München, Germany

www.ingramcontent.com/pod-product-compliance
Lightning Source LLC
Chambersburg PA
CBHW081432270326
41932CB00019B/3170